Collective Action in Organizations

Interaction and Engagement in an Era of Technological Change

Challenging the notion that digital media render traditional, formal organizations irrelevant, this book offers a new theory of collective action and organizing. Based on extensive surveys and interviews with members of three influential and distinctive organizations in the United States – The American Legion, AARP, and MoveOn – the authors reconceptualize collective action as a phenomenon in which technology enhances people's ability to cross boundaries in order to interact with one another and engage with organizations. By developing a theory of collective action space, Bruce Bimber, Andrew J. Flanagin, and Cynthia Stohl explore how people's attitudes, behaviors, motivations, goals, and digital-media use are related to their organizational involvement. They find that using technology does not necessarily make people more likely to act collectively but contributes to a diversity of "participatory styles," which hinge on people's interaction with one another and the extent to which they shape organizational agendas. In the digital-media age, organizations do not simply recruit people into roles; they also provide contexts in which people are able to construct their own collective experiences.

Bruce Bimber is Professor of Political Science at the University of California, Santa Barbara, where he is also affiliated with the Department of Communication and is founder and former director of the Center for Information Technology and Society. His interest in digital media and society arises from his training as an electrical engineer as well as a political scientist and from many years of observing the interconnections between social and technological innovation. He is author of *Campaigning Online: The Internet in U.S. Elections* (with Richard Davis) and *Information and American Democracy* (Cambridge 2003). Bimber is a Fellow of the American Association for the Advancement of Science.

Andrew J. Flanagin is Professor of Communication at the University of California, Santa Barbara, where he is also director of the Center for Information Technology and Society. His research focuses on processes of collective organizing, particularly as influenced by the use of contemporary technologies, people's perceptions of the credibility of information gathered and presented online, the use of social media and social metadata for information sharing and assessment, and organizational technologies. He has published extensively across a wide variety of academic fields on various facets of social relations as implicated by technologies and technology use. He is the coeditor of *Digital Media, Youth, and Credibility* (2008) and the coauthor of *Kids and Credibility: An Empirical Examination of Youth, Digital Media Use, and Information Credibility* (2010).

Cynthia Stohl is Professor of Communication at the University of California, Santa Barbara, and an affiliate faculty member of the Center for Information Technology and Society. Her work focuses on organizing and network processes across a wide range of global contexts, including corporate-NGO partnerships, activist organizing, and clandestine organizations. A signature of Stohl's work is global connectivity, and her empirical studies span several countries in Europe and Asia as well as New Zealand and the United States. Her interests in communication technologies arose from her studies of boundary permeability and emerging networks in workplace participation programs, organizational collaborations, and the contemporary global social justice movement. Stohl has published extensively in communication and organizational studies and is the author of *Organizational Communication: Connectedness in Action* (1995). She is a Fellow and the president-elect of the International Communication Association.

"This book ushers in a new era of theorizing on collective action. It turns contemporary notions of collective action on its head. First, this book brings the individual – and individual differences – back into traditional collective action by theorizing that people's contributions are shaped not just by demographics or an economically driven cost-benefit calculus, but more substantially by their interaction and engagement. Second, the book brings the relevance of the formal organization back into contemporary notions of collective action. Using compelling evidence, the authors argue that the advent of digital media enables formal organizations to offer much broader opportunities for people to define themselves and to establish their own participatory styles. By bringing to the fore both the individual and the formal organization, the authors offer a timely, balanced, and intellectually engaging corrective to previous undersocialized and oversocialized views of collective action."

– Noshir Contractor, Jane S. & William J. White Professor of Behavioral Sciences, Northwestern University

COMMUNICATION, SOCIETY AND POLITICS

Politics and relations among individuals in societies across the world are being transformed by new technologies for targeting individuals and sophisticated methods for shaping personalized messages. The new technologies challenge boundaries of many kinds – among news, information, entertainment, and advertising; between media, with the arrival of the World Wide Web; and even between nations. Communication, Society and Politics probes the political and social impacts of these new communication systems in national, comparative, and global perspectives.

Other Books in the Series

C. Edwin Baker, *Media Concentration and Democracy: Why Ownership Matters*
C. Edwin Baker, *Media, Markets, and Democracy*
W. Lance Bennett and Robert M. Entman, eds., *Mediated Politics: Communication in the Future of Democracy*
Bruce Bimber, *Information and American Democracy: Technology in the Evolution of Political Power*
Murray Edelman, *The Politics of Misinformation*
Frank Esser and Barbara Pfetsch, eds., *Comparing Political Communication: Theories, Cases, and Challenges*

(*continued after the Index*)

Collective Action in Organizations

Interaction and Engagement in an Era of Technological Change

BRUCE BIMBER
University of California, Santa Barbara

ANDREW J. FLANAGIN
University of California, Santa Barbara

CYNTHIA STOHL
University of California, Santa Barbara

CAMBRIDGE UNIVERSITY PRESS
Cambridge, New York, Melbourne, Madrid, Cape Town,
Singapore, São Paulo, Delhi, Mexico City

Cambridge University Press
32 Avenue of the Americas, New York, NY 10013-2473, USA

www.cambridge.org
Information on this title: www.cambridge.org/9780521139632

First published 2012

Printed in the United States of America

A catalog record for this publication is available from the British Library.

Library of Congress Cataloging in Publication data

Bimber, Bruce A. (Bruce Allen), 1961–
Collective action in organizations: interaction and engagement in an era of technological change / Bruce Bimber, Andrew J. Flanagin, Cynthia Stohl.
p. cm. – (Communication, society and politics)
Includes bibliographical references and index.
ISBN 978-0-521-19172-2– ISBN 978-0-521-13963-2 (pbk.)
1. Lobbying – United States. 2. Pressure groups – United States. 3. Associations, institutions, etc. – United States. 4. AARP (Organization) 5. American Legion. 6. MoveOn.org. I. Flanagin, Andrew J. II. Stohl, Cynthia. III. Title.
JF529.B585 2012
322.40973–dc23 2011032250

ISBN 978-0-521-19172-2 Hardback
ISBN 978-0-521-13963-2 Paperback

Contents

List of Figures and Tables

Figures

Tables

Preface

This book was from the outset a truly *collective* endeavor among the authors. We therefore chose the convention of listing the authors alphabetically, to convey that we are all equal contributors in this effort.

The project represents the nexus of our interests in technology, organizing, and social behavior. When we first began, a devastating earthquake and subsequent tsunami in the Indian Ocean had generated enormous global relief efforts. Protests against the U.S. war in Iraq were continuing across the globe, and economic and social-justice reform efforts were being waged at local, national, and international levels. Digital technologies, especially mobile ones, were a part of many of these stories of collective action. From Indymedia to smart mobs, videos on YouTube, and photos on Webshots and Flickr, pundits and scholars were heralding a new era of organizing, a time in which individuals no longer needed to rely on the formal apparatus of organizations of the past. Individuals could broker information through emergent and powerful social networks and bypass costly, ponderous infrastructures. To some, the end of formal organizations seemed near.

As we completed this book project, local and global responses to earthquakes in Haiti and New Zealand and rescue and reclamation efforts for the devastating earthquake and tsunami in Japan were underway. Multiple revolutions and uprisings in the Arab world were also unfolding. These events were not stories of how collective actions are no longer linked to organizations, but rather of events and organizing processes that take place at the nexus of organizations, networks, broadband and cellular access, Twitter and Facebook interactions, social media and blogs, search engines, and digital repositories. Organizations have not ceased to exist. Rather, organizations and their relationships with their members and civil society have changed, becoming less bureaucratized, more flexible, more subtle, and more readily constructed by individuals in a world in which people have a great deal of information at their fingertips and an essentially unlimited capacity to communicate with others, near and far, known and unknown.

It is the nature of these changes that have interested us throughout this project. Elsewhere, we have told parts of the story of what can be accomplished at present without formal organizations in the postbureaucratic era. Here we tell the story of organization in this same era, in which membership and involvement are entangled with technology and choice, and the style of participation that people construct for themselves is no less important than the kind of organization to which they belong.

Our account of organizations and collective action in this book would not have been possible without the involvement of key people at the three organizations we studied. Brad Pryor and his colleagues at The American Legion were extremely helpful, open, and accessible. Their commitment to the values and mission of The American Legion are apparent in everything they do and a credit to the organization. At AARP, Xenia Montenegro and her colleagues provided us with timely and expert information. In a time of transition they remained steady and dedicated to the work of AARP, one of the most important organizations in the United States. At MoveOn, Daniel Mintz and his colleagues gave generously of their time to talk with us about the special character of their organization. Their passion and dedication to MoveOn are impressive. We also thank the many members of these organizations who took their time to respond to our survey.

At the University of California, Santa Barbara, where we work, we wish to thank the Center for Information Technology and Society for supporting this project by providing valuable resources throughout the research process. The ideas for this book arose from a series of workshops sponsored by the center that were designed to foster collaborative research. These helped us discover that our interests in the subject matter that became this book were mutual.

This book has benefited from the comments of a number of colleagues: Eva Anduiza, Jennifer Earl, Dave Karpf, and Michael Stohl. We also want to thank those people who worked on the project while they were graduate students at UC Santa Barbara: Melissa Bator, Jennifer Brundidge, Pearl Galano, Alex Markov, and Rob Patton.

We would like to express special thanks to Robert M. Entman and W. Lance Bennett, editors of the Communication, Society and Politics series of Cambridge University Press. Lance especially supported and advised this project from the outset. His insights, constructive criticism, and wise counsel are greatly appreciated.

The project was funded by grants from the National Science Foundation and the University of California, Santa Barbara, and was also supported by a Fellowship for Bruce Bimber during this period from the Center for Advanced Study in the Behavioral Sciences at Stanford.

1

Involvement in Organizational Collective Action in an Era of Technological Change

A great deal of what people wish to accomplish cannot be achieved alone, either by private, individual actions or through markets and their modern instrument for aggregating private interest, the corporation. Only through some form of *collective action* can people realize important individual and group goals and produce the myriad shared benefits associated with social life. Acting collectively requires associating voluntarily with others who share interests or identities, and it can mean participating in solving problems at the local, national, or global scale. Collective action can involve advocating for causes or goals, recruiting others, and banding together to gain voice and representation before public institutions, corporations, and other bodies, or it can entail producing something of value that is shared beyond those who created it. Whether the goal is the creation of public parks or pathways, health care or human rights, environmental sustainability or electoral accountability, or information databases and communication systems, the need for at least two people to act together toward the establishment of some shared "public good" is an enduring fact of human life.

For a long time, scholarly literature placed organizations, not individuals, at the center of collective action. Olson's 1965 classic, *The Logic of Collection Action*, is an account of the choices faced by individuals to participate in collective efforts or not, and in his widely accepted view, it is organizations that solve the problem of individuals free riding on the efforts of others. Organizations act on behalf of groups of people, embodying and representing their concerns, empowering them as collectivities, and organizing them. Success at collective action in the end is not so much a function of the complexity or individualism of people's choices, which are constrained by the unvarying logic of free riding, but a function of how well organizations perform at overcoming that logic. Likewise, Truman (1951), in his own classic work, viewed latent interests on the part of citizens as being manifest only when expressed in organizational form. Similarly, Knoke defines an association, which can range from a trade association to a civic group, as "a formally organized, named group" and emphasizes the importance of the "acquisition and allocation of organizational resources to collective objectives" (Knoke, 1986, 2).

In historical and structural analyses of the growth and possible decline of civil society, organizational themes are crucial and often overshadow individual-level variation in citizens' outlooks (della Porta, 2007; Putnam, 2000; Skocpol and Fiorina, 1999). Putnam's famous *Bowling Alone*, for instance, is often read as a story of changes at the level of the individual citizen, but it is essentially an account of the causes and consequences of organizational change, as one class of organization in public life is replaced by others. Similarly, analyses of social movements typically focus on the strategies, tactics, and repertoires used to develop relevant organizational constituencies (Gamson, 1992; Tarrow, 1994), and the role of "social movement organizations" (Snow and Benford, 1992) has been identified as critical in understanding cycles of social protest (see Tarrow, 1983).

However, the place of the individual and the organization in the story of collective action and social change has been recently upended (Bennett and Segerberg, 2011; Earl and Kimport, 2011). The last two decades have been transformative for the state of collective action, often in ways that challenge the organization-centric view. Among the many interesting cases of collective action in recent years, those that tend to attract the most attention are those not closely managed by any formal organization or central organizer. These include Facebook groups for organizing revolutionary actions in the Middle East as well as protests over immigration policies and practices in Arizona, the use of Twitter to mount protests over election results in Moldova, and Meetups that bring together groups of people across a diversity of activities from hobbies and private interests to community service and various public-goods efforts.

As technologies of communication and information have proliferated and evolved, so too have opportunities among individuals seeking common goals. Chief obstacles to realizing collective goals, including locating a critical mass of people with shared interests, providing opportunities for meaningful forms of distributed contribution, and coordinating people's actions efficiently have all been diminished by technological tools that fundamentally enhance connectivity among people. Although some key challenges to successful collective action efforts endure as they always have, the novel capacities created by technological innovation have altered the structures and forms of collective action efforts today toward the direction of enhanced individual agency.

Many instances of collective action often lack not only the organizational command that scholars traditionally have believed should be present but also the identity and ideological agreement once thought crucial to such efforts. The cascading passions during late 2010 and early 2011 that grew into tumultuous protests for regime change in Tunisia, Egypt, and Libya were a result of diverse frustrations, not organizational strategy or control. In an iconic moment in January 2011, after the ouster of Tunisian President Zine al-Abidine Ben Ali, who fled into Saudi Arabia, protestors outside the Saudi Embassy in Washington displayed a banner thanking Facebook founder Mark Zuckerberg and vilifying Ben Ali (Madrigal, 2011). In Tunisia and in Egypt, digital media enabled citizens to coordinate among themselves and to communicate what was happening with observers outside their countries. The soon-to-fail Mubarak government in Egypt was sufficiently concerned about the enabling power of digital media that it shut down nationwide Internet service in late January 2011 – an unprecedented action for a nation of eighty million citizens.

Also prominent on the global stage of collective action have been the highly visible actions against the Iraq war and protests at key World Trade Organization (WTO) events, G8 and G20 summits, and the UN Climate Change Conference in Copenhagen. Among the more well-known and earliest of these actions was the 1999 "Battle in Seattle," in which a far-flung network of groups and organizations from several nations interested in everything from the environment to women's issues protested the policies of the WTO (Bimber, 2003; Kahn and Kellner, 2004). Similarly, as the U.S. government prepared to attack Iraq in 2003, antiwar demonstrations around the globe, representing not just traditional antiwar groups but also nonaffiliated activists and individuals who had never been involved in a protest before, reached a size and scale comparable to those of the classical height of U.S. protest politics during the late 1960s and early 1970s (Bennett, Breunig, and Givens, 2008). Protests against the repressive Myanmar government in 2007 brought more than seventy-five thousand civilians and Buddhist monks together in Yangon, making the event the largest Burmese antigovernment protest demonstration in twenty years (Global Voices, 2008).

Although many of these cases constitute ephemeral, one-off events, other examples of organizing that are more decentralized and less dependent upon formal organization show signs of greater persistence. The hundreds of Tea Party groups that began in 2009 to challenge the Democratic and the Republican establishments in the United States are a case of technology-enabled organizing that sustained itself and institutionalized into a meaningful political movement capable of electing officials to high office and shaping the course of public policy. The open-source software movement is not only well institutionalized but also has demonstrated some success at challenging dominant corporations as well as attracting corporations as participants. The user-generated and loosely coordinated content in the online encyclopedia Wikipedia – a public good created through several hundred million small collective actions – has likewise proven to be a vibrant and viable alternative to its more traditional counterparts and is among the world's most highly visited Web sites. In virtually any domain traditionally dominated by formal organizations, one will now find organization-less groups in which individuals construct their own interest-based collectives.

Cases of "organization-less organizing" have grabbed many headlines, as journalists demonstrate a penchant for stories of "online" accomplishments and novelties. Among scholars, one important strand of thought about digital media and collective action has emphasized the point that formal organizations with structures and incentives are no longer critical for accomplishing things collectively. Benkler (2006) has made this point about the social production of a diversity of resources, calling attention to a potentially fatal flaw in the fundamentals of economic theory, which is visible in the fact that large numbers of people are willing to contribute time and expertise to create things of public value in the absence of material incentives or a controlling organization. That the size of such efforts reaches commercial scale is a striking challenge to old economic paradigms. Shirky (2008) has highlighted the broad range of tasks that can be accomplished through self-organization rather than hierarchically. Many small challenges, such as recovering a lost phone, are problems of information or communication, and such problems can now readily be solved without central authorities. In many ways, the present period is a time of great choice among alternatives for how people can become involved.

In our own previous work, we have explored this issue in some depth, discussing the possibilities of organizing without organization. We argued the simple point that the fundamental solution to the challenges of collective action is not organization, but organizing. In a context of high costs of information and communication, which were nearly universal in large and complex societies until fifteen years ago or so, organizing typically requires organizations (Bimber, Flanagin, and Stohl 2005; Bimber, Stohl, and Flanagin, 2008; Flanagin, Stohl, and Bimber, 2006). Because technology places the requisite tools for organizing more fully in the hands of individuals and informal or semiformal groups, collective action can more seamlessly arise from those with an interest in shared goals, without necessarily requiring the substantial costs associated with the classical organizational apparatus that traditionally has served to facilitate shared action.

Even more fundamentally, the digital-media environment prompts new and unforeseen opportunities for collective action as people are increasingly immersed in an atmosphere in which it is their routine practice to share ideas, connections, and interests. Just as previous tools like the telegraph altered people's conception of time and space (Carey, 1989), recent technological shifts have prompted new understanding and assumptions about information and communication. These involve a vibrant culture of sharing among younger people, so widely on display at video- and music-sharing Web sites and in social media. It involves greatly weakened social and personal boundaries and diminished demands for privacy, which are the subject of so much discussion since the rise of social media. Among new practices and norms are a heightened emphasis on personal creation and initiative and expectations of choice among an array of informational and communicative alternatives. Living in a world in which two people wishing to communicate must choose among doing so in person, in writing, by phone, by e-mail, by text message, by Twitter, by wall post or message, by chat, or by video call, and in which most of these options are available on devices in their pockets, means that communicative practice and norms are undergoing great change, and with that social and political norms and practice will necessarily change as well. These developments are also contributing to the trend in citizenship practices away from institutions and norms of duty fulfillment and toward more personalized ways of being civic (Bennett, 2008; Dalton, 2008b; Inglehart, 1997; Zukin et al., 2006).

Although some observers might interpret these developments toward more individualized collective action and greater agency as marking the beginning of the end of formal organizations in public life, the complete picture is much more complex. Organizations in civil society are not dying wholesale or becoming obsolete. They are struggling in many cases to adapt, yet the result will not be the end of the organization in civic life but rather its transformation, especially with respect to the meaning and role of citizens and the forms of their involvement. As Michael Gilbert, a journal editor and consultant on technology and nonprofit organization, says,

> Is this the end of the organization? Probably not by name and certainly not in the broadest sense of the term. But the traditional, tightly controlled, top down, branded organization is finding itself having to adapt and change. Whether the organization as we know it survives or not, it is by studying the changing patterns of communication that we will discover the new shape of civil society. (Gilbert, 2008, n.p.)

It is not the case that formal organizations are being replaced by self-organized groups enabled by digital media. Activist networks and informal groups supplement formal organizations, enriching and adding complexity to the organizational forms rather than substituting the new for the old. All forms of organization, from rigidly bureaucratic and formal to loosely organized and ad hoc, are affected by the recent availability and adoption of tools enabling a wide variety of communicative options among those people whose shared goals are best achieved by banding together in some fashion. Organizations have choices regarding how they go about their business, activists have choices about what kind of organizational forms to develop, and people have choices about what forms their involvement in collective action will take.

In discussions regarding the new face of collective action, some observers have taken stark positions implying that organizations must either be always irrelevant or always necessary, but this rigid dichotomy is false. Social commentator Gladwell (2010), for instance, argued that real social change always requires thick social ties among participants and clear decision making and authority exercised by organizations. But no simple contest exists between networks and organizations, and neither exercises a monopoly over social change. Instead, what has happened throughout the last twenty years or so is that organizational forms and functions have expanded in number and richness, not shrunken. All sorts of organizational structures and processes are implicated in the new technological landscape for collective action, a state that Crowley and Skocpol (2001) refer to as "organizational fecundity." These include hybrid organizations (Chadwick, 2007), federated network structures (Flanagin, Monge, and Fulk, 2001), networks of organizations (Bennett, Breunig, and Givens, 2008; Stohl and Stohl, 2007), altered organizational strategies in public life (Bimber, 2003), and at the extreme, spontaneous, ephemeral, and large-scale organizing in the absence of the accoutrements of traditional organizations, such as the protests in Myanmar or the March 2006 walkout of thousands of Los Angeles high school students to protest the treatment of immigrants (Cho and Gorman, 2006). In many cases, formal organizations work alongside organization-less networks. In the wake of the devastating 2010 earthquake in Haiti, for example, social media such as Twitter, YouTube, and blogs were not only the major sources of initial information, but also many classic, formal aid and relief organizations found them to be the most effective means for managing information as well as for generating donations. Less than forty-eight hours after the earthquake, the American Red Cross had received more than $35 million in donations, including $8 million directly from text messages (Morgan, 2010).

Frequently lost in the excitement over new organizational forms as well as organization-less collective action is the story of traditional, formal organizations that can use digital media creatively, like the Red Cross. Organizations are increasingly recognizing that they can embrace a variety of methods for member engagement in their goals. At Amnesty International, for instance, an organization with more than two million members globally, people can join the U.S. chapter for thirty-five dollars. Or, without joining or making a donation, one can sign up to volunteer or take action online, receive an "activist toolkit," get updates on topics of interest to them, or link to Amnesty from Facebook or MySpace pages, Twitter, YouTube, or from mobile phone–based social-networking tools. Interested people can also find a nearby chapter at a school in order to connect with like-minded others on their own terms.

From the global scale to the local, Amnesty International, like virtually every major membership group, now offers a complex set of varying relationships and contexts for collective action, rather than a simple model of "membership" and "recruitment." An important feature of these practices of organizations – one that is central to what we have to say in this book – is that when organizations abandon old, constrained, limited definitions of membership in order to provide people alternative ways to affiliate, then they are engaging people's desire for choice. One result of people exercising choice when they act collectively through organizations is that understanding what they are doing requires more attention to individuals than was true in the past, when organizations were firmly the centerpiece of scholars' stories about collective action. Room exists for the new individualism and agency within organizations.

An unmistakable fact about the state of collective action at present is that formal collective action organizations are thriving, right alongside the profusion of organization-less forms of association that attract so much attention, as well as the many hybrid and mixed organizational forms and networks. A number of metrics indicate the strength of formal organizations of various kinds. According to the UN Department of Economic and Social Affairs, nearly one-fifth of the world's thirty-seven thousand nongovernmental organizations (NGOs) were formed just in the 1990s, in precisely the period that digital media arose and made organizing without organizations possible. Tarrow (2006) similarly reports that the number of transnational social movement organizations tripled between 1983 and 2003. The diffusion of the Internet, the expansion of organization-less organization, and the creation of new formal organizations have all moved together during the last two decades.

Within the United States, which is the focus of this book, the story of contemporary formal organizations in collective life is a vibrant one. The period between the 1960s and early 1990s is well-known as a time when interest groups multiplied rapidly. In the time since, the rate of founding of new organizations has slowed, but existing organizations remained stable and, in many cases, grew in size and infrastructure. For example, at the top of the scale of interest-group size in the United States is AARP, the organization for citizens more than fifty years in age.[1] It has thrived since the emergence of the Internet into civic life. In 1998, on its fortieth anniversary, AARP reported its membership to be close to thirty million, while in 2010 it was about forty million (AARP, 2010). This surge is due in large part to the aging U.S. population, as the baby boomers move through AARP. But as we will see in this book, the organization has been very successful at employing technology in order to expand and enrich membership, as well as to redefine it.

The Environmental Defense Fund had three hundred thousand members and 160 staff in seven offices in 1997, which is close to the time of the outset of the diffusion of the Internet into politics and organizing. Rather than shedding members or physical infrastructure in the presence of new communication tools, it grew to more than half a million members and 340 staff in eleven offices by 2009 (Environmental Defense

[1] AARP, with about 40 million members, and the American Automobile Association with about 50 million, are by far the largest interest groups in the United States, both about an order of magnitude larger than the next largest class of interest groups, which have a few million members.

Fund, 1997, 2009, 2010). It has benefited organizationally from the ability to communicate and inform people in new ways, at the same time that many citizens have also found new outlets for online environmental activism, such as Environment Online, also known as ENO, and the countless social media groups dedicated to green issues. Accomplishing this required considerable experimentation and adaptation (Bimber, 2003).

Another case is the National Council of La Raza, the largest organization advocating for Latinos and Latinas in the United States, and an example of a group formed during the heyday of organizing in the 1960s. In 2008, it celebrated its fortieth anniversary with a very traditional activity for formal organizations, the completion of a new building in Washington, D.C., near the White House. La Raza works through networks of community-based organizations rather than a large direct membership like the Sierra Club or AARP, and the size of its network grew from two hundred fifty organizations in 2000 to about three hundred in 2008 (La Raza, 2000, 2008). At the other end of the political spectrum, a wave of new antiimmigration organizations was established around the 1980s, and these remind us that not all immigration protest and advocacy is conducted through Facebook. These groups include Americans for Immigration Control, U.S. Border Patrol, and English First. The Federation for American Immigration Reform (or FAIR) was founded in 1979 and reported growth during the decade of the 2000s from about seventy thousand members to a quarter of a million (FAIR, 2001, 2008). The American Legion, which will be discussed much more in this book, continues to lose significant numbers of World War II veterans every day (in 2008 only 2.5 million out of 16 million World War II veterans were still alive), but since 2000 has recruited an average of 256,000 new members each year.

The growth and vitality of traditional organizations such as these is sometimes overlooked in the story of contemporary collective action across the globe. Some are doing old things in new ways, and some are doing entirely new things. The National Rifle Association (NRA), like many groups, exploits the Web to permit people who are not members and who do not contribute money to participate in its activities. Although it attempts to entice people to join with various member services and discounts, it also makes available to anyone many of its publications, blog, schedules of various programs, and news stream. In traditional theoretical terms, it is giving away for free some of the key selective incentives that it might otherwise use to overcome the free-riding problem associated with membership. Organizations are not supposed to do this, according to classical theories of collective action. The American Civil Liberties Union (ACLU) breaks theoretical rules further, not only posting reports and its congressional scorecard for the public but also "action alerts" that exhort the public to join petitions or send letters to officials regarding issues of importance to the organization. It provides a guide to activism with such tips as how to be an effective caller to talk-radio shows. All of these resources are directed toward the public at large, regardless of whether a citizen has "joined" or become a paying member. These efforts by the NRA and the ACLU, like so many other traditional organizations, suggest the weakening of one of the theoretically most important boundaries in traditional views of interest groups, the boundary between members and nonmembers.

In the contemporary culture, people's use of digital media breaks down boundaries within organizations in other ways as well. For instance, the children's advocacy group World Vision links its members to MySpace, Facebook, Twitter, Digg, and other media environments. This common tactic easily enables members to inform and enlist their personal networks in the organization's campaigns. The organization is seeking to exploit members' networks for communication and recruitment, and in doing so has shifted some impetus for organizing and activism to the members. Another striking example of old organizations doing new things involves AARP. At its Web site, it offers opportunities for members to interact personally with one another through social forums and discussion groups. In these contexts, which it calls an "online community," its members join support groups for health problems and grief, discuss aging issues, and exchange views about the politics of Social Security, health-care reform, and many other issues. AARP provides links to opportunities for volunteering and public service at the community level. According to senior staff at AARP, the volunteer program is very large and still growing, which may come as a surprise to observers who think of the organization as being entirely anonymous and mail-based. AARP is a large interest group and a large volunteer group. In these ways, it confounds decades of scholarship about what distinguishes interest groups, civic organizations, and other forms of personal and community association.

So, alongside the new forms of collective action, which emphasize social networks, organization-less organizing, and the social production of public goods facilitated by digital media, traditional organizations are enduring and innovating and are breaking scholars' rules. They are doing things that challenge how social scientists have traditionally understood what membership is, why people participate in groups, and what drives collective action inside formal structures. They are challenging how researchers classify organizations and draw inferences from those classifications about the consequences of people's participation. These developments raise the central question for this book: how do people experience collective action within formal organizations in the contemporary media environment?

Amidst the explosion in informal groups and self-organized collective action facilitated by digital media, in this book we will inquire about the experiences of people who participate in formal organizations of various kinds. We are primarily interested in technology as part of the environment in which people belong to organizations rather than in the specifics of which media tools are offered by which organizations, or how various tools are used in specific campaigns or episodes of organizing. This means we will not focus on decisions to use one or another technology by collective action organizations or examine how people use any particular technological tools that might be available to them. Instead, our interest is in situating people's experience of collective action guided by organizations in an environment in which high-profile alternatives to reliance on formal organizations exist. We will therefore focus on the core behavioral, attitudinal, and perceptual dimensions of individuals' relation to collective action.

A number of reasons exist as to why we will avoid an effort to undertake an exhaustive inventory of the specific uses of technologies in organizations. In a time of rapid technological change, any one tool is likely to be supplanted or modified by new ones in the space of a few years. Most careful observers of technology address that problem in one way or another, often quite successfully. But more importantly, people's experience of using media in connection with collective action goes well beyond the affordances and tools that any one organization makes available strategically. A person may follow a link from AARP's Web site to Twitter, yet they may also receive from a friend a "retweet" that originated at AARP. A person may watch a video while visiting MoveOn's Web site, or find that same video while searching the Web. Someone may read about The American Legion's latest advocacy effort at its Web site or be exposed to it through an independent blog that they follow, glean it from reading the daily news, or because a Facebook friend "likes" that effort. The technological routes to any one organization and its activities are many and changing.

A similar problem plagues efforts to use surveys in an effort to catalog how often people make use of specific technological tools in order to look for associations with behaviors. The number of ways that people use mobile technologies, social media, e-mail, the traditional Web, and audio and video are so many, so flexible, so integrated, and so ubiquitous that it is increasingly intractable to make thorough and fine-grained measurements of these common activities in the hope of finding out which ones are associated with collective action or civic engagement (Bimber and Copeland, 2011). Although we report in this book on some measurements of our own in that tradition, it is not our primary purpose to take a variable-analytic approach to technology use – to conceptualize digital media as tools whose differential use across people tells the important part of the story. We are more interested in digital media for having changed the environment for collective action by enhancing choice and providing alternatives to formal organization – by creating the context in which collective action happens in formal organizations. A similar conclusion about technology and collective action was voiced in the *American Prospect* by writer Nancy Scola, commenting on a debate about whether the ouster of Tunisian President Ben Ali constituted a "social-media revolution." She rejected the question of whether the revolt would have happened without the Internet as being wrongly framed. Scola quotes at length from the blog of *Foreign Policy*'s Evgeny Morozov, "Clearly, the Internet doesn't make the dissident. Rather, the dissident makes use of the Internet. What's happening in Tunisia isn't a Twitter or a WikiLeaks revolution. It's just what revolution looks like these days" (Scola, 2011, n.p.). Our objective in this book is to consider people who have chosen to affiliate with a formal organization in order to achieve their collective goals in a time when viable alternatives to formal membership exist and then to understand how they experience that affiliation.

Our argument about organizations and individuals will be a somewhat subtle one but with potentially far-reaching implications. We are convinced that formal organizations still matter and always will, despite people's ability to organize without them. Formal organizations remain an important part of the collective action landscape, and they have been largely overlooked in the literature on digital media in civic and political life. One goal of this book is to bring formal organizations into that literature on digital media.

At the same time, we believe organizations matter less than they once did, because people enjoy more agency that can shape their experiences of collective action and of the organizations. This agency arises from the structure and ubiquity of the media – from the ways these break down boundaries and create choices. When the classic collective action literature was formulated, organizational structure and resources were key, and members in many ways were reduced to simply fulfilling roles created for them by elites. In the most extreme caricatures found in some theories, citizens were interchangeable parts, differentiated only by rough demographic characteristics, location, ideology, level of identification, and issue interests – and perhaps not even by these. This raises another goal of this book: making organizational differences less exclusively the centerpiece of collective action by providing a greater appreciation of individuals and individual differences in collective action endeavors that are nonetheless sponsored by organizations.

The Three Organizations: The American Legion, AARP, and MoveOn

To accomplish these goals, this book considers the members of three quintessential organizations that are thriving in the context of digital media. These organizations are large and well-known, and in classical theoretical terms they are very different: The American Legion, AARP, and MoveOn. All three began during the twentieth century, neatly founded roughly a half-century apart: one in the Progressive Era during the dominance of newspapers, one midcentury as broadcasting was ascendant, and one in the late 1990s as an Internet-based organization. They grew up in dissimilar sociotechnical milieus, with radically different organizational designs and structures. Their memberships were constrained by different types of criteria, and the roles of members were conceived in vitally different ways. How their members experience these organizations today, in the contemporary media environment, is the focus of our attention.

The American Legion was created in 1919 by four U.S. Army officers and is a nonpartisan, not-for-profit organization dedicated to improving the lives of American veterans. Membership in The American Legion is restricted to those who actively served in the American military during specific periods of conflict. From its inception, however, The American Legion has sought to be an advocate for all American veterans' rights, provide tangible benefits to its membership base and their families, and become embedded in the social life of local communities, states, and the nation. Its first major success came in 1921 when the U.S. Veterans Bureau, forerunner of the Veterans Administration, was established as a direct result of the Legion's advocacy. The Legion exemplifies social-capital building organizations, rooted in locality and physical infrastructure but also with a national issue agenda and activities directed at national policy. Local posts are at the center of many veterans' social lives, organizing a great deal of community volunteer work and sponsoring a vast array of educational activities, oratorical contests, baseball leagues, and other activities. The American Legion is, for us, a thoroughly civic organization operating today in radically different circumstances than when it was established.

AARP, founded in 1958 by retired high school principal Ethel Percy Andrus, evolved from the National Retired Teachers Association, whose mission was to improve the health benefits and insurance availability for people older than sixty-five. In 1999, AARP stopped using the full name "American Association of Retired Persons" and now has only the former acronym as a name, in order to deemphasize "retirement" and reflect the changing choices and lifestyles of its expanded constituency, now anyone at least fifty years old. AARP aims to enhance the quality of life throughout the aging process by providing information, advocacy, and many services and special products, including health insurance and consumer discounts. Whereas The American Legion recruits veterans on the basis of a powerful common experience and maintains organizational affiliation with regularized personal engagement in local posts, AARP enrolls members and encourages continuing membership on the basis of broader interests and needs arising from one shared demographic: age. Typically within six months of Americans' fiftieth birthdays, they receive an unsolicited AARP application, accompanied by a list of material incentives for joining. This large-scale, impersonal mode of member solicitation reflects what has traditionally been the approach toward engagement of many large professionally managed advocacy organizations. In our story, AARP embodies the dynamics of the classic interest group, in which members do not see one another or interact and whose role historically has been simply to pay dues and then respond to exhortations to action by leaders. We will see how poorly that description characterizes the experiences of many members of AARP today.

MoveOn is the youngest of the three organizations we will consider in this book, having been founded in the late 1990s as an advocacy project by two software entrepreneurs to petition Congress during the Clinton impeachment and trial. The founders, Wes Boyd and Joan Blades, wrote to acquaintances by e-mail, urging them to contact Congress and encourage legislators to abandon the impeachment effort and move on to other concerns. They created a "MoveOn" Web site on which people could communicate their feelings to legislators and that, unlike most online petitions of the day, allowed Boyd and Blades to capture the e-mail addresses of participants. The effort caught fire politically among opponents of the impeachment and resulted in a large flood of e-mail to Congress that is variously estimated at 400,000 (Rohlinger and Brown, 2009) to 450,000 (Clausing, 1999) messages.

Today, MoveOn is comprised of a nonprofit advocacy organization working on progressive causes and campaigns of all kinds, as well as one of the largest political action committees in the country. Unlike the other two organizations in our study, membership is neither based on a demographic criterion nor an experiential one; anyone who agrees with MoveOn's position on a particular topic may join. Not only are there no membership criteria, but also there is no membership fee. One joins just by signing up electronically, and one belongs by virtue of being on its mailing list, which means that a "member" may be dedicated enough to host house parties and organize neighbors, or may only have signed up to receive e-mail. Variability in members' level of involvement is endemic to all organizations, regardless of their particular communication practices, and MoveOn is no different. MoveOn reports about five million members, which makes it the second-largest interest group in the United States, after AARP and somewhat ahead of The American Legion's 2.5 million. The election campaign of 2008 was an important moment in MoveOn history. As a result of its aggressive efforts on behalf of Barack Obama and other Democratic candidates, MoveOn added about two million members that year, diversifying its membership in a variety of ways. Among online interest groups, MoveOn has become a venerable and even traditional "old" organization, being more than a decade in age.

In examining these three organizations, our primary focus is on the perceptions, attitudes, and behaviors of their members, within an environment in which individuals have much greater autonomy and prospects to shape their organizational experience than ever before. It will not be our mission to describe the history of these organizations, their successes and failures, or their strategies and tactics. Other sources are available for that. We are interested in how people experience them.

For example, despite the traditionally impersonal nature of large interest groups, AARP members have opportunities to build personal profiles, share photos, and develop relationships with others – whom they may have never met face to face – through AARP's Web site. This means that the potential exists for social involvement and even social-capital building inside this quintessential interest group. This raises many interesting questions about AARP: What fraction of its members actually interacts personally with others? How many engage the organization, and with what impact on their relation to it? How many participate in calls for action, and what characteristics are associated with that kind of participation? Do those who use digital media more also participate more? What about identification – how does technology use affect people's group identity, if at all? The same questions arise for The American Legion and MoveOn. At The American Legion's Web site, members have the opportunity to follow national issues, voice their opinions in polls related to veteran issues, comment upon others' reactions, and interact with other veterans outside the local post structure. MoveOn's Web site provides the opportunity to participate in agenda setting for the organization and for members to join local councils in order to organize in their community.

In this manner, through various affordances of technology all three organizations offer their members some similar kinds of membership experiences by using menus of options for people to interact with one another and to engage with the organization. These menus look remarkably similar, despite the classic differences among The American Legion, AARP, and MoveOn. This fact suggests the possibility of a good deal of organizational similarity, despite formal differences. In addition, each of these organizations operates in a contemporary environment in which citizens are increasingly accustomed to high degrees of agency and individualism as they navigate civil society and the public sphere. Exploring what this means in terms of members' involvement with the organizations in our study provides much of the impetus for this book.

Individuals in Organizations: Interacting and Engaging

Understanding how the use of technology makes formal organizations relevant but also elevates individual-level differences within them requires a theoretical perspective that considers the role of formal organizations and individuals' experiences, against the backdrop of the contemporary digital-media environment. Our approach to this task is somewhat different from many perspectives on digital media and behavior, especially those that model relationships between how frequently people use e-mail or specific social media tools and how engaged they are civically or politically, or those that look specifically at the technologies that organizations offer for their members to engage with them. In such studies, which we as authors have contributed to previously, the assumption often is that variation in people's frequency or intensity of use of various affordances of digital media is predictive of certain behaviors, often in ways that are mediated by interest, knowledge, or other attributes.

Though we will look for such relationships in this book, these will not be our primary approach to technology. Instead, we will be chiefly interested in digital technologies as context. Technological context, we argue, provides an atmosphere for collective action today that is nearly ubiquitous for almost all organizations, groups, and individuals, regardless of how many hours any individual spends online, which specific affordances they use, or how adept any one organization is at adapting to the new environment. Whether any one person is online ten hours a day, once a month, or not at all, what organizations do today in organizing collective action is powerfully shaped by the digital-media environment, which among other things provides people many alternatives to formal organizations for collective action as well as other forms of association.

What is it about technological context that matters most? Some work has emphasized reduced costs of information and communication, which can alter the calculations that rational citizens might make about taking actions. This has been an enormously powerful, though simple, idea and has shaped a great deal of thinking and interpretation of the information revolution. In some ways, this forms a second stage of the rational choice revolution in the social sciences. The first was the assertion in the 1970s and onward that behavior might be modeled in terms of discrete choices about costs and benefits, where information was virtually always costly. The second stage, beginning in the 2000s, was the empirical realization that information can actually be essentially free and universal – a very disruptive notion for the original idea. Other scholars interpreting technological context have emphasized increased choice, rather than costs. Choice sounds attractive democratically, but perhaps as much research has identified its ills as its benefits: choice can lead to self-selection and polarization, decreased coherence of the public sphere, and increasing knowledge gaps (see, e.g., Prior, 2007 and Sunstein, 2009). These are important features of the contemporary media environment, but they are incomplete as a portrait also. Another vast body of work interpreting technological context has focused on decentralization of information and communication and the supplanting of hierarchy with networks. No doubt exists that horizontal interaction and network structures are increasingly a central feature of civic life, yet as we have suggested in the preceding text, organization and hierarchy are hardly dead. One of the most interesting features of a world filled with opportunities for network structures and horizontal interaction is what kind of practices people bring to their memberships in formal organizations, even as these organizations become players in networks of action.

In our own prior work, we have examined relationships of communication and information flows to institutional structures linking citizens to government, how people think about information, and how global collaborative processes are expanding across organizational sectors. All of these are relevant features of the technological context for human enterprise today. In the present work, our focus is on a different aspect of the media context: how the digital-media environment facilitates transactions at the level of individuals, and what this implies for how members perceive their ability to shape their own relationships with individuals inside organizations, as well as with the organizations. In the case of collective action, organizational leaders previously determined the nature of membership and opportunity. However, because digital media were designed and structured differently from broadcast media, and are significantly more available to individuals, they can significantly alter many aspects of human enterprise, including collective action processes. The chief design difference with digital media today is that they place power and agency at the ends of networks, in the hands of individuals, rather than in central locations like the leaders of formal organizations (Flanagin, Flanagin, and Flanagin, 2010).

We are interested specifically in how an environment with widespread end-to-end interaction and engagement, characterized by information processing and decision making that resides in network members rather than exclusively in central organizational leadership, breaks down boundaries among the members of our three organizations, and what this means for their involvement in the organizations of which they are members. By increasing the potential agency of individuals with respect to formal organizations, other members, and collective action processes, the presence of digital media breaks down boundaries previously established and maintained by organizations. This means that membership and participation in collective action can more than ever be communicatively constructed by individuals, rather than determined by the organization. We expect to find that, to some degree, people behave inside organizations like they do in informal networks, establishing personal ties of varying degrees of intensity and, in some cases, working to shape the direction of the collectivity. How often they do these things and how this shapes their relationship to the organization are among the questions we seek to answer.

The argument of this book is that people's contributions toward the construction of membership are found along two key dimensions of belonging. The first of these is interaction with other members. We argue that an important way that agency manifests itself is through people's capacity to interact personally with others in organizations of all kinds. This can be achieved with the aid of new technologies of communication or, more traditionally, through face-to-face meetings, social gatherings, and groups. To be sure, not all members of all organizations use digital media to build or form social networks among other members or to establish lasting personal relationships. This is certainly true of the organizations we focus on here. But some members do. The fact that some people may choose to do so while others do not gives rise to variation in the kind of experiences people have in organizations. This within-group variation in how people experience human interaction inside formal organizations is a central feature of our analysis. Digital-media use does not mean that everyone becomes an activist, despite the hopes of civic and political organizers of all stripes. Digital-media use does, however, signal a great deal of potential variation in what people can do, and therefore a greater role for choice, interest, and motivation. We suspect that the people inside organizations have always been more varied and diverse in their experiences than scholars have typically given them credit for.

The second dimension of belonging highlighted by the digital-media context is what we call engagement with the organization. This engagement is comprised of the ways that people are able to learn about the organization, its goals, and its successes or failures, and the opportunities for people to play a role in shaping what the organization does. Weak boundaries and high individual agency mean that, in many organizations, those people who are inclined toward entrepreneurialism can find ways to shape the experiences of others and influence the organization. Some are likely even to bring an expectation of networked entrepreneurialism with them from the rest of their experiences in the digitally connected society. For a classic civic association such as The American Legion, this is hardly new. For a direct-mail–based interest group like AARP, this is potentially revolutionary. Not all members of groups will take advantage of an altered environment of heightened member input generally, or digital media specifically, to become entrepreneurs within their organizations. But again, some will, while others will remain passive recipients of information and requests for activity driven entirely by their organization. This variation is important and is a key focus of our analysis.

These possibilities constitute one of our major themes. In the digital-media environment, individual agency and variation among people matters a great deal, and it deserves as much theoretical and empirical attention as has been given in the past to organizational-level characteristics and variation. Typically scholars have lavished elaborate analyses on structural and strategic differences among organizations involved in public life, classifying them as to their resources, internal structures and decision-making processes, and type – for example, interest group, civic association, social movement organization, and online organization – with little regard to the individual members' actual experiences within the organization.

Homogenization of members' experiences based on organizational structures is implicit in many traditional organizational analyses. Just as organizational structures were often defined in "either/or" terms – mechanistic versus organic, decentralized or centralized, specialized versus undifferentiated, loosely coupled or tightly coupled – individuals' experiences were expected to be similar within these constraints. Early on in the study of organizations, for example, Michels (1915) suggested that voluntary organizations are susceptible to nondemocratic tendencies ("the iron law of oligarchy") because the ruling elites or leaders curtail democracy in an attempt to consolidate power. The familiar argument is that, as organizational size and complexity increase, bureaucracy is developed to control the group and minimize threats to that control and identity. Working within bureaucracies requires detailed operational and political knowledge only available to a few organizational insiders; hence, in the traditional view, bureaucratic structures make effective involvement or even opposition from large numbers of members less likely. The communicative experience of most members is similarly structured and similarly experienced. Gamson and Schmeidler (1984) and Zald and McCarthy (1987) more recently suggested that the emergence of oligarchic structures may result in disengagement of members as their opportunities for meaningful participation become more bounded and limited.

In the case of voluntary organizations, Skocpol, Cobb, and Klofstad (2005) identify parallel processes at the macrolevel. She and her colleagues have traced the historical decline of popular membership-driven associations and the contemporary rise of professionally managed advocacy and nonprofit institutions. In general, literature about membership organizations suggests that members become less active over time and are usually content to leave the running of the organization to a minority of the members or managerial staff.

Across scholarly perspectives, the focus on organizational differences and features has often reduced the diverse memberships of organizations like The American Legion, AARP, and MoveOn down into statistical means. Large and often quite diverse memberships are too often characterized by their members' average age, ideology, education, or political interest rather than by the members' particular experiences of the organization. This emphasis on organizational-level analysis at the expense of individual-level dynamics was probably never adequate analytically in the history of scholarship on collective action, but the heightened level of agency and diminished boundaries implied by the contemporary media environment likely make it quite insufficient today, as people bring into organizations expectations and practices developed in the new freewheeling context for interaction and engagement outside organizations. As technology use changes expectations and weakens various boundaries, individuals are better able to negotiate them on their own terms and to shape their experiences of organizations to a substantial degree. This does not imply that all people will make the same choices about which boundaries to cross or how to situate themselves in organizational contexts that are more flexible. Rather, it implies a continual negotiation of boundaries in different ways as various members act on their own styles and preferences, rather than being so tightly constrained by those of the organization.

To focus on technology as context and on how it locates power at edges and ends of networks rather than at centers suggests that it will not be of much concern, in our perspective, whether members of the groups we examine are using YouTube or Twitter, connect from work or home, or connect through a smart phone. Thus we largely bypass measuring the technological features employed by organizations to capture their members' input in favor of measuring the ways in which they experience the organizations to which they have chosen to belong. What will matter in our account is that the flow of almost all innovation in digital media at present is in the same direction, as power is shifted from centers to ends; and when those ends are in the hands and minds of citizens, important things happen. For Castells (2009), it is that autonomy increases. For Barabasi (2002), Buchanan (2002), and other network scholars, small-world architecture is producing a new global world order. For us as behavioral social scientists, it is that the varying attributes of individuals take on much more significance to involvement in collective action efforts, while the specific attributes of organizations and other elites are less determinative. We expect this to be true even across organizations as different as ours, which we chose precisely because they represent "most-different" kinds of cases.

Explaining Collective Action in The American Legion, AARP, and MoveOn

Three organizations in public life that appear more different could scarcely be found than those we selected to study. From their original missions and structures to their contemporary positions and activities, each organization has a distinct and iconic identity in the landscape of American membership organizations.

The American Legion

The American Legion is nonpartisan and not affiliated with any political party but is generally perceived as conservative in orientation. It defines its mission around "Four Pillars": Americanism, children and youth, national security and foreign relations, and veterans' affairs and rehabilitation. Community service is central to the Legion's mission and is integral to its pursuit of each goal. It has a distinctive organizational structure for managing its 2.5 million members. Like many large U.S. membership organizations founded before 1940, the Legion adopted a federated structure in which three tiers (federal, state, and local) reflect the institutional structuring of the U.S. government (Skocpol, Ganz, and Munson, 2000). Headquartered in Indianapolis, Indiana, and Washington, D.C., the Legion is divided into fifty-five "departments" – one for each state, along with the District of Columbia, Puerto Rico, France, Mexico, and the Philippines. Most importantly for the traditional experience of membership, it has about fourteen thousand local chapters called Legion posts, the primary physical meeting place for social interaction among members. Posts are found in every state and in more than two dozen foreign countries.

The Legion has well-articulated, permanent administrative structures and formalized and clearly defined organizational roles. In addition to tens of thousands of volunteers serving in leadership and program implementation capacities in local communities, and dozens of standing national commissions and committees, the national organization has a regular full-time staff of about three hundred employees led by the national adjutant, the administrative head of the organization. The national adjutant supervises the national headquarters staff and is charged in the organization's by-laws with administration of the policies and mandates of the National Convention, the National Executive Committee, and the national commander.

As well as the national adjutant, there is a layer of officials roughly following a corporate model, often with military titles: the national commander (CEO) and five vice commanders, a treasurer, judge advocate, historian, chaplain, and paid staff, along with the many volunteers. The officers are elected or appointed for an annual term and in some cases can be reelected or reappointed. They attend an annual national convention that is typically attended by about ten thousand members and operates as the official governing body of The American Legion. This structure is constitutionally mandated to assure that The American Legion is a community-based, membership-driven organization.

The American Legion is congressionally chartered, and its basic purposes are defined by law.[2] It uses a well-structured process for making decisions. Proposals for national policy changes and position-driven initiatives begin with a member or members at the post level. If proposals are a local matter they can be passed at a local post meeting. If it is a topic that could end up shaping national Legion policy, the proposal is addressed at the National Convention or a National Executive Committee meeting. The resolution process follows the same cycle as Congress, and even-numbered years tend to have more resolutions because of the legislative cycle. What this means is that The American Legion is deeply rooted as a civic group in localities around the nation but also has highly articulated mechanisms for translating local concerns into national policies or decisions.

AARP

The story of AARP's structure and mission is quite different. It is also nonpartisan and does not affiliate with any political party. Its orientation is typically seen by outside observers as moderately liberal. It is historically a defender of Social Security and Medicare, as a reflection of the personal interests of its members, rather than from ideological positions about social policy, and it is widely regarded as one of the most powerful lobbies in Washington. AARP's most prominent position in years was its 2010 decision to endorse the health-care reform proposal of the Obama administration.

The CEO of AARP occupies a powerful position at the head of a twelve-member executive team reporting to a twenty-two-member

[2] "Patriotic and National Observances, Ceremonies, and Organizations." Title 36, U.S. Code, ch. 217.

volunteer board of directors that approves all policies, programs, activities, and services for the association. AARP had revenues of about 1.4 billion in 2010, and a large staff, most of whom work from an enormous headquarters in Washington, D.C., that occupies more than a city block (AARP, 2009). AARP offices are in every state, as well as the District of Columbia, the Virgin Islands, and Puerto Rico. State-level offices are designed to support volunteer and community service opportunities and to identify areas of AARP's legislative concern. AARP also has about 2,500 local chapters designed to engage members in community activities. One estimate from 1999 was that about 5 to 10 percent of members participate in the local chapters (Skocpol and Fiorina, 1999).

This is a considerable number in absolute terms given AARP's size, making it a very large community organization. However, local chapters do not serve as meeting places in the way that American Legion posts do, nor are they the point of entry for the organization in the way that posts are. In the Legion, all members join a post, becoming part of the civic organization, and those who choose become involved in issues of national scope. At AARP the process is reversed: all members join the national organization through direct mail or online enrollment, and those who choose become engaged in local chapters – and now, more recently, in various online forums and meeting places. Within AARP, the local and state chapter system does not provide mechanisms like the Legion's for advancing policy proposals formally upward from members to the leadership. Like almost all interest groups, AARP's leaders traditionally have made strategic decisions at the top of the organization, in light of members' positions, and then attempted to persuade the membership to support their lobbying. Campbell and Skocpol (2003) write that AARP lacks the structure to canvass opinion at the state and local level and channel it upward, which gives the leadership in Washington great autonomy and capacity to focus on opportunities for persuasion with public officials.

MoveOn

Like AARP and The American Legion, MoveOn is not affiliated with a political party, but its politics are quite unmistakable. It advocates exclusively on behalf of progressive candidates and issues, and it has a very broad agenda from environmental issues to immigration and health care. It is structured like neither of our other organizations and is like no other organization its size. Two key characteristics define MoveOn structurally. The first is its lean and minimalist infrastructure. With more than twice as many members as The American Legion, it has only about two dozen national staff, along with about a dozen field organizers who work with its volunteers. All MoveOn staff work remotely rather than in a headquarters or central office inside the Washington, D.C., beltway, so staff, volunteers, and regular members are spread around the country. MoveOn adheres to the philosophy of cofounder Wes Boyd that if not all employees can be in one place, none should share office space, in order to minimize the formation of cliques or internal alliances. Whereas the AARP headquarters on K Street would be suitable as the embassy of a major power, it is not possible for a citizen, reporter, or public official to visit the offices of MoveOn. In this way, MoveOn's internal operations are as Internet dependent as its relationship with its members. Its decision making is collaborative, under Executive Director Justin Ruben and a three-member board, and it moves with the speed one would expect of a small group.

MoveOn's second characteristic is its sophisticated strategy in conceptualizing its members and communicating with them. Because its messages to members are all distributed online, MoveOn is able to track which members respond to which messages and who takes which kinds of action. Its membership list is large enough that it can conduct many experiments with variations on message framing and targeting for a particular communication campaign, so that final messages that go out in bulk have often been vetted through subsamples and tests. It uses a similar approach to its political advertising by test marketing ads in local or regional markets before airing them more broadly (Karpf, 2009). It is also able to move with great rapidity, e-mailing members to ask them to make a phone call on a policy issue "today" or to respond in some other way to breaking news. For instance, in August 2009, Representative Joe Wilson broke tradition and decorum in the U.S. House chamber by shouting "You lie" at President Obama during his speech on health-care reform. The next morning, MoveOn distributed a message to members inviting people to donate to Wilson's likely opponent in the 2010 midterm elections. When Obama nominated Sonia Sotomayor for the Supreme Court, also in 2009, MoveOn e-mailed members the same day with a list of ten supportive facts about the judge, asking members to forward the list to ten friends "today." These are standard MoveOn rapid-response efforts aimed at organizing collective action as events unfold. By tracking the results of many efforts such as these, MoveOn has developed an understanding of subgroups of its membership that is probably unrivaled by any other large interest group.

Because of these very sharp differences in the structures of these organizations and the common and wide-ranging possibilities for member interaction and engagement embedded in the contemporary media environment, it is very instructive to look at interaction among members in each, as well as how members engage with the organizations. When we do so in later chapters, we will see that how people choose to interact and engage says a great deal about collective action, while which organization a person belongs to is considerably less important than one might expect. We will interpret this to mean that scholars should be more interested in understanding interaction and engagement within collective action organizations than with classifying them and scrutinizing their objective structure. We expect that the results of this most-different set of cases will be relevant to other cases, especially because we are concerned greatly with across-group and within-group differences. In a variety of ways, however, these three organizations do not and cannot "represent" other cases literally. We will return to this fact in the final chapter.

The Organizational Context for Collective Action

A great deal of behavioral social science that seeks to explain who participates civically or politically has taken membership in organizations such as these to be an outcome. In that view, to join an interest group is to participate: it is an expressive act, typically provides financial resources to the organization, constitutes a small act of standing up and being counted, and authorizes the organization to speak on behalf of the member. In these terms, to join a group that works toward goals in which one believes is to overcome the incentive to free ride on the actions of other joiners. Although we do not disagree with this way of thinking about membership as an outcome, in this project we emphasize what happens next. We view joining one of our three organizations as part of the context for collective action and the expression of procollective attitudes, rather than as an outcome.

Straightforward reasons for this emphasis exist. One is the Tocquevillian observation that most Americans are involved in various kinds of association or membership. An estimate using World Values Survey data shows that Americans averaged 1.98 voluntary association memberships per person in 1993, which is about twice the global mean (Curtis, Baer, and Grabb, 2001). To us, this makes the traditional question of explaining membership in groups rather less compelling in the United States than in nations in which many people belong to none, which is the case in developing nations as well as in places in southern Europe, for instance.

Even accounting for some overlap among them, the memberships of our three groups together outnumber the population of any state in the United States and many nations around the world. Rather than being concerned with who has joined and who has not, we want to know what happens after people have joined. Another reason for this emphasis is that we are concerned with people's direct engagement in political and civic affairs through their organizations – with their own actions to express views, make demands, and become involved – and with how they identify and trust political elites. This makes us less interested in passive membership that funds professional lobbying than with membership that leads to further action.

In pursuing this, we will devote little attention to traditional objects of study by scholars of organization: internal structures, strategic choices, and resources. Interesting stories could be told about these aspects of each of our organizations, but we set those aside to shine our spotlight instead on the dynamics of members, who have often been left in the empirical dark in organization-centric scholarship. The analysis will show that the three organizations look much different from the perspective of their memberships than one might expect.

Outcomes: Involvement in Collective Action

In this book, studying collective action will mean studying three things. The first is participation. We will inquire about who free rides on others' contributions and who is active in calls for letter writing, petition signing, or other formal actions on behalf of the organization. This first outcome therefore is behavioral: who contributes to the collective goals and activities of the organization? In answering this question, we will want to see what factors predict participation in The American Legion, AARP, and MoveOn and how these might vary within as well as across the organizations. We expect to find that within-group variation is quite high compared to across-group variation, despite the differences in objective structure and purpose of these groups.

The other two collective action outcomes of interest to us are attitudinal. We will be interested in matters of trust in the organization and in organizational identification. We want to know how trusting people are of the three organizations for several reasons. Organizational trust is an attitude rooted in people's communicative experiences. At the organizational level, trust can be conceived as a collective commitment to cooperate in order to achieve organizational goals (Puusa and Tolvanen,

2006). At the individual level, organizational trust means that people expect their organization's future actions to benefit them or at least not to harm them. Where trust is present in greater supply, people are thought to be more likely to act in concert, according to a wide range of scholarship. It is especially interesting to consider how trust may work for people who have chosen to participate in formal collective action organizations, in a time when so many alternatives to formal organizations are available.

Identification is related but is new to the study of collective action. As conceptualized by scholars like Simon (1976) and Kaufman (1960), organizational identification is a relational construct formed in interaction with others through a process of ordered comparisons and reflections. Consistently linked theoretically and empirically to decision making, persuasion, and compliance, organizational identification guides members to see issues in particular ways and to evaluate options in terms of the consequences for themselves and the organization. One of the attributes of formal organizations that differentiates them from informal networks, single-event actions, flash mobs, Twitter protests, and other organizationless instances of organizing is that organizations provide a durable brand, an object for the potential development of sustained trust and identification by members and participants.

When one conceptualizes collective action this way, rather than in the more atomistic approach in which multiple organizations in effect compete with each other to mobilize individuals to join or to do something together, it becomes clear that collective action entails more than just participating at least once in some effort. It requires more than a series of one-time calculations of whether to contribute or free ride. It entails the development of positive cognitive and affective orientations toward the individual-organization relationship. Such orientations promote and sustain relationships and future behavior on behalf of the organization. So in addition to inquiring about who participates, we want to know how these two key attitudes work across our organizations. For example, do its members trust MoveOn, the relatively new online organization, as much as Legion members trust their venerable organization? Who develops the strongest identification with their groups? We will refer to contributions to collective goals and activities, trust in the organization, and organizational identification together as *involvement* in collective action. By focusing broadly on these three components of involvement, we will emphasize how there is more to organizational collective action than simply a series of choices to participate.

As we explore involvement in collective action in this book, our analysis will take place at the individual level but within the context of our three organizations. Our data come from surveys that we conducted of their memberships. We worked with leaders of each organization to obtain the information necessary to conduct probability samples of members, using telephone surveys and e-mail invitations to an electronic survey. We collected a total of about five thousand survey responses across the three organizations, and these allowed us to analyze and compare the memberships of each in some statistical detail. The core empirical part of this book involves the analysis of these survey data. We also spoke with officials in each of the organizations in order to ask them about their organizations, membership, involvement, technological context, and visions for the future.

Contributors to Involvement: Technology, Motivation, and Goals

The theory we develop in the following chapters leads us to look for several factors that may shape who contributes to, identifies with, and trusts in their organizations. We examine people's use of technology, and a striking pattern emerges. For the most part, across the Legion, AARP, and MoveOn, how intensively people use digital media in general has little relationship to their participation in these groups and even less to how well they trust and identify with them. We take this as an indicator that technology is in part context; it is background. To conceptualize technology as context is to say that the presence of technology in people's lives affects what options are available to them, what they do, or how they experience the world around them, regardless of whether they use particular tools a great deal or a little. Whether a person is an experienced "power user" of the Internet or someone who dabbles online infrequently, the Internet has affected the context of civic and public life. A person who is not often online may not receive a particular message directly from AARP but may hear about it from their neighbors or friends at church. The agenda of the organization may be shaped by the presence of digital media, just as the agenda of news organizations is influenced greatly by the twenty-four-hour news cycle and the interplay between the blogosphere and traditional news businesses. Even the offline person who avoids the Internet entirely is likely to receive old-fashioned direct mail from their organization that is shaped powerfully by the ability of the organization to target messages to individuals – an ability arising from technology.

Technology matters indirectly to the individual, in these and other ways, by creating an environment that is information rich and communicatively intensive.

We will also consider concepts relatively new to the empirical study of collective action: motivations and goals for belonging. Human motivation is tightly coupled to action. However, for the most part scholars of collective action and related topics such as civic engagement do not attempt to measure it. Though a number of adjacent concepts are often measured and employed, such as interest, motivations are generally not analyzed or are simply assumed. We are interested in three possible motivations for belonging to a collective action organization. The first of these is instrumental. As economic theories of collective action suggest, some people join organizations because they expect some direct return – information and news that they care about or discounts and financial perquisites of belonging. Among our organizations, AARP is well-known for its extensive array of financial incentives for membership; MoveOn offers no such material gain but may attract people seeking its aggressive channel of information about breaking political developments.

A second and different motivation for belonging is social. It is quite plausible that some people belong to each of our organizations because they seek social interaction with others, such as the opportunity to work together or socialize with like-minded others. These people are likely to join and remain a member because of the social and civic context it provides for them to act socially and express themselves. This is very different from belonging because of material or informational benefits. This motivation has, in our view, been given short shrift in scholarship on interest groups, though it has played a more prominent role in research on civic associations.

A third motivation for belonging is because people wish to be represented by the organization about issues that matter to them. All three of our organizations advocate for issues of various kinds. Despite the prediction of traditional collective action theory that incentives for being represented by an organization are not sufficient to overcome the temptation of free riding, we expect that at least some people belong because they expect their organization can influence politics or society in ways that they seek.

The situation is similar for goals, our second concept. From its inception, collective action theory has in some ways been a theory of goals, a theory of people acting collectively in pursuit of common objectives. Yet it is almost unheard of in quantitative models of collective action for researchers to actually measure goals, because these vary so greatly from person to person. It is typically not feasible to measure the various weights that people attach to social order versus liberties, environmental protection and health care, immigration and tax reform, fixing potholes, and reducing federal debt. Moreover, agenda-setting effects mean that people's civic goals across such values at any one time may to a degree reflect the elite messages to which they have been recently exposed, rather than enduring and stable underlying priorities. Again our analysis at the level of the individual in an organization allows us to skirt some of these problems by examining how well people perceive that their own goals – whatever those are – align with those of their organization. We expect to find that, for many people, the various components of involvement will be associated with how closely they perceive their organization's goals to correspond with their own.

Participatory Styles

When people in organizations are conceptualized in these terms, rather than simply as bundles of socioeconomic characteristics that are invariant across each person's various memberships and affiliations, it becomes clear that goals, motivations, and other factors are unlikely to work the same way for all people. A one-size-fits-all model, in which each of these is of equal importance for everyone, is hardly appropriate. Everyone knows some people who are more goal-driven and some who are more social. Some people care more about process and some care about outcomes. A theory of collective action in organizational contexts should account for variation in this way, rather than assuming a single model applies to all people. Making this problem tractable requires a theoretical starting point that provides reasonable a priori expectations about what might differentiate groups of people within an organization in a systematic way. In the following chapters, we draw on several literatures to observe the repeated appearance of two crucial dimensions of the collective action experience. We use these as the theoretical starting point to look for empirical evidence about how goals, motivations, and other characteristics may work differently for different people. Our approach is therefore theoretically driven and empirically exploratory.

Our first theoretical dimension, interaction, involves the level of personal interaction that members of the organizations have with one another. The extent to which people interact personally with each other is a concept that appears time and again in the social sciences across many contexts. For our purposes, it is a crucial feature of the experience of collective action, and we expect it to have considerable bearing on differences in people's involvement in their organizations – though just what those look like in our three organizations must await the analysis of data. The second dimension is engagement, which involves how much people perceive that they are able to shape the agenda and direction of their organization. This concept captures ideas from several strands of thought about organizations: hierarchy, centralization and decentralization, and size. It separates, to a degree, people who might be thought of as active members from those who might be considered passive, but it focuses this distinction not on interaction with others but on people's orientation toward the organization.

In our previous writing, we have advanced the idea of interaction and engagement as orthogonal concepts that form the two-dimensional collective action space (Flanagin, Stohl, and Bimber, 2006). In this book we develop that idea further, and then use our survey data to place the members of The American Legion, AARP, and MoveOn in this space. We use the Collective Action Space framework to classify people across the organizations, and then see how goals, motivation, and other characteristics are associated differently with collective action as a function of their location. For some people, it matters less to their involvement that their goals are aligned with their organization, while for others this matters more. For some people, participation in other civic or community groups carries over into their involvement in our three organizations, while for others their activities within the Legion, AARP, and MoveOn are insulated from the rest of their civic life. Some people exhibit the classic relationship in which age and education predict participation, but some do not. These differences, and others, are a function of their location in collective action space. This is to say that these differences are connected to people's choices about interaction and engagement and, to a large degree, are unrelated to the organization in which they are members. We refer to patterns in these relationships as *participatory styles*.

The existence of differing participatory styles in the three organizations has implications for several bodies of thought. One of the central precepts of collective action theory is that collective action typically entails formal organizations, which are viewed as a chief mechanism for overcoming the problem of free riding (Olson, 1965). By accumulating resources, acquiring expertise, setting direction, and attracting members, organizations help solve a wide range of social dilemmas associated with collective action efforts (Walker, 1991). Our findings refine this old story by looking at the variation in what happens across members inside organizations once those resources have been accumulated and spent. We find strong reasons to reject the implicit premise in much work on collective action that members are essentially interchangeable, while organization-level variation in skills, resources, and strategies tell the bulk of the story.

A second tradition implicated in our findings is work on social capital. Putnam's (2000) influential formulation of the social-capital paradigm is, as we suggested in the preceding text, really a claim that a certain class of organization has the benefit of building social trust and norms of reciprocity and exchange among its members, and these bring powerful benefits, including helping people solve collective action problems together. The organizations that accomplish this remarkable task must have certain properties that are readily operationalized, namely regular, face-to-face interaction among members who know one another. In this formulation, Putnam's historical story is that this special class of organization has been in decline in the United States since the 1960s or so. Meanwhile, other classes of organization that are growing more populous, such as interest groups and support groups, do not produce the same effects. The social-capital thesis is as much a claim about categories of organization as it is about trust and civic skills on the part of individuals. Our argument is that the neat system of classification underlying social-capital theory is inadequate to the changes occurring in organizational forms. Interaction among people can occur in a variety of contexts – online, offline, and both – and The American Legion, AARP, and MoveOn can each offer their members and participants a range of interaction, from the personal to highly impersonal. Social-capital theorists' identification of a historical trend toward the depopulation of traditional social-capital organizations has crashed abruptly into a newer trend: the diversification and blending of organizational forms, driven by increased agency on the part of individuals and the presence of multiple participatory styles, in which the relationships between individuals' attitudes or characteristics and their involvement varies across people.

The same phenomenon affects another classic and closely related body of scholarship, namely, interest-group theory. A hallmark of the U.S. public sphere in comparison to those of virtually every other industrial democracy is its vibrant and extensive population of interest groups. These groups direct democratic processes toward pluralistic sets of interests and away from views and demands of large coalitions of citizens or the public good defined in terms of the majority (Arnold, 1990; Lowi, 1979; Schattschneider, 1975). In the traditional formulation, interest groups are commonly rooted in formal membership, either on the part of individuals or other organizations, and these exploded in growth during the second half of the twentieth century. In this view, it is impossible to understand how the U.S. government acts or why it makes the policies it does without conceptualizing American society as organized into its array of interest-group organizations.

In this book, we acknowledge that membership-based interest groups are alive and well, but show that they may be less easily classifiable than at any time in the past. The people who associate with them may or may not be anonymous individuals responding passively to calls for action by central leaders. They may or may not be people who have paid dues to "join." In 1998, Baumgartner and Leech wrote, in their widely read book on interest groups, that "as groups make use of new fund-raising and mobilization techniques, they blur some common distinctions between members and non-members" (Baumgartner and Leech, 1998, 31). In the years since that analysis, those distinctions have grown only more blurry as the boundaries that define groups and the meaning of membership have faded. For people with certain participatory styles, interest groups may function more like the social-capital building organizations of the first half of the twentieth century, while for others membership-based interest groups may remain very traditional and true to classic form. Our story of the memberships of The American Legion, AARP, and MoveOn is intended as a kind of remedy to those scholarly traditions that viewed membership primarily in terms of macrostructure, in which people's roles and opportunities, as well as their relationships with one another, were defined exclusively by the structure of their organizations.

Plan of the Book

In several ways, our approach to these issues is equally theoretical and empirical, and so the chapters that follow give similar attention to each. Our search for individual-level variation in participatory styles begins with considerations that culminate in what we label the *collective action space*. We use this framework in the second half of the book to model involvement in collective action. So, rather than using theory to produce a model that we then subject to a traditional empirical "test," we intend the book as a set of theoretical rationales for some novel empirical explorations by looking at variation within and across organizations. Most of our empirical evidence comes from our surveys among the members of The American Legion, AARP, and MoveOn, which we describe further at the beginning of Chapter 4. We also conducted telephone and in-person interviews across the span of the project with about two dozen senior personnel in the three organizations. Our interviewees are responsible for membership, research, mobilization, information technology, digital communication and Web strategies, and campaigns, and we refer to their observations and comments throughout the book.

We start in Chapter 2 with the contemporary media environment as a context for collective action. That chapter makes the case that two features of technology are key: the power it places in the hands of organizational members and its ubiquity. These in turn weaken boundaries of all kinds. Social life is a web of various boundaries, and many boundaries that structure public life are changed because of the end-to-end power of ubiquitous technology.

The idea of weakened boundaries then leads us to ask in Chapter 3: what do changed boundaries mean specifically for collective action within organizational settings? Our answer will be that two specific features of collective action within organizational contexts are affected by weakened boundaries, interaction and engagement. In that chapter we show how interaction and engagement can be combined into collective action space. This framework permits two things: it allows us to classify people theoretically as to potential participatory styles and to see later what this can tell us about actual behavior and whether coherent participatory styles exist along the lines that we expect. Approaching collective action this way allows us to declassify organizations, in the sense that organizations of all kinds can be placed together in the framework, in which we expect to find a good deal of within-organization diversity in members' experiences along with a great deal of across-organization similarity. Specifically, in declassifying organizations, we will quickly move beyond traditional categories like "civic association" and "interest group," and beyond distinctions such as "online group" and "offline group."

In Chapter 4, we begin looking at involvement in collection action through our empirical analyses by asking: How are the members of The American Legion, AARP, and MoveOn situated in collective action space? What factors predict who will participate in these organizations and how people's identification with and trust of them varies? The analysis in that chapter is organized around the three organizations, and it shows several things. The first is that factors that scholars traditionally use to explain behavior, such as age, education, and participation in other civic associations, indicate very little about variation in people's involvement in these organizations. When we add into consideration our measures of goals and motivation, as well as interaction and engagement, then involvement comes into much sharper focus. Chapter 4 examines our ideas about within-group variation and across-group similarities and develops a basic model that can explain involvement in the organizations.

In Chapter 5, we take that model and use it to explore participatory styles across The American Legion, AARP, and MoveOn. To do this, we combine their memberships and compare across and within them, statistically. We explore how technology use matters and examine how motivations and goal alignment contribute to involvement in collective action. Most importantly, we explore how the answers to all these questions vary across people, not as a function of what organization they belong to but as a function of where they locate themselves in collective action space, through their choices about interaction and engagement. The main analytic focus of that chapter is an exploration of four participatory styles, which we call *individualists*, *enthusiasts*, *traditionalists*, and *minimalists*.

In the conclusion, Chapter 6, we elaborate on what our findings about participatory styles mean. We explore the three aspects of involvement articulated in that chapter – contributions to collective goals and activities, identification with the organization, and trust in the organization – and we examine how participatory styles interact with them. We propose that alongside the importance of looking at organizational memberships in a more fine-grained manner through participatory styles, it is critical not to neglect formal organizations, which we situate in this richer context. We also consider the role of technologies in contemporary collective action efforts, along the lines of the arguments that we develop more fully in Chapter 2, and situate the individual's place in the organization, consistent with our focus on the question of how individuals experience collective action within formal organizations.

2

The Contemporary Media Environment and the Evolution of Boundaries in Organization-based Collective Action

An understanding of collective action in the contemporary media environment requires a way of conceptualizing technology that is relevant to collective action. In our case, that means technology that is rapidly ramifying and collective action that takes place within organizational contexts. As we suggested in Chapter 1, it is important to avoid the pitfalls of attempting to theorize connections from such fine-grained matters as how frequently people use e-mail or a particular social-networking tool to hypothesize about a variety of behavioral outcomes. A good deal of analysis has theorized that technology use affects behavior by reducing costs or increasing choice, but those theories have typically not conceptualized behavior as being structured through organizational membership, and they also provide little purchase on differences among so many technologies, all of which in one way or another reduce costs, facilitate communication, and distribute information more widely and seamlessly. Our interest in this book is in theorizing how the digital-media environment affects behavior as well as attitudes – involvement – in a way that is not dependent on solving intractable measurement problems and that is also specified precisely to take place in organizational contexts. This will require conceptualizing technology in organization-relevant ways. Our main theoretical task is therefore to trace how features of technology shape people's experience of organizations. We will do this in several steps in this chapter and in Chapter 3 by identifying two general aspects of the contemporary media environment relevant to all collective action regardless of context, showing how these affect human boundaries of all kinds and what that means for collective action theory generally, and focusing on what these aspects of the media environment and boundaries mean inside organizations, through interaction and engagement.

Without too much loss of precision, one can divide much thinking about the media environment into two large camps, one operating at a high level of abstraction with whole societies as the unit of analysis and one addressing individuals and their use of specific technological tools. Among the prominent work at the high level of abstraction are such ideas as "the post-industrial society" (Bell, 1974), "the knowledge revolution" (Drucker, 1999), "the informational age," the "network society" (Castells, 1996), or such trendy concepts as "globalization 3.0" (Friedman, 2005). These monikers reflect the multiple meanings of change and the multiple scales on which it is occurring, from the personal to the global. This level of theory tends to focus on the large social, economic, political, and cultural changes prompted by modern technological change.

Several themes drive this work including, for example, control. Beniger (1986) situates the origins of the contemporary information age in the period of industrialization, which constituted a revolution in the need for control and means for exercising it. Carey (1989) notes that, with the invention of the telegraph, symbols were able to move independently of time and geography, and this separation enabled new mechanisms of control in the conduct of commerce, civic life, government, and the military. "Information" and "networks" have been the basis of another theme. Castells (2000a, 2000b) argues that contemporary communication and information technologies have ushered in an informational age in which the global economy is characterized by rapid information flows that privilege certain groups over others, in which political phenomena routinely play out in the media and electronic information networks serve as the basis for modern society. Although this work has implications for collective action, within organizational contexts and outside of them, it is often too abstract to connect directly to the core theory of collective action.

A great many other insightful interpretations at this level of theorizing have also been offered, but for understanding the involvement and varying experiences of members of organizations such The American Legion, AARP, and MoveOn, as well as for many collective action issues more broadly, such high-level abstractions frankly shed little light. They are often difficult to operationalize and connect to the theory of free riding. One can rightly observe that MoveOn is a product of the information age because it was created specifically to exploit information technology for political advocacy. One can also note that The American Legion was originally an industrial-era association born after World War I, and AARP is a mid-twentieth-century organization created just as television broadcasting and direct mail were about to explode into American life. However, situating these organizations, or most others, in this context does not help us much in understanding how people experience them differently.

The second large theoretical camp has sliced into the contemporary media environment in a very detailed way, focusing on how the use of specific technologies matters – for instance in the transition from Web 1.0 to Web 2.0 or in differentiating the civic consequences of Facebook as opposed to Twitter. Often these studies make comparisons between "older" and "newer" technological forms or argue for or against the importance of some evolving feature of contemporary tools, such as the extent of interactivity. A central question has been the debate over the last decade and a half about whether Internet use promotes political participation. During the late 1990s it was appropriate to ask, as the National Election Studies surveys did, a single question about whether people saw any political information online and look for associations between that and various political acts (Bimber, 2003). Early in the 2000s, scholars had shown convincingly that different uses of the Web had different implications for civic engagement and attitudes (Shah, Kwak, and Holbert, 2001), and so measurement of media use became more fine grained. By the mid- to late-2000s, two empirical facts had become clear. The first was that media use matters because it interacts with motivations and interest, and these interactions may be more important than the main effects scholars have been debating for years (Boulianne, 2009; Prior, 2007; Xenos and Moy, 2007). The second fact is that very high percentages of people less than sixty-five years of age are online, and among those under thirty, Internet use is nearly as common as television ownership. These facts have rendered simple questions about correlations between Internet use and political or civic engagement less than satisfying. This way of conceptualizing the media environment does provide testable claims in a way that the highly abstract theories do not, but it has two major limitations for the issues that interest us in this book.

The first is that it can be quite limited in its capacity to make lasting conclusions about rapidly changing digital media in society. It is often difficult to identify what the central consequences of technologies will be and which features are merely part of the ebb and flow of specific products and (re)configurations. The second is that this level of analysis has not yet been connected adequately to the theory of collective action or to an alternative to it. If it is simply that the use of specific technological tools makes acquiring information and taking actions less expensive, thereby altering the cost side of cost-benefit calculations about contributing to a public good or free riding, then changes in behavior should be dramatic because so much information is now free and so many actions are only trivially difficult to undertake. Although relationships do exist between the use of technology and various forms of participation in the United States and other developed nations, these are not dramatic or commensurate with a revolution in the costs of information and communication. Alternative conceptualizations of the relationship between technology use and civic or political behavior have focused on the contingencies of people's interest, motives, and context (Bimber, 2003; Xenos and Moy, 2007). Although these are empirically and theoretically more satisfying than instrumental theories, just how they connect to collective action theory generally or to organization-driven collective action has not been shown definitively.

All three of the organizations in our study offer interactive and social features of various kinds, and interestingly, their technological portfolios are similar but not identical. The American Legion offers its own discussion forums on such topics as health-care reform, Boys' State, and "Americanism." It also links members to Facebook and Twitter, as well as its YouTube channel, from a prominent location on its home page. AARP does essentially the same. MoveOn, renowned for its technological savvy, links to Facebook, Twitter, and YouTube as well, but conspicuously it does not offer discussion forums. Is that fact important? Will it be so in five years? We are doubtful of this and skeptical of any effort to connect people's use of specific tools, such as a link to Facebook from the Legion's site, to enduring features of collective action. We eschew making inferences about the nature of collective action for members of an organization like MoveOn from an inventory of the specific tools and features present at its Web site at the particular moment that we are writing about it.

We therefore do not focus on this level of technological description in our analyses, opting instead to emphasize the experiences of members operating within a technological environment characterized by a few key features that we believe are connected theoretically to collective action and organizational structure, through the nature of boundaries. For understanding the experience people have of organizations involved in collective action, it is preferable to talk to people directly. This is especially a concern if one expects, as we do, a great deal of variation across people in how they interact with Web sites and use the changing mix of online tools that organizations provide.

Interviews with officials in The American Legion and AARP, as well as conversations we have had with leaders of a wide range of advocacy organizations beyond our three main groups, have confirmed this. Commonly, organizational leaders acknowledged that it was not clear to them exactly how to use social media strategically, whether Facebook is consistently more important than Twitter and for what types of collective action, or what constitutes the core technologies of communication and information. Many of the stories we heard from activist groups were idiosyncratic: Twitter seemed to be successful in one case but not another; in another instance, "old-fashioned" e-mail was most successful at mobilizing people. In other cases, people noted that they think about digital media as a system of interconnected parts rather than simply as a set of discrete tools for different tasks.

For example, in one of our interviews a senior staff person at The American Legion noted the relationship between viral communication among Legion members and topics of interest to the national leadership. He stressed how, in a seamless manner, messages at the Web site, members' posts in the Legion's blog, formal newsletter communication, and messaging on Facebook all move together. Referring to a recent campaign that began on the national Web site and was subsequently taken up by individual members, he noted that "We see this on Facebook, we see it in our blog comments, we see this all over, that members will buy into something, and they will drive it in their local posts and their departments." In this way, compelling issues and members' interests drive communication, and the various technologies support this process in an interconnected way. "When we post a really riveting controversy on our blog site and maybe even a fundraiser... other blog sites will pick it up and of course it goes viral and then all of a sudden we've got a $10,000 donation." Thus The American Legion does not appear to think about technology in terms of separate strategies for e-mail, the Web, social media, and so on, but rather in terms of the rapid, rich communication that members have at their disposal. Even their staffing choices reflect this position. Those who produce content for online and offline venues are not hired as media specialists but rather are expected to understand multiple distribution channels, including video.

At AARP, channels of communication are increasingly interconnected, from the organization's and the members' points of view. A senior staff person told us, for example, that members "are starting to use the Web site like they use the call center, and the expectation says when you call with a question or a concern you expect it to be resolved. They come a lot to the Web site even about things that aren't on the Web – they come because they know someone is listening. It's another communication vehicle for them." She also indicated that AARP uses "social media to get our message out about a lot of different things."

The picture is somewhat different at MoveOn, which has a special approach to online organizing. MoveOn still relies chiefly on e-mail for communicating with members and uses social media for somewhat special purposes. In an interview, we learned that MoveOn views social media as good for sharing content easily and rapidly but not for organizing, which requires targeted communication rather than unpredictably viral messaging. Twitter, a senior campaign director told us, is good for a very small set of real-time communication, but its lack of persistence makes it poor for many kinds of communication with MoveOn activists. Among our three organizations, MoveOn not surprisingly evinces the greatest subtlety in its understanding of technology. Yet MoveOn also knows the limits of technology. "There is a deep recognition that particularly for our nonvolunteers, which is the vast majority of MoveOn members, e-mail and Twitter and Facebook and all of the electronic means we have at our disposal are very light-touch tools. It is very hard for me to get you to do something you don't want to do only via e-mail. If I pick up the phone it is easier to get you to do it, and if we are in the same room together it is even easier."

The message we take from our conversations with various organizations is that digital media matter most often as a collectivity of tools and as the context for organizing, but it is not often the case that any one tool is supremely useful or consistently crucial across time and across events. At MoveOn, we learned of how the organization is always looking beyond the current tools: "We have been talking about e-mail dying – what's the next e-mail? – since about 2006."

One of the implicit messages of current social science dealing with technology, which echoes lessons from the study of previous technological revolutions, is that too close a focus on individual technologies is especially limiting in times of rapid change. A theory of e-mail from 1993 or chat rooms from 1995 is hardly adequate to the dynamism and multiplicity of alternatives for communication available now through our organizations and others. Just as feudalism cannot be understood from a theory of irrigation, or the Industrial Revolution from a theory of threshing machines or looms, understanding the information revolution requires more than a theory of how organizations use Facebook or Twitter.

The telegraph and the railroad highlight the timeless character of this challenge. The telegraph, which stands out historically for its short life and wholesale replacement by subsequent technologies, is significant not merely for its appearance and then disappearance, but for what it wrought in terms of changes in the communicative framework in which social life was ordered. Undoubtedly, some tools of computing, information, and communication are destined for obsolescence like the telegraph. But as with the telegraph, featuring those technologies as independent artifacts is less meaningful than considering the ways in which the technologies entrench themselves in organizing practices across social domains.

Consider the significance of the railroad. Unlike the telegraph, which it accompanied in the nineteenth century, the railroad survived to the present and remains vital to economies. But it grew embedded in an increasingly complex matrix of technologies. To understand its significance requires not simply a theory of the standardization of track gauges or an account of labor coercively imported from Asia but also an account of transportation, movement, infrastructure, and industrial power – theory at a level of abstraction well above the specifics of particular episodes of innovation. The danger is that moving to this level of abstraction risks also becoming overly vague and general. To call the late nineteenth and early twentieth centuries in the United States the "railroad age" would not be particularly instructive.

So as researchers committed to the need to understand relationships between technological change and social innovation in collective action organizations, we are cautious of focusing too sharply on the specifics: on cell phones and mobile social networking, the presence or absence of discussion forums or Twitter streams, or whatever new techniques for organizing that will arise in five more years. We are just as wary of formulating a grand theory of technology that implicates everything from economies to culture on a global scale. Doing so runs the risk of losing specificity in the pursuit of explanations for social phenomena.

A way forward is therefore required that identifies connections between enduring features of digital media and the experiences people have of organizations and that shows how these connections are theoretically relevant from the perspective of collective action. This path should illuminate what is most important about the context in which people choose to be involved civically or politically through formal organizations rather than in some other way. Much of what is occurring today as a result of technology with regard to the social, economic, and cultural landscape can often be better described as a change in scale than in kind (see, e.g., Bimber, Flanagin, and Stohl, 2005). We are sensitive to the irony that theories of technology and social change that focus too closely on technologies may end up saying the least in the long term.

Two Capabilities of Technology Relevant to Collective Action of All Kinds

To understand the relationships between technological change and features of collective action relevant to The American Legion, AARP, and MoveOn, we begin with the observation that some general trends currently exist across technologies, and that these appear to promote and privilege certain capabilities over others. These capabilities enable social participation on a greater scale than in the past, changing its meaning and form. They disrupt structures of control, organization, and coordination that have long remained relatively static and predictable. As a consequence of these affordances, ways of participating in collective action efforts and ways of organizing them are undergoing a fundamental transformation in concert with social and economic shifts prompted by technological change. We therefore focus throughout this book on this level of change, rather than on the specifics of how organizations use Web 2.0 or 3.0, social media, tablets and smart phones, cloud computing, and the like. Similarly, we avoid formulating a grand social theory of technological change.

Two major features of the contemporary technological atmosphere stand out. The first is the capacity of the technological environment to involve people with one another, socially, politically, and intellectually. This capacity arises primarily from recent changes to technological structure, and it involves changes in the capacity for people to easily share information, experiences, desires, and knowledge (Flanagin, Flanagin, and Flanagin, 2010). It captures what happens in social forums, Facebook, e-mail forwarding, and many other specifics. The second major feature is ubiquity, which is relevant because of its influence on people's psychological orientation and to the social practices that result, as well as with how organizations perceive their environments.

Structure and ubiquity are not sufficient for a theory of collective action, which ultimately requires a view about the problem of choice, decision, the achievement of public goods, and a view of organization, which are matters to which we will turn in Chapter 3. But structure and ubiquity establish a useful foundation for the theory that connects features of technology with the conditions or circumstances in which collective action takes place. These phenomena exist at a level of complexity precisely where we believe specific sociotechnical developments accumulate into lasting trends and where the interactions among multiple developments occur, even as specific developments come and (occasionally) go, and as compelling macroforces are also at play.

The Implications of Structure: End-User Enterprise

The theoretically most significant feature of contemporary technology for collective action is among its oldest: how the technology is structured. Engineering design choices matter (Feenberg, 1995) in lasting ways. Design choices do so not because they determine the future, as some strands of technological determinism would maintain, but because they can create critical moments in path-dependent courses of history, making some sets of subsequent choices and actions much more likely than others. The key decision in designing the Internet, which by now is quite well-known, was to follow a set of network principles called the end-to-end arguments or end-to-end structure (Blumenthal and Clark, 2001; Saltzer, Reed, and Clark, 1984). Many later decisions, and many of the Internet's novel features about which one may be tempted to hypothesize specifically, follow naturally from this first, founding choice. The defining characteristic of an end-to-end system is that network "intelligence" in the form of discrimination and processing functions exists primarily at the periphery of the network, while the network pathways remain neutral, handling all data traffic identically. This end-to-end structure is in direct contrast to the design of the old telephone network or of a network of satellite terminals connected to a mainframe computer, for example, where the core processing functions are performed centrally and the devices at the edges of the network have a limited functionality that is wholly reliant on central processing.

Extension of the basic data-processing principle of end-to-end design resulted in the familiar evolution from centralized, data-processing–intensive networks to the largely distributed, decentralized structure of the Internet. "Peer-to-peer" technologies, for example, have relied on this fact in order to provide wide information sharing among individuals who manage their own storage and processing devices residing at the periphery of the network. In contrast to the technologies of the industrial era (e.g., telegraph, train, telephone, and mainframe computer), which needed formal hierarchical systems for coordination, technologies of today (e.g., personal computers and cell phones) have reduced the need for coordination by hierarchy, centralized decision making, and expensive bureaucracies and hence have reduced the cost of coordinating, making individuals' experience of formal organizations less determined by the human and resource capital that reside within formal organizations and more on their own desires about what membership should be like. Centralized computers at AARP may still manage mail lists and subscriptions, but at the same time some degree of control and power has shifted outward, away from centers, toward individuals who decide whether to read or post on a blog, share information or videos relevant to an AARP goal, take a poll about their views, or sign up to volunteer in their neighborhood toward a community project. "We have thousands of groups [on AARP's *Online Community*]," one senior AARP official told us, "and these groups are primarily created by the user. There are some AARP-created groups, but they number in the tens, maybe ten to twenty groups that AARP has created, versus the thousands that have been created by the community themselves."

Likewise, members can access rich sources of information about The American Legion through its own Web site and in the rest of the online environment. A Legion official says that the organization is delighted to be able to get more information into the hands of members, especially about its activities at the national level. One example of this involves the Legion's presentation of testimony about veterans' issues in Congress and in meetings at the White House. The Legion used to struggle, often unsuccessfully, to attract media coverage of these activities, so its members could follow and be engaged in the process. As he noted, "the media are not going to cover some boring hearing about veterans' benefits." Now, however, the Legion posts what it is doing on its Web site, including details of testimony and messages. "We put what-we-are-doing-for-you-today on our Web site. Even if it is just that today we are meeting with VA Secretary Eric Shinseki to talk about his plan to eradicate homelessness among veterans in five years. You click on that and you might get a link to a story, it may have a link to our testimony, it may have a link to his statement." He concludes, "We are opening up so many valves of communication." The value of this, according to him, is that all members can find something to satisfy their level of interest, from those with a deep "academic" level of curiosity to those just seeking to know generally what is happening. In turn, members whose interest is piqued by what they see have multiple digital venues in which to discuss what is happening with others, bring conversations into their posts or onto Facebook pages, and decide whether to respond or act. Technological choices made by the builders of the Internet during the 1960s and 1970s set the stage for AARP and the Legion to offer their members these kinds of opportunities in the 2010s.

The end-to-end nature of the underlying architecture of physical connections and intelligence in technology was a design choice made without an inkling that organizations such as MoveOn would exist, as was the nonlinear nature of the infrastructure for human content, in the form of hyperlinks. Such design choices make the Internet infrastructure ideal for innovation through flexible and programmable technical standards that support end-user modification, control, and interconnectivity (see, e.g., Lessig, 1999). This inherent flexibility, coupled with a reduction in communication costs, lowers the risks associated with innovation on the Internet because failure is not as devastating for an individual as it would be if greater investment were required at the outset. The negligible price of failure and the potential cache of personal rewards for success serve as powerful incentives for individuals to continue to experiment with new, still highly unstable and sensitive organizing tools that are more likely to fail than succeed. The same holds true at the organizational level. MoveOn, for example, may continually experiment with new forms of action and connection because of the low cost and ease with which it can segment its membership, personalize its interaction with members, and rapidly change requests and responses to fit a turbulent and often-volatile political environment. It is central to how collective action organizations work that their members are increasingly authors of their own membership experience.

Put another way, the Internet's end-to-end structure is especially well suited to innovation and customization at the scale of the individual member. Because the network is largely indifferent to specific data content, and the information-processing functions reside in the hands of interconnected users, its design suggests an enormous capacity for personalization, through customized information seeking and specific information provision facilitated by the sheer scale of users online. This suggests a kind of "end-user enterprise," in which people have an enhanced capacity to initiate and sustain collective actions based on their personal goals, given the migration of more information, by more people, to more places than ever before.

As a function of these features, organizing of collective action has been made increasingly feasible by small groups that can sometimes reach audiences larger than their own memberships, self-organizing groups whose reach is defined by the logic of viral, exponential growth rather than by membership size, and the many other organizational forms now present in the collective action landscape. Organizations such as MoveOn do not turn over their membership lists for members to use as they see fit. But by giving people choices about what issues to follow and how, and by giving them opportunities to be organizers within the organization, MoveOn exploits the structure of the technology to shift discretion and some "authorship" into the hands of its members. One of the best examples of this transfer of initiative is SignOn.org, a petition service that MoveOn released in 2011. SignOn allows anyone to create a petition about nearly any topic, using tools provided for free by MoveOn. MoveOn is explicit about the fact that it offers these tools without endorsing the content of any particular collective effort that people might undertake. MoveOn promises not to remove petitions simply because it does not agree with them, and it likewise reserves the right to promote those that it does support and to keep for its own purposes the e-mail addresses of petition signers. With this tool, in effect MoveOn has made its agenda open-source: anyone can pursue petition-based collective action on topics of their own choosing, and MoveOn has the discretion to integrate these actions with its own as it chooses. This radical departure from centralized decision making is possible on a large scale only through the end-to-end structure originally designed into the Internet and reinforced through decades of ongoing choices about how best to use and develop technology.

It is worth acknowledging that this shift, while enabling and empowering individuals to more easily act on their own interests and styles of participation, paradoxically may also disenfranchise them in certain ways. For example, the structure of the technology enables personal information to be readily available to public audiences without people's awareness. Further, chat rooms, bulletin boards, and discussion forums present public or quasipublic archives of conversational communication that until recently would have evaporated immediately. Where historically the chief problem to overcome in information sharing was how to publicize information effectively, individuals must now take affirmative steps to maintain privacy and control of their personal information. Not only can Web-based information constitute a public good that can be readily harnessed by motivated individuals or groups for specific ends, but it is actually difficult to inhibit. The contribution to information-based public goods online can often be unintentional, unwitting, or unknowing (what we have described elsewhere as "second-order communality"; see Bimber, Flanagin, and Stohl, 2005), as when a person posts feedback on a Web site about a product or person, provides an opinion in a public forum online, or fails to guard personal information from technologies that routinely gather and organize the various traces people deposit online daily. Many new forms of social practice actually require greater effort for people to achieve privacy than publicness. From the standpoint of collective action efforts, this suggests that even relatively "innocent" instances of information provision, such as posting a comment to an online forum, can be readily transformed into meaningful bases for collective action by their ready availability and permanence. From the perspective of public goods provision, one might evaluate these possibilities very positively, while from the perspective of privacy, one might be less sanguine about some of them.

Ubiquity of the Sociotechnical Infrastructure

In addition to the capacity for the Internet and associated technologies to promote and support new forms of information sharing and enterprise, a second critical feature for contemporary collective action efforts is the ubiquity of the technological environment that supports this range of diverse practices. Ubiquity of technology is a common theme in commentary on new media, but it is not always clearly conceptualized. Ubiquity is sometimes discussed in quasieconomic terms, as the endpoint of a process of diffusion or the saturation of a market. It is also commonly described in technical terms, when some threshold of interactivity and technological intensiveness has been reached. For the purposes of understanding collective action, a more psychological and subtle consequence of ubiquity is important: through the Internet's incredible variety and centrality of applications and capabilities that capitalize on it, it has become unremarkable, commonplace, and routine. The result is that the Internet and associated tools have in some sense disappeared while nonetheless being wholly embedded in pervasive everyday practices.

We are not suggesting that people are unaware of their use of technology, but rather that it has quickly become unremarkable in the sense that it is taken for granted and neither surprising nor worth noting as something special. This evolution of a technology in the mind has been addressed by other authors occasionally, for instance by Weiser (1991), but its implications have been noted more often among those concerned with designing or marketing technology than those interested in understanding its effects. To quote Zander (n.d.), former CEO of Sun Microsystems, on the Internet's evolution:

> The Internet is going away in the same sense that electricity and plumbing did in the 20th century – out of sight and out of mind.... The net will assume an always-present, behind-the-scenes quality. No longer will you tell a friend "get on the Internet and compare air fares to Bora Bora." You'll just say, "Compare air fares to Bora Bora." Who today ever says, "Activate the plumbing and pour me some water"? And like plumbing, the Internet will be everywhere, but largely invisible. (n.p.)

By what process does some technology become "unremarkable," and what are the implications of this change? The Internet has evolved along a pattern common to many technological innovations, from substitution to enlargement to reconfiguration (see Malone and Rockart, 1991). Its first-order effect was largely substitution for the already common functions of communication and information dissemination, through such specific features as e-mail, simple Web sites designed to pass information unidirectionally, and electronic data interchange. In this capacity, the Internet did little to alter existing social relations, economic structures, or power arrangements, but it was noticed mainly because it required new and unfamiliar routines. This meant, for example, that AARP could reach its members much less expensively than by mailing paper to their homes. In 1996, for instance, AARP was online with a simple Web site describing its issue positions and providing a way to join and by 2000 was distributing its newsletter from its site. This early stage of the Internet was "remarkable" insofar as it was conceived as a new way to do something old and people were aware that they could now "do the same with less effort." In this early stage, the average person was amazed at what was possible, whether that be sending an e-mail to someone more efficiently than it took to phone him or her or finding a needed reference by using a search engine rather than spending the time going to the library and looking in the card catalogue.

Second-order effects are characterized by attempts to use technologies "to do more with less effort," for example, to reach more people than traditionally possible and engage in more technologically mediated communication as people conduct routine organizational activities. Second-order effects expand capacity through processes of enlargement, often by several orders of magnitude. The technology, however, is still not taken for granted; it remains notable and central to new processes, and the criterion for evaluating success remains increased efficiency. The classic paradox of costs associated with the investment in technology is recognized and discussed strategically as organizations choose whether to adopt the technology. The resolution of the paradox recognizes that organizational outcomes are enhanced not simply by the adoption of technologies for substitution or enlargement of existing social and task practices, but also by the opportunities they offer to reconfigure the communicative and organizational environment. MoveOn was initially notable to scholars and journalists, as well as public officials, more because it did things exclusively online than for what it did or did not accomplish; after all, the House of Representatives did not "move on" but rather impeached President Clinton.

It is important that in these first and second stages, the use of technology can be adequately characterized in terms of conscious choices. Technology is remarkable when one can choose to use it because it is efficient or less costly than alternatives. In these stages, people's use of technology remains coherent in economic terms of utility and cost. On The American Legion's "Find the Reunion" Web page, for example, there are explicit remarks comparing the efficiency and low cost of utilizing the Web to publicize activities to the inefficient time lag when using traditional communication channels. Similarly, after years of discussion, The American Legion provided a "Post Locator" online to make it easier and more efficient for veterans who were traveling to be able to locate and visit American Legion posts anywhere in the United States. Previously, veterans had to contact The American Legion headquarters in Indianapolis directly for this information.

The recognition and exploitation of users' individual resources, in a manner that capitalizes on their aggregation and combination, eventually resulted in the Internet's third-order effect, most obvious in a host of new social, economic, and political structures. In this reconfiguration phase, individuals and organizations use technologies "to do more with different effort," and the criterion for evaluating success is increased effectiveness and opportunity rather than just increased efficiency. As "Web 2.0," social computing, and other new technologies became an essential part of reconfigured everyday practices, the technology grew unremarkable inasmuch as these new ways of organizing become routine and are no longer compared to old ways of doing and organizing. At this stage, when explicit comparisons to old ways are no longer made, it is not helpful to think about people's actions exclusively in terms of choices, intentions, costs, resources, and the related theoretical apparatus traditionally associated with collective action theory. Rather, the ubiquity of the sociotechnical infrastructure changes normative expectations for what is and should be possible. By about 2004, for example, MoveOn was no longer a novelty worth attention because it was an online organization but was judged a player in national politics because it had become influential and could compete on substantive political grounds with other organized interests. MoveOn is now relevant for what it can do, not because of how it goes about its work.[1]

For Weiser (1991) what matters about this seeming disappearance of technology is that its use ceases to be a goal, so that people are able to think in a more unobstructed way about what they want to accomplish rather than focus on the means they are employing to do so. As he suggests, "The most profound technologies are those that disappear. They weave themselves into the fabric of everyday life until they are indistinguishable from it" (94). Examples of this third level of development are increasingly common. For example, MoveOn members are likely to believe they can have some say in the goals of a several-million-member organization or locate and activate strangers with shared political

[1] At first blush, the age differences across the organizations' populations in this study belie the notion that new technologies and Internet-connected mobile devices are becoming similarly routine and unremarkable among the organizational memberships. However, a close examination of the samples, as well as the recent "2010 Generations Report," sponsored by the Pew Internet and American Life Project, supports the plausibility of this argument. Not surprisingly, the typical AARP member is, on average, 7 or 20 years older than the average American Legion or MoveOn member, respectively. However, 99% of American Legion members in our sample and 95% of MoveOn's membership were born before 1979, the latest year of birth in our AARP cohort. The earliest years of birth are not very different either. The oldest Legionnaire in our sample was born in 1900, the oldest AARP member was born in 1912, and the oldest MoveOn member was born in 1918.

Moreover, the "2010 Generations Report" indicates that "certain key Internet uses are becoming more uniformly popular across all age groups" (2), including utilizing e-mail and search engines, getting health information, following the news, making purchases and travel reservations, conducting online banking, supplying reviews or ratings, donating to charity, and downloading podcasts. The Pew study also suggests that social networking for those older than 74 years has quadrupled in just the last 3 years and 55% of people between 45 and 55 access Web sites or other digital media or services using a laptop, cell phone, or other mobile device. Finally, the Pew data suggest that even if an organizational member is not partaking or even consciously considering the opportunities afforded by new technologies directly, their friends and other organizational members are and, hence, the information, framing of possibilities, availability of resources, and repertoire of behaviors associated with contemporary media have become part of the context in which they operate. According to AARP, more than 70% of their members go online regularly. Thus it is not surprising, as we shall see in Chapters 4 and 5, that there are only small differences in technology uses among our samples.

interests with relative ease, though each of these would have been nearly unthinkable even as little as fifteen years ago. This behind-the-scenes quality is important because technologies take on new features and functions and enjoy new capabilities as they tend in this direction. Before technological disappearance or ubiquity occurs, the use of the technology is the focus of social action, thereby constraining individuals' imaginations. This is a crucial point because traditional collective action theory entails explicit choices over means to accomplish given ends. Once the requisite tools for collective action fade into the "fabric of everyday life," however, people are increasingly freed to focus on their collective goals over the technical means required to achieve them.

As this happens, efforts by social scientists to measure how many hours people spend online, which tools they use, and how these correlate with collective behavior become less important and less meaningful than attempting to understand how they experience the totality of the media environment. One of the best antecedents to this is the telephone, which initially diffused largely for business purposes, then among a small number of geographically isolated individuals, then to the vast majority of households, and most recently in cellular form to a significantly larger number and wider variety of people. Around the globe, there were about five billion cell phones in use at the end of 2010, enough for three out of every four humans (ITU, 2011). In each step in the diffusion of telephony, more people were included as users, new uses were invented, and social connections, expectations, and possibilities evolved. Importantly, the phone became a basic technology that was largely assumed to be available to most people for point-to-point communication, especially in developed nations but also increasingly in developing countries. This presumption of availability – the phone's attendant taken-for-grantedness – and its unremarkable nature are important features. With regard to collective action, these meant that people could rely on the ability to reach one another directly, cheaply, remotely, and quickly. They did not have to think about this resource. They could do something that, prior to telephone diffusion, was a critical obstacle to collective endeavors ranging from organizing a political meeting or rally to constructing a product boycott effort. This new ability, premised on the phone's ubiquity, changed the way that people thought about organizing their efforts, the costs associated with doing so, and the likelihood of achieving their desired goals. There is little point, however, in asking whether telephone use is associated with increased civic engagement or political action on the part of citizens who use it more intensively. By the same logic, we do not expect in our study that measurements of people's use of their organization's various online tools will be an important part of the story of their involvement.

Explanatory Models in an Era of End-User Enterprise and Technological Ubiquity

Understanding the implications of technology that provides new agency and has become subconscious in its presence requires new approaches to explanation. These should emphasize context over technological features. In traditional theories, specific technological features stand out against the background of the human environment. In our view, these remain important, but the context in which they exist, and the social features that they cumulatively prompt and alter, are more compelling, particularly in the long term.

For example, the long tradition of scholarship about interest groups in the United States has treated technology as essentially an economic tool. Theories of interest groups typically remark how technologies of database management and mass mail for recruiting and mobilizing citizens enable groups like AARP to manage large memberships. In an earlier era, these technologies meant large mini-computers or mainframes organizing direct mail delivered by the postal service. Those technologies were adopted by organizations with the resources to afford them, who exploited their affordances to overcome citizen inertia and produce collective action. In a world in which technologies of communication of this kind are expensive and available only in proportion to organizations' abilities to accumulate resources, traditional models of recruitment and mobilization give some insight into the relationship between organizations and members. But in a world in which technology is ubiquitous, citizens are embedded in continuous flows of communication and information, and "choices" to use one means of communication or another are not obviously discrete, old models connecting resources with organization and organization with capacity to employ technology tell us little. When virtually everyone can communicate with everyone, technology recedes into the background.

Imagine, for example, the citizen who receives an e-mail message from a colleague at work who tells her that MoveOn has a petition to Congress about an issue that she cares about, perhaps immigration. She reads this message on her smart phone, which she then uses to look at the Facebook page of MoveOn. There she "likes" the petition, identifying herself publicly as supportive, and follows a link to MoveOn's Web site where she joins the petition and also decides to donate a few dollars to the cause. She concludes her episode of civic activism by Tweeting to her network of friends that she is appalled at all the immigrant bashing she reads about in the news. As researchers, how shall we tally her uses of digital media? They cannot be readily disentangled. She is acting with enterprise in an environment of ubiquitous media and in which discrete "choices" to act or free ride are embedded in her social and communicative practice. The context for her actions matters greatly, while her choice of one tool or technology over another is not so significant.

To take another example of how traditional thinking about media is challenged by the new context, scholars of communication have often applied theories of uses and gratifications in order to explain people's habits of media use. Developed in an age of mass media that could be categorized simply in today's terms – newspapers, broadcast news, and entertainment television – uses-and-gratifications approaches to media postulated a body of needs met variously by choices among media, from escapism to surveillance of the environment. But uses-and-gratifications approaches provide little insight into technology that is ubiquitous, is highly assimilated, and offers an enormous and nearly continuously varying range of affordances. Under such circumstances, the paradigm is helpful only to the degree that specific technologies can be cleanly separated from others, an increasingly rare event possible primarily at the earliest stages of the diffusion of new technologies.

A critic might object that not everyone has access to these technologies, and so to speak of ubiquity and enterprise is to ignore digital divides; one merit of traditional approaches that measure who uses which tools is that they readily highlight these inequalities and exclusions. It is certainly true that within the United States, some people are offline (currently just more than 20% of adults and declining) (Internet World Stats, 2010; Zickuhr, 2010), and this is particularly true of older people – the key demographic differentiating the online from offline. However, technological systems and practice can take on features of ubiquity without being used by everyone. The United States, for example, has exhibited a "car culture" for many decades, though not everyone owns an automobile. At the turn of the twenty-first century, about ten million households in the United States were without an automobile, according to the Department of Transportation (2003), yet the character of America as a car-based society is without question. So many social, personal, and economic practices are organized around the automobile that they are uncountable; car-based transportation is one of the most salient features of society, regardless of who owns a car or how many cars a person has. This is true despite the millions who rely exclusively on public transportation because they live in a city, cannot afford a car, or are unable to drive one for various reasons. Television culture is equally deeply embedded in the United States. Broadcast and cable television exerts a deep and broad influence on life and culture, though not everyone watches television to the same degree, and for decades a few percent of people have not owned a television set.

Although the proportion of people offline is greater than the number without a television or a car, digital media are arriving at the threshold where the systems, practices, and context they create affect essentially everyone. Dutton (2007) has compared the emerging system to the Fourth Estate of the news media. The presence of the Fourth Estate is vital to democracies as a means of public information and accountability, Dutton reminds us, and all citizens experience its effects regardless of whether they attend to news. Digital media are forming, he argues, a new Fifth Estate, involving changed practices and institutional arrangements that shape context for nearly everyone. It is lamentable that not all are online. It is more lamentable that those offline are, in some cases, people who have been disadvantaged in many other ways historically, though it is increasingly less the case that access to the Internet is a function of simple socioeconomic advantage. These normative problems, however, do not change the increasingly ubiquitous systemic effects of digital media.

It is a counterintuitive feature of the state of modern affairs that theories placing technology most consciously in the foreground of explanation appear not very capable of explaining technology in the context of ubiquity and assimilation. In the survey work that we describe in Chapters 4 and 5, we will pay special attention to these issues. We will, as is customary, measure a variety of aspects of people's use of technology, such as their skill and the number of hours they report spending online, and we will look to see how much these measures can say about their participation in collective action. The results will show general support for the idea of technology as context and as a tool. The theoretical challenge for now is to develop a clearer picture of collective action in organizations in which the specific medium seems no longer to matter. We turn next to considering more specifically what this might mean for collective action inside organizations.

The Implications of End-User Enterprise and Technological Ubiquity for Organization-based Collective Action

The contemporary media environment provides a widely available, popular, and flexible infrastructure that often acts as the basis for collective action organizing and, at other times, alters expectations and experiences of collective action efforts that exist largely apart from it. The end-user enterprise inherent in modern technological tools can serve to connect individuals to one another, by promoting information sharing, point-to-point communication, and opportunities for coordination of people's collective efforts – inside and outside of formal organizations. The enhanced capacity of people to connect in meaningful ways with one another suggests tremendous opportunities for innovation on the part of individuals and organizations, particularly as the fundamental tools that support social interconnections become increasingly commonplace in their use and acceptance.

Important features of a relationship or an entire social structure are often apparent only after the relationship has ended or the structure has changed. The emerging possibilities created by technology illuminate vividly just how great limitations historically have been on people's capacity to obtain and manage information and to communicate with few constraints. Only with the new hindsight gained from actually using technologies that would have been science fiction not long ago does it become clear how impoverished public life has been with respect to information and communication. The recognition that public life is emerging from that state of paucity to one of much greater abundance of information and communication raises a host of questions about how human processes and organizations are adapting. It also prompts questions about the extent to which the social, political, and economic arrangements of two decades ago were adaptations to the previous regime of information and communication (Bimber, 2003).

These questions are as relevant to processes of collective action as to any other domain of human activity. By placing the requisite tools for organizing more fully in the hands of individuals and informal or semiformal groups, collective action can more seamlessly arise from those with an interest in shared goals. This can occur with or without the substantial costs associated with the organizational apparatus that traditionally has served to facilitate shared action. For example, in organizations such as The American Legion, AARP, and MoveOn, the membership experience can be reconfigured in several ways. As the preceding anecdote about

The American Legion testimony before Congress shows, technology places information about the organization and its practices in the hands of members. This information comes from the organization, as well as through the wealth of online resources outside each organization that describe its history, strategies, successes, and failures. The new environment expands the means that members have to engage with the organization: to express views, give feedback, comment, participate in polls, and make suggestions. It also places members in touch with one another, allowing those who are interested to get to know others, share private or public interests, and self-organize within the organization around issues of mutual interest. For instance, when AARP endorsed health-care reform legislation in 2010, several Facebook groups were started by members to protest the organization's position and encourage others to quit the group. Though these were tiny in number and did not influence the stance of the organization, they demonstrate the capacity of members inside an organization to find one another and organize against it. Even more fundamentally, the digital-media environment prompts new and unforeseen opportunities for collective action as people are increasingly immersed in an atmosphere in which it is their routine practice to share ideas, connections, and interests. Just as the telegraph changed people's perceptions of their world, current technological shifts have prompted new understandings and assumptions about information and communication, which can serve as the bases for collective action in a variety of contexts – within organizations and in instances not (wholly) reliant on them.

E-mail, for instance, has revolutionized the ability to reach large numbers of people rapidly, cheaply, and directly. The ease with which message recipients can forward messages to others has further expanded this ability, resulting in "viral" e-mails that perpetuate and diffuse quickly outside, within, and across the boundaries of organizations. Other tools that blur traditional models of point-to-point or group communication, such as blogs, Twitter, wikis, and community-based forums such as Google groups or portions of Craigslist, further expand individuals' capacity to communicate broadly and share information quickly. What often matters most is that this frequently occurs across social and practical lines that in the past would have been difficult or impossible to cross. In such cases, people are able to act with enhanced agency by working in concert with others in order to achieve collective goals.

The Web, generally, and social media, in particular, coupled with indispensable search-engine and social recommender technologies, have similarly expanded information-sharing capabilities by enhancing the ability to navigate information online. In the traditional search model embodied by Google, the vast array of anonymous information online provides the basis for powerful tools of information discrimination and location. In the newer social model embodied by Facebook and Google+, the information associated with a person's comparatively small network of acquaintances is the basis for identifying information of all kinds that is likely to be relevant and meaningful. An enormous part of contemporary social life involves the production and sharing of information in repositories, databases, and archives. Some is produced intentionally, such as when someone edits Wikipedia or posts a video. Some is produced secondarily, such as when someone "friends" another person, which signals some increased probability of shared interests or tastes. Such resources create tremendous opportunities for collective action efforts by putting information directly in the hands of those for whom it is most critical, making organizations and the work they do more transparent, and giving people alternative information sources that often reveal networks of shared interest.

Other forms of collective endeavors made possible by technology have not reached the level of regular social practice but may well do so. Flash mobs (see Rheingold, 2002) and their derivatives are an example. Exploiting a combination of mobile telephony, e-mail, and Web technologies, these groups coalesce in the most ephemeral of ways. For example, in May 2008, organizers of "Day of Silence" demonstrations for gay rights in Russia organized small flash mobs in Novokuznetsk and Yaroslavl. Participants coordinated by social-networking technology, in part to avoid repression by the state. In both instances, the groups were met with violent responses by other citizens, who apparently had also observed the call to assemble and acted in parallel. The capacity to mobilize people to gather at a particular moment for a common goal on short notice involves solving information problems unfamiliar to most traditional organizations – identifying people proximate to a location within a span of only hours and contacting them with an appeal for action tailored to the specific interests or personalities of the participants. Flash mobs permit ongoing, decentralized communication among participants in ways that facilitate individual agency and a level of coordination rarely achievable even by formal organizations with considerable resources at hand.

Moreover, as technological tools become increasingly ubiquitous, a number of possibilities that were until very recently unthinkable become prominent. In an atmosphere in which these tools are being used by a large proportion of the population, considerable opportunities exist to discover what others think and do, conduct informal research at trivial cost on a wide range of phenomena, and locate and connect with others with relative ease. Such emerging social practices have many implications for collective action, by establishing procollective habits and norms, altering people's very understanding of private and public information and knowledge, or literally creating public goods of various kinds.

More generally, human practices can be understood to emerge from familiarity with ways of acting, from literacy with particular techniques, and from a normative orientation toward some actions over others. Practice is social when it involves people's relations with one another, and it is social practice that bears on changing conditions for collective action. A number of observers have noted that technology is altering social practice in the direction of less boundedness and greater continuity across time and domains of action, or what Katz and Aakhus (2002) call "perpetual contact." Humphreys (2007) characterizes perpetual contact as giving rise to "microcoordination" combined with spontaneity, increased importance of serendipity in social interaction, social exhibitionism or performance, and the custom of documenting or cataloging social relations. When people coordinate with one another about social goals not previously articulated, or when people maintain frequent if not perpetual contact with one another not to achieve goals but because it is their practice to do so, the very possibilities of social interaction and collective organizing are altered within organizations.

In our terms, an environment in which individuals at the periphery of a large network are able to share ideas, coordinate, and communicate with one another nearly seamlessly suggests changes to collective action and membership in collective action organizations. The foundations of successful collective action efforts are fourfold: people making their preferences and desires known to others, locating others with shared interests, connecting with them, and facilitating coordination and communication. When a tool endowed with the Internet's basic capabilities – communication, connection, information sharing, and bridging – becomes ubiquitous, each of these abilities is enhanced and made more a routine part of life and less a discrete and conscious choice about means-ends relationships. It also becomes part of life inside organizations, just as it enables actions outside them. The fact that such abilities become more routine affects not just individuals initiating collective action efforts without the aid of formal organizations but also the experience of members of collective action organizations, who are influenced by the evolving expectations, norms, and possibilities of these technological tools.

The end-user enterprise inherent in contemporary technological tools, coupled with their increasingly ubiquitous nature, might at first appear to be detrimental, and even destructive, to formal organizations such as AARP or The American Legion. When individuals are able to act nearly autonomously in order to enlist the aid of large numbers of others, who share an interest but retain other individuating features, it would appear that organizations can in large part be rendered inconsequential or unnecessary. Much of the current rhetoric on self-organizing advocates such a view, proposing in the extreme that (at least theoretically) an individual can in such circumstances comprise "a one person company" (Nohria and Berkley, 1994) capable of achieving what in the past required highly resourced, formal, and tightly structured organizations to accomplish (Shirky, 2008). Across the world, and as the examples in Chapter 1 show, formal organizations such as Environmental Defense Fund, La Raza, and the Federation for American Immigration Reform, as well as the three groups we are studying, are actually thriving in the digital-media age, often with increased memberships and staff. Whatever the consequences of the ability to organize without organization, the irrelevance of formal organization to the public is not among them. So the questions become, what do these changes mean for organizations, and how can these be conceptualized not as a contest between formal and informal organization, but in more subtle ways? There are many approaches to this question. Ours is to focus on the concept of boundaries.

The Evolution of Boundaries and Organization-based Collective Action

Strong and difficult-to-cross boundaries have traditionally existed around people's private interests, separating these from public view and consideration, including from others with similar interests. Successful collective action efforts have typically entailed overcoming these boundaries, through methods for finding and coordinating a variety of people with sufficiently high interests in the public good and sufficiently high resources to help to achieve it. Affiliations with relevant organizations that might signal mutual interests, social networks of relations among like-minded individuals or those sharing some relevant and identifying trait, and strategies that publicize collective action efforts broadly are effective means by which to find the right set of potential contributors and to stimulate interest in the formation of public goods.

Each of these means of facilitating successful collective action efforts is altered by the existence of ubiquitous tools that enable broad information sharing among individuals. In earlier work, we have argued that focusing on public and private boundaries helps situate technology properly in a larger picture (Bimber, Flanagin, and Stohl, 2005). We suggested that much traditional collective action theory is limited to conditions in which private-public boundaries are firm and comparatively impermeable, such that individuals' efforts to cross them (e.g., by contributing private resources toward the realization of some public good) are characterized by discrete free-riding calculations in the context of high personal costs. Such conditions are widespread and important and will likely remain so. However, they no longer constitute all the relevant circumstances in which public goods are pursued. Many uses of technology confound categories of public space and private space, public communication and private communication, and one individual's social space from that of the next.

Weakening boundaries enable greater independence and opportunities for diverse entrepreneurialism on the part of individuals and have important implications for collective action within the context of formal organizations. Where boundaries are permeable and easily navigated implicitly or explicitly, such that costs of contributing to public goods are trivial or unobservable, then the choice to participate in collective efforts is no longer the sole useful rubric to understand collective action. When boundaries are easily crossed, the definition of organizational "membership" becomes a fluid and fuzzy notion. What does "membership" mean for those who contribute to communal information repositories, whether they are entries in Wikipedia or posts to AARP's online communities? Does participating in online "credentialing" activities of various forms or revealing the identities of networks of friends and common interests in social-networking environments make one a member? People who post comments on The American Legion's Burn Pit section of its Web site are not necessarily members, yet the Legion sees the blog as a way for people to "get on and start communicating and being part of this social organization," according to one person we interviewed. People do not pay to "join" MoveOn; so are its five million "members" not really members in the traditional sense?

When people have a great capacity to act freely and without constraints by larger social structures or formalized rules of belonging, their negotiation of a boundary typically involves less intentionality and calculation. The creation of deliberative public spaces, for example, is often seamless, emerging from activities associated with goals such as sharing photos online and not from the intentional objective of creating a space for political discussion. Yet the tagging of these photos and the commentary it engenders provide a public space in which diverse voices may be heard, interpretations are contested, expertise is reconstituted, and deliberations are not controlled by others.

It is not just these boundaries that are of relevance for understanding collective action. The entire human environment is composed of boundaries, at some levels clear and distinct, at others fuzzy and overlapping. Easiest to observe, yet rarely considered any longer because attention is increasingly directed toward digital technologies, are physical boundaries like mountains and rivers that separate geographic regions. These tangible boundaries separate groups of people physically, influence the types of economic and social practices that may emerge and constitute society, and powerfully shape the trajectory of language and culture. Political and sociocultural boundaries (often less obvious) divide nations, communities, and individuals but are even more consequential for people's identities and the ways that they organize and approach social life.

Although more difficult to recognize than even those defined by political institutions or cultural practices, the boundaries that are constituted by arrangements of communication and flows of information also powerfully influence and shape people's behaviors. Communication and informational boundaries separate what is private from what is public, what is "here" from what is "there," what is personal from what is social, what is "mine" from what is "yours" and what is "ours," and importantly for our present purpose, who interacts with whom and who is able to engage with which social or organizational processes. The permeability and relative strength of communicative boundaries contribute to the separation as well as the integration of individuals and groups, enhancing or mitigating physical and sociopsychological boundaries and defying or reifying the political and social boundaries defined by institutions. Paradoxically, once an individual has crossed a permeable boundary, it often becomes more difficult to go back than it was to cross it in the first place. In the case of the private/public boundary for example, a senior AARP official observed that people are more likely to return to an organization's Web site and maintain connection to the organization once they have set down roots with that Web site: "by roots I mean you uploaded your pictures, and your videos, you now have friends on this site, that you talk to every day, that you play games with every day you also have groups that you created so it becomes much harder for someone to leave . . . to give it up would be a big behavioral change."

Boundaries are at the core of collective action, and boundary-spanning tools ranging from the material to the ethereal suggest ways in which collective action processes are evolving. Physical boundary-crossing mechanisms like bridges and tunnels, for example, span geographic boundaries and connect previously distinct locations of interaction, thereby enabling people to congregate together in the same space at the same time. The capacity to interact directly with one another lays a foundation for collective action through the identification of common interests and the ability to act on them together. This capacity also sets terms for the ease and cost of collective action.

Like physical boundary-crossing tools, communication and information technologies accomplish similar tasks, allowing people at a distance to discover mutual interests and act together toward them where they are so inclined. The communicative and informational functions of postal services, the newspaper, the telegraph and telephone, as well as later technologies, all broke down boundaries not just of distance but also of personal, professional, and civic activity. Not coincidentally, the rapid expansion of the telephone during the early twentieth century – described as a "technology of sociability" (Fischer, 1992) – is associated with one of the most "organizationally fecund" eras in American history (Crowley and Skocpol, 2001). The technological changes of the last several decades have consolidated and accelerated many historical boundary-spanning developments. Organizations and organizing flourish when spatial contexts and time frames become reconstituted within webs of increasing connectivity.

Examples of digital media weakening what have traditionally been difficult boundaries to cross within and outside formal organizational contexts are plentiful. For example, viral e-mail and other forms of networked communication illustrate the ease with which what is located within the personal domain, such as an individual's private address book or list of friends in a social media site, readily becomes part of the public domain. Individuals receive a message from someone they know or from the organization in which they are a member, and without much effort forward it to other people in their own social network, some number of whom will forward it to people the original sender does not know, inside or outside the organization. Some of those people will repeat the cycle, and the message moves across network and organizational boundaries as easily as within them. The indifference of the message to organizational boundaries is crucial. Sometimes the originator of a message is later forwarded his or her own message by someone else, outside the initial network. In such cases, not only has the communication flowed effortlessly back and forth across personal boundaries, but the boundary between sender and receiver is conflated. Traditional collective action theory, which we will review in Chapter 3, would attempt to conceptualize this process as a series of decisions not to free ride. At best this is a strained and impoverished way to understand what people communicating in such an information-rich environment are doing. It is more informative to say that they are navigating back and forth across personal and organizational boundaries and across boundaries between the private and public.

Various discussion tools offered by groups such as The American Legion and AARP, including discussion boards, chat groups, and personal blogs, weaken boundaries between members and nonmembers, and between private and public domains. In discussion boards, small groups of members may hold conversations in public, as if speaking with raised voices on a crowded street for anyone to listen, but with the key difference that conversations are recorded for those not present to witness later. The "water cooler discussions" found on The American Legion's Burn Pit are explicitly personal opinions and do not necessarily reflect or represent the views, policies, or positions of the organization. Not surprisingly, The American Legion, like many other organizations, reserves the right to use its own discretion when determining whether to remove comments or images that it finds offensive. Yet the more important point is that the technologies used by the Legion facilitate public conversations that fall outside its agenda and organizational boundaries in the first place, even as they take place technically within them. SignOn, the petition site of MoveOn, is also a related example of boundary spanning. Those not affiliated with MoveOn are as welcome to use the site as those who are. By using the site, activists and petition signers create their own network of action and bring that network into view of MoveOn, which may attempt to recruit people from it in its own future actions.

File sharing, or the exchange of private collections of material with anonymous others across the globe, is one of the most powerful and institutionally disruptive general examples of boundary crossing. The end-to-end structure of the Internet enables the publication and sharing of previously privately held and privately controlled material to wide audiences that are typically unknown to the original information holder. Because individuals are able to manage their own content from their perspective at the periphery of networks, they are able to transfer digital data and images at will. What any one person "owns" at one moment can in another moment become an essentially public or organizational resource shared by many and "owned" exclusively by no one. When individuals post personal videos of their latest vacation on AARP's online community site, the boundary between organizational and personal identity becomes difficult to delineate. In this manner, the conversion of private to public information is seamless and permanent.

Another important domain of boundary weakening associated with features of digital media involves the hierarchical control of information by organizations. The evolution of data sharing, processing, and storage from centralized to largely decentralized peer-to-peer technologies empowers individuals to utilize and easily process information across multiple contexts in ways never before possible. As people have the ability on their own to access readily and interpret complex and diverse information about their organization and its goals, successes, or failures, their individual sense making becomes personalized across a greater number of contexts, and some people will become less reliant on established organizational authorities (Metzger and Flanagin, 2008). When news and independent commentary about the organization is available to members with a few clicks, information ceases being a tool exclusively of the powerful and becomes a resource that is shared. Informed decision making becomes possible at all levels of the hierarchy.

In this regard, the search engine, in some ways the sine qua non of the Web, is one of the ultimate mechanisms for transcending boundaries of time, space, and control. The Internet's end-to-end structure allows people to design idiosyncratic searches that produce a wealth of information, while freeing individuals from the constraints of their own locations and the flows of information directed at them from the organizations with which they are affiliated. Search engines enable people to "see" inside the walls of archives, libraries, institutions, and organizations of all kinds, as well as into the conversations, thoughts, photo collections, opinions, and music libraries of others. The hallmark of the classical search is that it functions without regard for the many potential boundaries between collections of information, thus making information that was inaccessible in the past readily available. Social search and recommendation systems extract information from specific networks of relevance to the searcher, but also cross boundaries in different ways. These mean that within "memberships" of organizations, traditional boundaries among hierarchical levels are diminished, command control structures are modified, and entrepreneurial activities are reinforced, whether people are using this power to increase their voice within the organization or to skirt it entirely.

Under these circumstances, organizational boundaries are porous in the sense that an organization's infrastructure can – with virtually no cost – be used by individual members for entrepreneurial activities not officially sanctioned by the organization. For example, postings on AARP's online community Politics/Current Events group often contain personal pleas by members to take part in some collective action, whether it is the support of an initiative or policy, the boycott of a practice or business, or the adoption of a particular viewpoint and action consistent with it. At the blog "BoycottAARP," a group self-described as "Christian, conservative, and libertarian, but not necessarily in that order" posts remarks about AARP destroying American values because of its health-care position and urges people to boycott the organization. A link from one contributor leads to a set of wall posts on Facebook in a group calling for the resignation of President Obama, which attracts a variety of conservative positions on issues beyond health care, such as immigration. In 2009, an Ohio Tea Party group attempted to organize a nationwide AARP membership card burning through its blog "The Tea Well," which mobilized AARP members from inside against the organization. The ease with which members of an organization can find and reach others inside and outside the organization is striking, not only because of the low financial and social costs of this entrepreneurial activity but also because of the seamless ability to cross organizational boundaries and pursue private or semiprivate interests in a public space.

Other scholars have noted that the low transaction costs and sheer scale and ease of connectivity embodied in technology significantly alter the boundaries between and among individual and organizational networks. Early studies of the global social-justice movement (e.g., Bennett, 2003; Gerlach, 2001) demonstrate the ways in which activist networks are mediated by digital communication and enacted through loosely coupled rather than tightly bound networks. Whereas previously only organizations had the necessary assets and capital to occupy global brokerage roles and bridge structural holes – by creating links among disconnected parts of a far-flung network (McAdam, Tarrow, and Tilly, 2001) – individuals can now readily engage in brokerage activities without organizational resources. Today, global social-justice networks are comprised of multiple, emergent, transient hubs that are not necessarily defined around organizational leaders. Instead, they are centered on the fluid and personal linkages made possible by the end-to-end structure of the Internet (Ganesh and Stohl, 2010). Network linkages reference and reflect multiple identities and entrepreneurial activity rather than ideology or organizational affiliation. In these networks, organizational and individual roles are blurred, and individuals are not bound or controlled by particular organizational identities, even though the organizations may remain vital. In the domain of global contentious politics, Bennett and Segerberg (2011) use the concept of "the logic of connective action" to describe how organizational strategies are changing to reflect these new conditions. They write that organizations are "morphing from being hierarchical, mission driven NGOs in some settings to being facilitators in loosely linked public engagement networks in others" (Bennett and Segerberg, 2011, 17). This reflects adaptation on the part of organizations to the reality of people's empowered, personal choices, which they write "are motivated less by altruism than the interest of sharing one's own ideas or appropriated content and seeing how others respond" (Bennett and Segerberg, 2011, 30).

People's involvement in collective action within organizations such as The American Legion or MoveOn can emerge in this context rather than strictly from explicit, bounded choices about whether to participate or free ride. Whether they experience their organization as highly social and networked or as individualistic is no longer solely a function of the structure and strategy of the organization but is also a function of their own choices. It is important that the practices associated with informal structures and networks do not simply replicate the conventional view of organizational functions or practices because costs of traditional information, communication, and coordination functions are lower. In some cases, the functions of these emergent networks surpass what is possible by the kinds of organizations that early statements of collective action theory intended.

So far we have suggested that people's engagement in collective action inside formal organizations transpires in part through a process of interaction and negotiation of their communicative and informational environments, just as it does in cases of organization-less organizing. Under these circumstances, although strictly speaking the choice to act toward an organizational collective action effort or not act often remains a binary decision (i.e., contribute or free ride), it also involves considerations and interactions not well characterized by the traditional, reductionist view of the organization. These include defining roles and boundaries and offering members choices to participate, mediated perhaps by levels of identification or other attributes that influence the decision calculus. Contrary to traditional theoretical formulations, the perceived cost of contribution to collective actions by using contemporary electronic tools is either a relatively weak factor (Fulk et al., 2004) or is unimportant (Yuan et al., 2005) in explaining individuals' decisions to contribute to information repositories. This confirms the intuition that the conversion of private to public resources has become relatively simple when using these tools. Other work on collective action has recognized the interactive, affective process involved in crossing boundaries between private and public. For instance, Melucci conceptualizes contemporary collective action as "the outcome of complex processes of interaction mediated by certain networks of belonging" (1996, 18). Technologies help people develop collective identities and identify a common complaint or concern. This does not simply alter the calculus of participation, but also it enhances the public expression of new kinds of private interests.

Positing boundary crossing as central to collective action implies that any set of conditions or influences on human societies that weakens or strengthens boundaries – especially between private and public, among individuals, and between individuals and organizations – should shape collective action. Historically, the nature of private-public boundaries has proven variable over time as societies evolve. Much classic scholarship on the industrial age, for instance, argued that the rise of industrialized, urbanized societies entailed the erection of barriers between the private and the public. The work of Tönnies, Durkheim, Weber, and others interpreted the modern age as a time of sharply defined boundaries. The private-public boundaries of the modern age arose from the structural and economic nature of society, its physical organization, and the reliance on comparatively costly and ineffective technologies of communication and information.

Preindustrial societies, especially small-scale agricultural and rural communities, exhibited comparatively porous boundaries of all kinds. Heavy reliance on interpersonal communication for exchange of information and for coordination, high levels of familiarity among members of communities, and high social interdependence meant that, within external boundaries, the public sphere intermingled closely with what would be more private domains in the later age. Theoretically, these conditions were actually superior to those of the industrial period for facilitation of collective action within the scale of these communities, although collective action across communities would have been typically harder. From this perspective, a close examination of collective action in preindustrial societies would also reveal sets of social practices that are procollective, rather than sets of distinct participation choices framed by elites.

Similarly, the structure of states and the nature of their public policies may affect the nature of boundaries, thereby influencing the extent to which collective action exhibits discrete decisions or more continuous, nondiscrete boundary crossing. Most recently, postmodern theory posits a contemporary collapsing of distinctions such as private/public that traditionally have shaped modern societies and identity (Taylor, 2004). Focusing on boundaries helps situate technology properly in this larger picture. It is not sufficient to say that contemporary forms of collective action are strictly technological in nature; instead, they are the product of conditions in society that can arise in various ways, but that at this stage come from the influence of people's use of particular technologies in ways that weaken industrial-age boundaries of many kinds.

The organizations in our study have a range of reactions to this sociotechnical environment in which agency and opportunity are manifest through weakening boundaries. AARP, for instance, has in recent years capitalized on the use of "online community" tools and the like, in order to facilitate direct interactions among its members. These resources enable AARP members to share everything from opinions to photos across a diversity of topical interests relevant to the organization and to themselves. In this manner, the organization has made it easier for members to connect with each other, yet under the banner of AARP and thus within the space of a shared identity based on the criteria that define organizational membership. Like many other prominent collective action organizations, AARP has thus made it more convenient to locate "like others," even though tools exist to do this independent of the formal organization. In this way, AARP and other organizations retain some "control" over their members, even as they offer them tools for independent communication and interaction.

Similarly, The American Legion has created an online environment in which members can "get connected" with other members who are neither a part of their local post nor participate in national conventions, two traditional channels for enabling member interaction and the development of a committed and active membership base. In the words of an American Legion staff person: "What I think is happening is that by having a Web site and a social network and a robust Facebook presence, ultimately those who don't want to go down to the post, don't want to go to the bar, don't want to go to the meetings – or maybe they can't because they are disabled – will have an opportunity to participate in The American Legion electronically. That's an important aspect of all this, that we give them a way to engage the organization if they are not inclined to get up and drive down to a bricks and mortar structure and work their way through the system." Online polling results and members' posted comments provide nonmember visitors to the Web site a sense of the diversity and activity within The American Legion. Besides having a Web site hosted by the national headquarters, which provides information about an array of services and a forum for members and others to connect directly with The American Legion and with veterans across the country and world, The American Legion has developed www.mylegion.org, a Web site designed to connect members with their own local post and department leadership. The American Legion has also recently begun to take advantage of a wide range of online tools in order to connect veterans to the activities of the organization. Thousands of members have signed up for The American Legion Online update on Facebook and follow it on Twitter.

Given its exclusively online presence, MoveOn clearly differs from most other organizations with regard to its use of communication and information technologies. In some ways, it has taken boundary breaking further than other organizations. For example, in 2003 MoveOn sponsored a political advertising contest called "Bush in 30 seconds," in which the public contributed original thirty-second ads against the policies of President George W. Bush. Winning ads were narrowed down from several hundred submissions by public voting in which about one hundred thousand people participated, and a panel of celebrity judges decided the winner. MoveOn then aired that advertisement nationally. It repeated the process in 2008 by soliciting advertisements in favor of the election of Barack Obama and selected a winner based on the votes of more than five million people. MoveOn commonly polls its members online to determine which issues its members want the organization to pursue. This type and level of information sharing creates ripple effects across the organizational landscape. For instance, online petitions are effective tools of political mobilization that encourage people to bring their personal networks to organizational or political business, while implying less organizational control over members' actions. In these and other cases, MoveOn clearly takes advantage of a range of technical tools to involve and engage its members directly in organizational goals.

From the perspective of organizational members, several questions arise: Given the range of organizational reactions to the current technological environment, and the diversity of options available to individuals for initiating and participating in collective efforts, how do members view collective action organizations and their utility? What is their relation to the organization and to other members, and the specific affective and organizational outcomes that stem from these? What are the dynamics of collective action in the contemporary technological context when people choose to act within organizations rather than outside them?

Our argument about technology up to this point has been that the key sociotechnical trends relevant to collective action are the design of the Internet and associated tools such as its end-to-end structure, which alters possibilities for individual enterprise, and the ubiquity of the Internet, which affects intentionality and choice, the presence of opportunities, expectations of engagement, and orientations toward social practice. This in turn can be understood in terms of weakened boundaries. In making these observations, we have eschewed listing specific technologies or attempting to differentiate the effects of one online medium from another, in favor of making the case that technologies matter because they provide a context in which boundaries of all kinds are diminished. For collective action, the implication is that across many dimensions of social life, boundaries are becoming less important in constraining behavior, delimiting spheres of interaction or communication, dividing the private from the public, defining people's choices, and constraining the roles that people play within organizations. This is the case within and outside of formal membership in organizations such as The American Legion, AARP, and MoveOn.

The presumption of access on a large scale to contemporary technologies raises questions about how well traditional theories can illuminate collective action now. Elsewhere, we have argued that focusing on the relationship of technological structure to emerging social practices brings to light changing foundations for collective activity. These cannot be explained adequately by the traditional emphasis on organizations like AARP or MoveOn as solving free-riding problems by creating opportunities for action and recruiting people who decide whether to participate or free ride (Bimber, Flanagin, and Stohl, 2005; Flanagin, Stohl, and Bimber, 2006; also see Lupia and Sin, 2003). Likewise, traditional social-capital theory has held that only community-based organizations such as The American Legion can build social capital by creating opportunities for personal interaction, but this presumption flies in the face of the levels of the entrepreneurialism and interaction that people can experience in virtually any organization now. In Chapter 3, we explore these problems in more depth and work toward a reconceptualization of collective action as a boundary-crossing phenomenon, against the backdrop of a technological environment that enhances individuals' and organizations' options with regard to collective action efforts.

3

The Collective Action Space

Conceptualizing technology as creating a context for collective action where boundaries are easily crossed provides a way around the problem of taking too fine grained a view of technological tools and their use in a period in which technology is ubiquitous and rapidly changing. If the observations in Chapter 2 are right, then we have moved a step forward in thinking about collective action in organizational contexts. Completing that task, however, will require a clear view of the theory of collective action, against which the significance of diminished boundaries can be examined; this is the first goal of Chapter 3. We begin with a review of the key elements of collective action theory, consider further what diminished boundaries imply for this body of theory, and then focus on two particular boundaries: among members, and between members and organizational processes and decision making. This leads to the chapter's second goal, presenting our main theoretical framework, collective action space, which provides a way to conceptualize and measure people's experience of two important kinds of boundaries within collective action organizations.

Traditional Collective Action Theory and Its Modifications

Theories of collective action have a special place and rich heritage in the social sciences. *Collective action* is one of relatively few broadly discipline-spanning ideas, with important contributions from economics and political science (e.g., Chamberlin, 1974; Downs, 1957; Olson, 1965; Ostrom, 1990; Samuelson, 1954), sociology (e.g., Coleman, 1990; Marwell and Oliver, 1993; Oliver, 1993), communication (e.g., Connolly and Thorn, 1990; Fulk et al., 1996; Markus, 1990; Monge et al., 1998), and ecology (e.g., Hardin, 1982) among other disciplines. Collective action theory has been subject to a great deal of critique, modification, and elaboration. Much of this body of reaction to the basic theory of collective action was powerfully symbolized by the 2009 Nobel Prize in economics, which went to Ostrom for work showing how common pool resource problems, a form of collective action challenge, can in practice be solved through adequate institutional arrangements – that is, forms of organization. Because processes of collective action lie at the heart of so many social phenomena, they are an important part of the fabric of societies. People's involvement in community affairs, voluntary and charitable activities, larger social and political associations and identifications, levels of social trust, and participation in democracy are all connected to matters of collective action.

Traditionally, collective actions, or those "actions taken by two or more people in pursuit of the same collective good" (Marwell and Oliver, 1993, 4), are framed as resulting in some shared outcome, or "public good."Public goods may consist of traditional, physical goods like parks, bridges, or libraries, or less tangible goods like databases of information or communication systems (Connolly and Thorn, 1990; Fulk et al., 1996; Markus, 1990; Rafaeli and LaRose, 1993). They may even consist broadly of public policies or political outcomes that affect all the members of a constituency or polity regardless of who advocated or contributed toward them as, for example, when The American Legion lobbied Congress to develop the Veterans Administration or AARP added its voice to the debate over health-care reform in 2010. Consequently, collective action perspectives have been applied to a great diversity of phenomena. These include classical problems such as voting participation, membership in interest groups, the course of social movements, and the success of international alliances. They also include problems such as the establishment of electronic bulletin boards (Rafaeli and LaRose, 1993), the formation of interorganizational relationships (Flanagin, Monge, and Fulk, 2001), and bidding behaviors on eBay (Kollock, 1999).

It is central to the theory that public goods are nonexcludable and nonrival. Nonexcludability stipulates that relevant people or groups cannot be excluded from enjoyment of the public good, regardless of their own contributions to its provision. The benefits of public goods accrue automatically to all. Nonrivalness means that one's use or consumption of the good does not reduce the amount available to others (Hardin, 1982). In reality, few goods are perfectly nonrival. Even the public good of clean air, for instance, is functionally limited due to automobiles, factories, and even breathing. In addition, most public goods are prone to some form of "crowding," whereby use of them by too many effectively limits their use by others (Barry and Hardin, 1982). Accordingly, it is common to emphasize public goods that are held in relatively joint supply, as opposed to being perfectly nonrival (Chamberlin, 1974; Hardin, 1982; Head, 1972), a reality reflected in the study of "common pool resources," in which some potential beneficiaries are excluded from obtaining the benefits of the public good.

Public goods theory proposes that early contributors to collective actions enjoy smaller marginal rates of return in the early stages of public goods provision (Markus, 1990; Marwell and Oliver, 1993), and once public goods are established, early contributors receive benefits that are only equal to those of the other participants (Oliver, Marwell, and Teixeira, 1985). This exacerbates the key problem in the successful establishment of public goods, "free riding," in which the greatest disincentives to contribute occur during the early phases of public goods provision.

The concept of free riding is central to our concerns about boundaries. Free riding occurs when people enjoy the benefits of the public good without contributing to its establishment or maintenance. Although some theoretical and experimental work has challenged the magnitude of the free-rider problem (Bagnoli, Ben-David, and McKee, 1992; Bagnoli and Lipman, 1989; Bagnoli and McKee, 1991; Marwell and Ames, 1981), it remains the central theoretical concern for theories of collective action. Early formulations, such as Olson's (1965), argued that group size is negatively related to the likelihood of collective action, due to the diffusion of responsibility within larger groups. This proposition reversed some earlier thinking on public association, notably that of Tocqueville (1945), who argued that a person's willingness to participate in groups is positively related to size, because people perceive larger groups as more likely to accomplish significant goals. Olson, among others, claimed that collective action would be crippled by individuals' tendencies to free ride on the efforts of others, particularly in larger groups, where it would be assumed that sufficiently motivated and resourceful others would take charge and where scale conceals free riding.

Subsequent views, however, suggest a more complex relationship. Larger, heterogeneous groups may actually supply nonexcludable public goods better, due to the smaller critical mass of contributors required for successful collective efforts (Marwell and Oliver, 1993; Oliver and Marwell, 1988). Moreover, reliance on group size to explain the likelihood of collective action is a rather crude measure of several important social phenomena that bear on collective action efforts, including the conspicuousness of individual contributions, social connections that foster action, and the complex nature of perceptions of the good.

Disincentives to contribute in the early phases of collective action are particularly strong for many types of public goods because returns to early contributors are deficient: early contributors must invest in the absence of investments by others, and thus receive little direct, immediate benefit from their contributions. In essence, the incentive system rewards each participant for waiting until others contribute, thus serving as a disincentive for early contributors. Consequently, the public good is not created unless there are some especially interested and resource-rich participants who are willing to pay the substantial start-up costs without receiving corresponding benefits. Even if such early contributors exist, marginal returns are low because the benefits of the collective action are divided equally among all participants, regardless of one's level of investment.

The challenge of collective action in these traditional formulations may be understood as generating sufficient interest among a subset of the public to contribute adequate resources toward a shared goal. Obstacles to effective collective action include the temptation to free ride on others' efforts, difficulties in locating appropriate contributors, challenges of motivating individuals to contribute under conditions in which individual costs seem to outweigh personal benefits, and the substantial burden of coordinating contributions effectively. Overcoming these obstacles often falls to organizations, whose role is to forward agendas and use tactics designed to address these challenges.

In this classic view, the key element in collective action is the individual's choice made in relation to requests and opportunities, often authored by the organization driving collective action. These choices involve free riding: discrete decisions by potential participants regarding whether to contribute to the provision of a public good or just take advantage once it is established by the actions of others. This is one of the best-conceptualized ideas in the social sciences; it is not only the bedrock of formal collective action theories and many models of cooperation but also is a very common informal heuristic in a wide range of conceptions of human behavior. The underlying frame to this core issue is a vision of the individual as respondent and decision maker.

Volumes of criticism have gone into the rational model of collective action and need not be recapitulated here. As Chapter 2 suggested, in our own previous work we have argued that this tightly constructed model of collective action is confounded by the collapsing boundaries of the contemporary technological atmosphere. In that work, we focused on the point that the choice to contribute to collective action efforts, or to free ride on the efforts of others, is most explicit where costs of action are obvious and nontrivial and where boundaries between action and nonaction, or between private and public, are clear and not easily crossed. When boundaries are permeable and easily navigated implicitly or explicitly, such that costs are trivial or unobservable, then choice is no longer the sole useful rubric to understand participation in collective efforts.

Throughout the literature, many of the largest obstacles to collective action are assumed to be problems of organizational communication in support of individuals' choices: locating and contacting appropriate participants, motivating them to make private resources publicly available, persuading them to remain involved despite short-term setbacks and long-term risks, and coordinating their efforts require a costly and elaborate communicative infrastructure. Olson conceptualized people with common interests in a public good in terms of "latent groups" that confront the logic of collective action. A latent group is not only a state of common private interests not yet publicized but also is a collection of individuals without the organizational structure to solve communication and coordination problems. Olson argued that "most (though by no means all) of the action taken by or on behalf of groups of individuals is taken through organization" (Olson, 1965, 5). In this manner, organizations are the central coordinating mechanisms through which individuals recognize and assess their mutual interests, create and sustain motivation to contribute to these shared visions, and develop ways to act together. Moreover, legitimacy for collective action is situated within organizational identities. Issue entrepreneurs, advocates, movement leaders, and others accumulate resources and expertise, organize structures for the purpose of recruitment and mobilization, and facilitate collective action through organizational means. Collective action has been generally understood to be most successful when it is well resourced and involves proximate participants, central coordination, clear leadership, and recognized organizational structures and roles.

The diminished boundaries associated with features of digital media are crucial to the assumptions of collective action theory. Diminished boundaries not only necessitate a reconceptualization of the basic tenets of collective action theory but also suggest that the requirements for organizing collective action efforts can be met by a complex array of organizational arrangements, within and outside a formal organizational rubric. When boundaries are weakened, the complexity of organizing is magnified and organizational dynamics belie the classical, narrow view of organization associated with traditional views of collective action, such as that of Olson.

First, there is an assumption that we can clearly distinguish who and what is inside the organizational boundary as opposed to outside it. Classically, organizations are positioned as empirical objects embedded within larger ongoing systems or fields in which groups of individuals exchange resources and information across clear boundaries. However, consider the individual who is not a member of AARP but whose personal YouTube video critiquing some relevant public policy is linked to the AARP Web site by a member of AARP. Where is the informational boundary? Does the video information help enhance AARP's utility for its members? Similarly, when American Legion members forward calls to action from the organization to their personal network of friends, and those friends act in accordance with The American Legion's wishes, where is the organizational boundary to be drawn? The same problem arises in the case of MoveOn's political advertising contests, and in many other situations.

Second, traditional views presuppose that the interests of each group are known and distinguishable and that individuals within a bounded group or role are more or less functionally homogeneous. Clearly the forty million members of AARP are a diverse lot. Even a brief perusal of local American Legion posts' Web sites shows that relationships among members are established in qualitatively different ways and reflect varying norms. In some, social-capital building is infused throughout a Web site filled with personal stories, opinions, and connections to others. For other posts, the Web is simply a means of exchanging news. There is potentially a great deal more variation in approaches to goals, in motivations for belonging, and in styles of membership than in the ideal-type portrait of collective action theory.

Organization Theory and Boundary Crossing

The richness of the organizational experience apparent today not only challenges classical collective action theory's conceptualization of the organization as controlling boundaries and authoring requests to members but also raises interesting issues in organization theory and how relevant boundaries are conceptualized. The central points of contact between collective action theory and organization theory are related to organizational boundaries. Where classical collective action theory places formal organization at the center of organizing, organization theory traditionally differentiates the concept of formal organization and social organization. Formal organizations are those deliberately established for specific purposes, such as serving a particular population or producing a good. In contrast, social organization refers to the patterned network of social relations and shared values and orientations that emerge as people interact and go about their daily lives. Both not only have relevance for collective action, but as we have seen when it comes to social practice, they can no longer be easily separated.

In their classic text, Blau and Scott (1962, 14) characterize formal organizations as having "explicit goals, an elaborate system of explicit rules and regulations, formal status structure, and clearly marked lines of communication and authority." Organizations are created to resolve tensions between collective needs and individual desires, with the systems for doing so formalized in advance and administered operationally.

Today, organizational theories vary widely in their view of organization, from rationally designed linear systems, with the concomitant concern for environmental fit, efficiency, and effectiveness (e.g., bureaucratic theory and contingency theory), to nonrational asymmetric systems of power and unobtrusive control (e.g., neoinstitutional theory, critical theory, feminist theory, and cultural theory). Some theories approach organizations as discrete entities with clearly drawn organizational boundaries and tightly defined membership separating what is internal and what is external. Other perspectives view organizations as loosely coupled network structures of changing resources and forms of exchange (Stohl, 1995). Challenging the container metaphor of organizations (Axley, 1984), many of these theories eschew structural categorizations completely, conceptualizing organizations and groups as emergent, communicatively constructed, and embedded discursive formations (Cooren, 2006; Putnam, Stohl, and Baker, 2012). Some theories are organizational-centric, such as theories of the firm, whereas others see organizations as ecological fields of activities in which organizational capacity is rooted in interorganizational relationships rather than the internal features of the organization, such as size or complexity (e.g., coevolutionary theory and resource dependency theories). From a collective action perspective, organizational theories and typologies may vary on the degree to which they address organizational dynamics under strong or weak boundary conditions, but they all address the basic dimensions of formal organizations: (1) classifying organizational purposes, (2) discriminating among the types and nature of member relations, and (3) distinguishing among organizational structures that, among other functions, limit roles.

Central in organization theory, as well as theories of collective action, interest groups, and social capital are classic cui bono typologies, which are based on identifying who is the prime beneficiary of organizational activity – that is, whose interests the organization is expected to serve, whether it be the mutual benefit of the members, business concerns of owners, welfare and interests of clients, or welfare of the public at large (Blau and Scott, 1962). One of the most prominent areas of scholarship on collective action within this tradition analyzes interest groups such as AARP as a form of nonstate organization in which the membership is expected to be the prime beneficiary. Interest groups that exemplify collective action, such as MoveOn or the NRA, are conceived as having clear purposes and defined goals as well as discrete and well-bounded contours. In the membership model, individuals are imagined to choose consciously and rationally whether to join and remain "in" the organization and to conform to an explicit set of organizational rules and normative expectations. It is crucial to this view that the boundaries associated with these roles are defined by the organization for members, not by members. The literature on interest groups generally focuses on the structures and processes associated with emerging goals and identities of organizations, mobilizing people and resources, building alliances, and shaping ideologies and cultural frames to support and sustain collective action.

Organizational scholars have tended to focus on two interrelated issues facing interest-group organizations: the challenges of membership apathy and free riding (Knoke and Wood, 1981) and the general tendency for oligarchic control, or the tendency for organizations to move toward centralization and hierarchy as they attempt to meet their goals efficiently (Barasko and Schaffner, 2008). The first challenge of membership apathy is rooted in the bounded dynamics among participants and the organizations. The claim is that organizational members need to maintain the sense that the organization is serving their interests and not other conflicting interests. Organizational identification is considered a primary mechanism of initial and continuing membership and commitment within the interest group (Knoke and Wood, 1981). When the organizational mission is not perceived to represent the values, goals, or motivations of the member, organizational identification is weakened, and it is less likely that the individual will be active or remain in the organization.

Because membership may have a specific and nontrivial cost to the individual, as well as to the organization, a great deal of study has been dedicated to understanding free riding and member apathy, as well as the organizational effort expended to persuade members and potential members that the activities and everyday practices of these public organizations are beneficial to the private interests of their members. From this perspective, it is the organization and its strategies that receive focus, rather than the perspectives and agency of members. Organizational identification and commitment have traditionally been reinforced through formalized efforts at socialization and communicative mechanisms such as membership booklets, news releases describing organizational actions, initiation rituals, and symbolic tokens of membership, such as pins, backpacks with insignias, and mailing labels disseminated among members. In this sense, organizational identification is a strategic resource that organizations create through interaction and communication with members.

But today these relations are far more diverse and complex. What does it mean to be a member of MoveOn when one does not have to pay dues? In its brief history, MoveOn has mastered the art of specialized mobilization, whether it is in phone banks, marches, virtual primaries, or bake sales. Members can contribute in multiple ways through multiple media. AARP and The American Legion are dues-paying organizations, but even here contributions to collective action transcend traditional relationships between organizations and their members. Every time a member logs on to a Web site and posts a comment, he or she is not only creating a form of personal connection with other members but also is participating in the development of a deliberative public sphere – the act of communication is part of a collective enterprise. These networks of interaction simultaneously free individuals from organizations, institutions, and material and physical constraints, but also link and connect the individual to the organization in new ways. Sharing one's opinions or resources builds networks that might later be activated within and outside organization control. These new Habermasian public spheres of deliberation and public opinion construction change the relationship between organizations and their members, by capturing such interactions as part and parcel of the organization and by extending its boundaries well beyond its traditional locus of control.

The question for collective action in organizations is how weakened boundaries affect people in MoveOn, AARP, or The American Legion. How does the end-to-end structure of technology, as well as its ubiquity, affect members' boundaries with respect to each other and the boundaries that define their roles with respect to the organization's decision making and direction? How does an environment in which information availability and sharing have been radically altered during the last few decades affect organizational members' expectations about their roles within the organization? Our approach to answering this question is nontraditional: it lies in the person's experience of the organization not in its objective structure.

Traditional collective action theory is focused at the individual level, which is appropriate. However, when scholars interested in collective action examine the organizations that are so vital, they typically shift focus from the individual, making the organization the unit of analysis. Although there is a great deal to be learned that way, what is missed is how people experience objective organizational structure and process, and especially how that experience varies within the membership of a particular organization. In circumstances in which boundaries are not firm and are easily negotiated by members, communication among participants is less controlled by the organization, communication outside the organizational boundaries is inexpensive and easy, and types of participation may be more spontaneous, more idiosyncratic, and overall less similar across members. As Chapter 2 suggested, members are freer to interact with one another, the organization, and actors in the organizational field and to do so more on their own terms rather than strictly on the terms of the organization. This is the first consequence of diminished boundaries within an organization – heterogeneity among members' experiences. It means, for example, that one cannot assume a modal set of member experiences are attached to AARP because it is an "interest group" or to The American Legion because it is a "civic association."

The character of relationships among members and their organizations under conditions of weak boundaries is calling into question long-established linkages in the literature on organizations. Civic associations are commonly understood to produce social capital and be distinguished from interest groups not in terms of whose interests are served, but rather on the relations among the participants. Rooted more in the tradition of Tocqueville than Olson, the social-capital literature concerns itself with associations exhibiting a crucial difference from interest groups: regular, personal interaction among members. The face-to-face engagement of neighborhood associations, fraternal organizations, and other organizations like The American Legion has traditionally created the basis for a sharp theoretical distinction from interest groups, which feature clear boundaries separating members from one another. Robert Putnam has been unequivocal about this assumption. Referring to AARP explicitly, he writes, "For the vast majority of their members, the only act of membership consists in writing a check for dues or perhaps occasionally reading a newsletter. Few ever attend any meetings of such organizations, and most are unlikely ever (knowingly) to encounter any other member" (Putnam, 1995, 70). Yet, as the data we will present in Chapter 5 show, 40 percent of the members of The American Legion (a traditional social-capital building organization) and AARP (a traditional interest group) report finding the contacts they made through the focal organization to be at least sometimes useful to them in ways not associated with the organization. Regardless of the type of organization, we see that social capital is developed through organizational membership, and these resources transcend organizational boundaries.

Although the logic of interest groups is believed to rest on the need by organization leaders to overcome incentives to free ride by anonymous members, the lynchpin of civic associations is the capacity for building trust and developing norms through interaction in the absence of strong boundaries between members. The trust and "norms of reciprocity" that people develop in such associations then feed their participation in collective action more generally. It has long been empirically demonstrated and accepted that social contact among members exerts considerable influence on the degree to which members identify and are active in organizational activities. The early work of Spinard (1960), for example, established that union activity was positively correlated with the frequency of interaction, positive identification, and homogeneity among workers rather than the dissatisfaction with management.

It is no surprise that this classic distinction among anonymous and nonanonymous forms of association does not hold up well in an environment in which boundaries are less obvious. Just as boundaries between public and private domains are blurred in the modern technological context, so are boundaries among kinds of experience in organizations. Diminished boundaries mean that, in theory, members of AARP who so choose can use social media tools to develop personal relationships with others. Likewise, people belonging to The American Legion may use technology to organize and coordinate across communities for larger-scale collective action, within The American Legion and beyond it, which may include disparate others not known in advance. These types of enhanced connection are prone to affect members' experience of their organization in significant ways.

A related implication of weakened boundaries inside organizations relates to the universal concern by organizational theorists regarding the conditions under which varying organizational structures emerge. A fundamental principle in organization theory is that structures arise from the complex and diverse interactions among members and their organizational environment. In this sense, structure refers to two aspects of experience, the structuring of the activities of members with one another and with the organization, and the concentration of authority and decision making (Pugh et al., 1968). Within the organizational literature, theories of structure are most often rooted in some form of contingency model in which technical (e.g., environmental uncertainty, organizational size, and technology) or nontechnical aspects of the context (e.g., culture, legitimacy, or trust) shape organizational structures, and the "fit" between structure and environment predicts organizational efficacy.

Although typologies of organizational structure are useful, they are challenged by cases in which boundaries are not strong and members play a substantial role in situating themselves within the organization, as suggested by the idea of AARP or MoveOn members building social capital with one another and American Legion members organizing nationally around issues of concern. Traditionally, however, environmental complexity is conceptualized as separate from organizational members who are assumed to be socialized into the organization, identified with the goals and tasks of their particular units, and part of the design structure. Clegg and Hardy (1999) describe implications of boundary breakdown:

> On the outside, the boundaries that formerly circumscribed the organization are breaking down as individual entities merge and blur in "chains," "clusters," "networks," and "strategic alliances," questioning the relevance of an organizational focus. On the inside, the boundaries that formerly delineated the bureaucracy are also breaking down as the empowered, flat, flexible, post-fordist organization changes, or to be more accurate, *loses shape.* (8)

In the case of collective action organizations, it is membership that is losing shape or, more accurately, taking on more complex and heterogeneous shapes as boundaries weaken and individuals are better able to negotiate them on their own terms. This does not imply that all people will make the same choices about which boundaries to cross or how to situate themselves in organizational contexts that are more flexible. It implies a continual negotiation of boundaries in different ways as various members act on their own styles and preferences, rather than being so tightly constrained by those of the organization. When organizations are spontaneous, open, and self-organizing, as well as deliberate, closed, and formal, the result is less homogeneity among individual members' experiences. To understand this theoretically, and in later chapters empirically, we need a specific conceptualization of how people's communicative styles inside organizations might translate into variation in their experiences of being involved.

The Two Central Dimensions of Boundary Crossing

Which boundaries associated with people's experience of organization-based collective action are most important? One fundamental boundary regulates the degree to which people interact with one another personally or impersonally. The literature on interest groups, for example, has in a sense codified the power of bounded, impersonal relationships. Interest groups like AARP are believed to be successful because they mobilize large numbers of citizens beyond the scope and range of their personal networks, multiplex ties, and other manifestations of local community. They aggregate impersonal relationships and amplify people's voices before the state and other actors in civil society. The power of an interest group lies in the highly circumscribed, bounded member roles and relations that permit scaling to large numbers. Interest groups work in this view by recruiting as many interested people as possible across external boundaries into membership; once inside, members are generally separated from each other but readily accessible to the organization for recruitment and calls to action. Organizational resources are directed toward strengthening the organization/individual relationship, providing incentives for identification with the organization writ large, and developing organizational trust. Little, if any, effort is expended in activities designed to facilitate member relations with one another.

In contrast, the social-capital literature has codified in theory the importance of personal ties and interaction in groups like The American Legion. Groups with personal interaction can offer significant advantages of attraction, motivation, and rhetorical sensitivity but are limited in size to the scope of people's ability to manage interactions and relationships. Groups not dependent upon personal interaction are free to scale much larger, with resulting gains in clout but, social-capital theorists argue, at the cost of cohesion, trust, identification, and other prosocial consequences of personal interaction. Social-capital theory is, at its most basic level, a theory of how organizational structure affects personal interaction, and Putnam's argument about the United States reflects the concern that organizations offering only impersonal interaction in public life are supplanting those offering personal interaction. It is not that organizations fostering personal relations among their members do not develop large membership bases. Rather they are fundamentally different in that the organizational mission and a great deal of effort and resources are devoted to organizationally sponsored activities that bring members together in social and interpersonal contexts. This in turn spawns corollary benefits to members, the organization, and society.

Although interest-group theory and social-capital theory each directly address the issue of interaction, traditional collective action theory has been largely agnostic about it. From Olson forward, decisions to contribute or free ride have not traditionally been understood as dependent upon whether people know one another or remain anonymous. The logic of exploiting the contributions of others by free riding on the production of a public good as well as the individual's calculus derived for participation is largely indifferent to whether others are known or unknown, although Olson and others do note that smaller groups are more likely to discover free riding by an individual. Thus even within traditional collective action theory, there is an implicit connection between the nature of communicative relationships and collective action. People are more likely to free ride as part of large groups, typically comprised of impersonal interactions, rather than as members of small groups, in which interaction is more likely to be personal and individual action may be more readily attributed to particular persons.

In this space between collective action theory's relative indifference to personal ties, and the distinct concerns of interest-group theory and social-capital theory with the impersonal and personal nature of ties, theories of networks make the general relational dynamic explicit. Strong ties built on trust and personal interaction can be productive, norm-enforcing, and persuasive in many ways that facilitate cohesion and collective action, as can the relative freedom and power of aggregating the voices of many people unknown to one another. Weak ties, grounded in impersonal member relations, are untethered by old routines, relational expectations, and redundant information. Power, opportunity, and creativity lie in the information and communicative capacity of larger, diverse, and fairly unconnected networks of people who add value to a person's strongly tied, personal relationships and who are tied just enough to rise above anonymity (Granovetter, 1973).

Despite the absence of specific attention in traditional collective action theory to the question of boundaries between personal and impersonal interaction, one variously finds the character of collective action portrayed theoretically by strong or weak boundary conditions that facilitate impersonal membership, personal relationships, or a range of ties in between. By explicitly recognizing that boundary permeability and the nature of people's interaction with one another are central features of collective action, it becomes clear that individual communicative experiences are likely to be at least as salient as the traditional factors scholars turn to for explanations of participation: demographic characteristics and a person's general propensity to be involved civically. Within organizational contexts of all kinds, from The American Legion to AARP, boundaries between personal and impersonal interaction are easily navigated. The affordances of technology hardly compel people to act personally, but they do provide opportunities to do so regardless of the structure of the organization, just as they provide people opportunities to find like-minded others at a distance and to aggregate their resources in impersonal ways. In the organizations from two decades ago, whether members' experiences were personal or impersonal may have been largely a function of boundaries created by the organization and reinforced by their explicit structural features. Today, whether they do so reflects the nature of the organization as well as the personal choices, interests, and styles of members – that is, how they communicatively construct their roles in the organization.

Interacting: From Personal to Impersonal

Within any organization today one is likely to find some members who interact very personally, some whose interaction is less personal, and some who do not interact at all. Rather than forming the basis for differentiating types of organization from one another, variation in interaction is a feature likely to be found within any organization. Viewing interaction as a continuous variable at the center of organizational life is necessary if one is to account for people's experience of collective life in an age of fluid boundaries, where people shift readily between private domains and public domains and where a person's experience of a collective action effort may entail a wide range of ties and relationships with nonobvious boundaries among them.

We take this idea as a central proposition to be explored and tested in our three organizations. We define this concept as "interaction," and in our surveys of the organizations' memberships, measuring interaction was a key task. Theoretically, we think of interaction as a continuum, where one endpoint is defined by personal interaction and the other by impersonal interaction. Personal interaction is just as it sounds: it describes repeated, intentional interaction with known others over time and the concomitant development of interpersonal relations. Personal interaction is centered on sustained relationships with others whose specific identities or personal attributes matter. Such sustained contact may generate "strong" ties among interactants, which typically embody mutual trust, shared norms, reciprocity, and close identification (Granovetter, 1973). Strong ties tend to be homogeneous along relevant attributes, embody additional shared links with significant others, and are multiplex, thus including mutual involvement in other personal and organizational contexts.

For people whose interaction is skewed toward the personal end of the interaction dimension, the development and maintenance of individual and group relationships often takes precedence over other types of collective activities, although social and relational motives may not be the only reason for engagement. Within The American Legion we expect there to be members who join and remain members for the tangible benefits they receive directly from the organization and the informational resources that are made available to members, in addition to the cultivation of useful connections and the opportunity to serve the larger community or to help increase the influence of the membership organization.

The other end of the continuum of interaction is impersonal. This type of interaction emphasizes the expression or pursuit of interests and concerns and involves no personal, direct contact with known others. Consequently, individuals remain largely unknown to each other in spite of their shared affiliation and interest. Individuals are often recruited into collective action through sources such as mass mailings, television and Internet advertising campaigns, news articles, and public service announcements, rather than through direct solicitations in contexts in which people meet and socialize. The historical direct-mail campaigns of AARP are paradigmatic cases. The organizational design and media possibilities of the 1960s, 1970s, and 1980s made it unlikely and certainly unnecessary that people who participated in the organization's efforts had direct personal contact with one another, except incidentally.

These types of impersonal connections are often forged through participation in large-scale campaigns sponsored by organizations. For example, MoveOn routinely solicits its members to call Congress expressing opposition to or support of one or another policy or issue or to sign petitions. In such instances, members' identities or personal characteristics are irrelevant to other members, and their actions are coordinated by MoveOn as a central organizer of relatively anonymous individuals. The power in achieving collective actions in such instances lies not in the social capital built across interpersonal connections, but rather in the sheer number of people expressing a position in common, by making their private preferences public en masse.

Any social benefit or development of personal relationships from happenstance face-to-face contact, such as might occur at a protest or on a march, remain secondary to the goals of the group and its members. Such impersonal contact is sometimes deemed a "weak" tie (Granovetter, 1973) although, theoretically, weak ties are structurally defined within a particular network and represent acquaintances who are not linked or associated with other links in the focal actor's network. It may be preferable therefore to identify these impersonal relations as "affiliative" ties, rather than weak ties, in order to indicate a sense of common connection that occurs absent of direct communication or other known linkages among individuals.

Organizations typically have tended to structure around specific locations along the interaction dimension, with an aim to define a particular kind of interaction for their members. But these boundaries can increasingly be overcome as members use technology to locate themselves where they wish on the interaction dimension. To some degree, such boundaries have always been navigable in some organizations. For instance, federated organizations such as The American Legion may be national or international in scope but also have local or state chapters. The Surfrider Foundation is a nonprofit grassroots organization dedicated to the protection and enjoyment of the world's oceans, waves, and beaches. With more than fifty thousand members across many coastal countries, Surfrider Foundation asks its thousands of unacquainted members to become involved in large, isolated, noninteractive activities that are anonymous to other group members. These actions include letter-writing campaigns and making individual financial contributions to their strategic initiatives. It is in the traditional classification scheme an "interest group."

At the same time, however, Surfrider Foundation chapters, like the local chapters of Amnesty International or the posts of The American

Legion, are central to the organization. Chapters act locally to protect their community's coast. Members may volunteer for organized beach "clean-ups," be present at city council and other community meetings when environmental topics are on the agenda, and attend civic events like farmers' markets and summer festivals, as an organizational representative to sit at a booth and meet and inform the public about the organization. During these activities, and the many more that are undertaken, community members get to know one another, share interests, and may develop strong ties. A number of federated interest groups, such as the Sierra Club, have relied on a chapter-based structure that provides opportunities for regular face-to-face meetings and outings with other members who would otherwise be anonymous. These personal relationships can be more than ancillary to the functioning of the otherwise impersonal group at the national or international level as it pursues its interest-oriented agenda.

In the contemporary media environment, collapsing boundaries separating personal from impersonal interaction mean that many organizations can operate across scale, or can strategically change scales between local and supralocal levels – what Tarrow (2006) calls "scale-shifting." Other new and compelling examples of hybrid modes of interaction are in evidence, and these should be expected to increase in number with the increasing ubiquity of end-to-end technology, evolution of new forms of collaboration and social practice, and changing nature of boundaries. Social-networking Web sites, for example, are infamous for their blurring of the private and public – for offering hybrid experiences in which people are immersed in interaction that ranges across the spectrum from personal to impersonal. Just as these practices are disruptive to traditional notions of privacy, they are disruptive of traditional ways of discretely categorizing social interaction and collective action.

The fluid nature of boundaries suggests not simply increasing flexibility, multiple strategies, or "hybridity" on the part of collective action organizations but also increasing complexity and heterogeneity of individuals' experience of others. Conceptualizing interaction as a continuum reflects the fact that no clear demarcation point necessarily separates wholly personal from wholly impersonal interaction in collective action contexts. The structure and strategy of group leaders or activists in response to specific events or goals, as well as the technologies of communication and information sharing available, shape the opportunities and context for participants to interact with one another, but in practice individuals' experiences are subject to vary, sometimes greatly, even within a single group. Focusing on the experience of interaction as an individual-level phenomenon, rather than simply as a product of group type such as "interest group" or "civic association," helps bring this fact into sharper relief. Measuring the extent to which this is true empirically for our three organizations will be a major task of the empirical analysis when we turn to it in Chapter 4.

Engaging: From Institutional to Entrepreneurial

Another important boundary within collective action organizations is the degree to which individuals participate in organizational agenda setting and decision making. In most traditional organization theory, the normative model of collective action includes a highly institutional organizational structure (Walker, 1991) in which individual choice is tightly constrained by reified hierarchical levels. This type of organizational design sets firm boundaries that constrain opportunities for individuals to influence an organization's agenda and to participate in decisions regarding organizational forms, strategies, and tactics. At the same time, the traditional mass media environment made it difficult for people to obtain information about the specific context in which any organization operates. One reason why people belonged to an environmental or civil rights group was to learn from the organization about issues and developments of interest to them, in the absence of good alternative sources of specific news. This meant that organizations could benefit from large information asymmetries with respect to their own members about what issues or projects the organization decided to pursue, as well as information about their efficacy.

In conventional bureaucratic organizations, participatory structures and processes are designed by those at the top to "enable employees to identify with organizational goals and collaborate as control agents in activities which exceed minimum coordination efforts 'normally' expected at work" (Stohl and Cheney, 2001, 350). Not surprisingly, collective action organizations often exhibit the same predictable structures within some broad parameters that are roughly hierarchical and bureaucratic (Bimber, 2003), thereby limiting member participation to formally designed and sanctioned activities in a well-bounded environment. From the Veterans of Foreign Wars to the National Organization for Women, Weberian organizational modes have several classic characteristics, including central leadership that can make decisions and rules for the group, the accumulation and expenditure of resources on costly efforts to recruit and mobilize participants, employment of staff in various specialized and fixed roles, from substantive experts to financial managers to legal staff, formal coalitions and institutional commitments, and the attachment of priority to protection and maintenance of the organization over time.

The digital-media environment breaks down some of these boundaries, just as it does boundaries around member-to-member interactions. People have ready access to up-to-date information and opinions about the organization from external sources of all kinds, and they often have opportunities to provide feedback to leaders, participate in internal polls, and even to organize like-minded members for action or advocacy inside the organization. At The American Legion, members develop resolutions to be considered for adoption at the post level, department (state) level, or National Conference. Comments on its Web site "certainly influence our enthusiasm to proceed with various initiatives," according to one of our interviewees, but he does not see members "getting resolution concepts from interactive media exchanges – more likely from something that has struck in their hometown, news, chats."

At MoveOn, a great deal of the general direction of the organization and tactics in the field come from collaboration between the national staff and members. The campaign director with whom we spoke confirms this: "Agenda and issues come from the members entirely, whether it is through formal processes where we ask the whole membership, or through our testing of positions with subsets of the membership." Some of MoveOn's tactics, especially in the case of what it calls "scalable actions," are also collaborative. MoveOn staff members distribute to field volunteers an outline of what they seek to accomplish and then tell those volunteers to figure out how to proceed. "We tell them: 'Here's the tool kit, now you go figure out how to implement it in your community. What does this look like? Where does it happen? What exactly is the program? Who are you going to invite?' All that comes from the local level, from members themselves."

Boundaries around decision making involve what we will call "engagement." People engage with their organizations, while they interact with one another. Engagement may at first appear simply to constitute "decentralization" or "centralization," but it is different. Engagement entails the extent to which participants are offered opportunities to shape the organization's direction, regardless of where in a hierarchy decisions are finally made. We call engagement "entrepreneurial" when individuals have a high degree of autonomy and may design collective organizational action efforts in ways that are not sanctioned or controlled by any central authority. In entrepreneurial cases of engagement, organizational members do not act within constraints or rules of action associated with the organization or group. In the extreme, member coalitions based on agendas, strategies, or tactics outside any official organizational framework can form idiosyncratically within the organization or network, and may be short-lived. Self-organizing mechanisms predominate. Individuals move easily in and out of organizational roles, and they are more likely to bridge the divide between the private and public realms. The iconic example of entrepreneurial engagement is the network of protestors that converged on Seattle in 1999 during the meeting of the World Trade Organization (WTO). This loose coalition of environmental, human rights, antiglobalization, and antiestablishment supporters had the goal of expressing common opposition to trade policies pursued by the WTO but lacked a central organization, consensual agenda, or consistent set of rules for engagement.

By contrast, classic engagement in bureaucratic organizations involves a patterned set of normative rules and practices that are expected to be followed by all participants. We label this "institutional" engagement. When engagement is institutional, individuals' access to organizational processes is strictly bounded in a system that defines and controls opportunities. Organizational hierarchy, such as the classical Weberian ideal type, plays a key role in influencing the shape and form of engagement while serving to reduce volatility and increase predictability.

Institutional engagement situates members' actions in the framework of "what is good for the organization" as it is determined by central leadership rather than by members. When Amnesty International sends out an "urgent alert" and issues a direct call for members and interested citizens to send a letter to a particular governmental representative in a particular country, the group is providing a formalized role for participants. Similarly, when AARP requests that its members take some direct action on its behalf, it does not provide space for members to guide or alter the request for action. This kind of collective action involves little initiative, creativity, or control on the part of individuals, and is best thought of as collective action that works by people responding to centrally initiated requests.

Collective actions that fall at this end of the continuum are more likely to have well-developed organizational routines, procedures, and artifacts that are intended to introduce members to the official organizational mission and standards of procedure. This is in contrast to entrepreneurial engagement in which members develop innovative repertoires of response, experiment through trial and error, and rarely develop stable routines and procedures. Institutional engagement is most often coupled with formal communication artifacts such as magazines, newsletters, and annual reports that socialize members to the values, rules, and obligations of membership. Informal communication mechanisms, such as organizational stories and rituals, help develop an organizational memory that is collectively shared, mutually accepted, and a stable and influential force on member practices.

Institutional engagement also tends to develop enduring coalitions with other organizations for the purposes of furthering the organizational agenda. These institutional commitments often mediate organizational communication practices, constraining what members can do. For example, if a group is registered as a nonprofit or nongovernmental organization (NGO) it is often subject to federal regulations regarding donations, expenditures, reporting procedures, and organizational transparency. The Nuclear Age Peace Foundation, for instance, a registered nongovernmental affiliate, has consultative status to the United Nations and is designated by the United Nations as a Peace Messenger Organization. Members of this organization have severe restrictions on how to develop their own agenda or practices. Prior experience and expertise become more salient under these circumstances, as organizations need to maneuver within an interorganizational bureaucratic environment that requires special skills and knowledge.

Most of the examples above fall very clearly on one end or the other of the engagement continuum. This type of bifurcation is clearly present in the way scholars and practitioners often conceive of organizational engagement: mechanistic and organic, democratic and autocratic, centralized and decentralized, and tightly coupled or loosely coupled systems are just a few of the many organizational dualities that have been developed. But collective action has often simultaneously exhibited both types of engagement. More permeable boundaries suggest more variation within an organization.

Clearly, evolving boundary conditions along the engagement dimension do not mean the end of institutions or organizations. Rather, increased flexibility in boundaries enhances people's capacity for a greater repertoire of engagement. Presidential campaigns offer an illustration. Recent presidential campaigns combine the classic form of central campaign staffs, a hierarchical structure of roles and responsibilities, central strategic decision making, and a very important resource-accumulation effort with a more freewheeling, network-based periphery, which is often formally dissociated from the "official" campaign effort. In many cases, centrally controlled campaign efforts embrace, without necessarily endorsing, the emergent campaign efforts of individuals that are facilitated by Facebook, MySpace, Meetup, coalitions of poorly bounded local and regional groups, and blog communities. This model can even be evident in the explicit goals of traditional organizations, such as the AARP Divided We Fail Campaign begun in 2007 to advocate bipartisan approaches to health-care reform, and what the Global Policy forum describes as Generation X NGOs: the small, nimble charities that rely on blogs and social-networking sites. These groups may complement the goals and activities of – but are not dependent on – more established institutional processes associated with traditional NGOs. Rather than constituting mere outliers that do not fit theories, these hybrids represent an important area of change and development in collective action today. Such possibilities for change in the modes of interaction and the mode of engagement set the stage for more accurate conceptualizations of contemporary collective action.

Viewing organizations involved in collective action in terms of interaction and engagement means that they are not distinguished primarily by their formal or informal characteristics, but rather by the ways in which personal relations and activities are enacted by members. Our theory of the "organization" of collective action focuses on what people do and how they communicate rather than on organizational structure per se. It is the key characteristic of collective action in the contemporary environment that form is more flexible and may be adapted to fit context, and it may vary across individuals within a single context. Most traditional conceptions of structure emphasize semifixed, predictable organizational structures and examine how these shape behavior. Contemporary collective action requires working as much the other way causally: emphasizing what people are doing, how they are relating to one another, and what opportunities are afforded them, and from these examining what organization and structure fit their behavior and help facilitate collective action.

The Collective Action Space

Interaction and engagement are thus key features of organizational life in the realm of collective action, and each has become more highly variable as a function of recent technological change. Although it remains to be seen empirically how common various combinations of these dimensions are, for theoretical purposes they are orthogonal to one another:

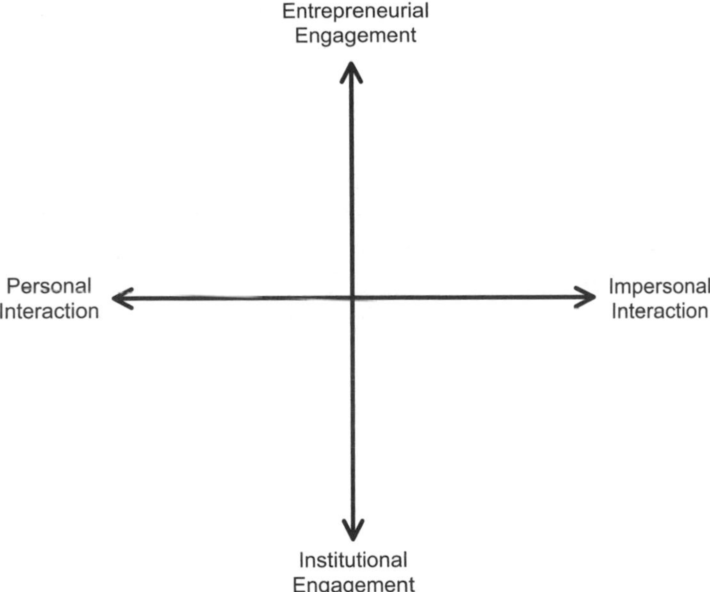

FIGURE 3.1. Collective Action Space

a member of an organization may experience any combination of interaction and engagement, which are theoretically independent. In principle, personal interaction can accompany either institutional or entrepreneurial engagement, just as institutional engagement can accompany personal or impersonal interaction. We can therefore array them perpendicularly to form a two-dimensional collective action space, as depicted in Figure 3.1.

In the collective action space, we arbitrarily designate interaction as the horizontal dimension, with personal interaction at the left and impersonal at the right. A member of an organization involved in collective action can in principle be located anywhere along this dimension. Engagement is depicted on the vertical dimension, and we place entrepreneurial engagement at the top and institutional engagement at the bottom. A person might be located anywhere along this dimension as well. The result is four quadrants, each representing a specific combination of interaction and engagement.

By depicting these dimensions this way conceptually, it is possible to identify the locations of people belonging to very different organizations. People belonging to interest groups, civic associations, informal networks, and any other organizational form can be compared by focusing at the individual level on where organizational members are located, as a function of their personal experience of the organization. For example, the median participant in Meetups, in which people use a Web site to find and meet others interested in similar activities, would likely fall toward the upper left, where interaction is more personal and engagement more entrepreneurial. Toward the lower right, diagonally opposite, would be many participants in RightMarch.com. Membership in this conservative online organization is largely anonymous, and engagement almost exclusively involves responding to centrally directed calls for action on such topics as limiting immigration. If one had surveyed participants in the massive 2010 Copenhagen climate conference protest, the result would likely be that they fall all across the entire collective action space. Many formal organizations mobilized people to participate, but many activists freelanced, creating messages and acting out in ways they saw fit. Many were clearly there as part of large networks, and some were in smaller groups.

Location in collective action space does not necessarily imply anything about technology use, though it might be tempting to imagine the upper quadrants as more highly "technological," due to apparently enhanced opportunities for providing organizational feedback. In principle, however, people could be located anywhere regardless of how intensively they use technology for their interaction or engagement. For example, some groups exhibiting primarily entrepreneurial engagement have traditionally done so without reliance on modern technology, such as the Grameen Bank, established in 1983 in Bangladesh in the absence of access to new communication technologies. That organization, like others, relies almost exclusively on informal networks and personal interaction for their entrepreneurial engagement (see Bornstein, 1997).

Collective action space helps shed light on the unresolved relationship among size, organizational dynamics, and free-rider issues within collective action theory. Olson (1965) claimed that free riding would be more rampant in large groups in which it would be assumed that sufficiently motivated and resourceful individuals would take charge and where free riding would be difficult to observe. Marwell and Oliver (1993; Oliver and Marwell, 1988), however, suggest that larger, heterogeneous groups are actually better able to supply nonrival public goods, due to the smaller critical mass of contributors required for successful collective efforts. In collective action space, group size is important only to the extent that it affects interaction and engagement, which can be mediated by technology use. The issue of the visibility of individual contributions, for example, becomes salient only when interactions are predominately impersonal and institutionalized. In the entrepreneurial/personal modes, by contrast, social connections will tend to minimize free riding because of increased visibility and responsibility.

If all organizations had homogenous memberships, collective action space would be useful for distinguishing among organizations as points in space, but it would indicate little about what goes on inside them. Changing boundary conditions, which make it likely that groups have heterogeneous memberships, however, mean that within an organization members are likely to be distributed along the axes. This means that an organization is best represented by an area, or a "footprint," in collective action space. Organizations occupying larger footprints have more diverse membership experiences, while more experientially homogenous groups demonstrate smaller footprints. In a small-footprint group, most participants interact with one another and engage in the collective process in similar ways, with the limiting case being a point at which all participants have identical forms of engagement and interaction. Many classical interest groups, such as the World Wildlife Fund (WWF), are good examples in theory of small footprints. WWF membership is anonymous, and the group has traditionally offered no substantial opportunity for participants to interact in any personal way. Members were also afforded few entrepreneurial opportunities because the group established opportunities for engagement only through donating or contacting public officials. Similarly, the Citizens Flag Alliance provides resources for individuals who support the passage of the Flag Desecration Amendment to the U.S. Constitution, without providing mechanisms for interaction among these individuals or any entrepreneurial means of action, goal formulation, or articulation.

An example of a group with a theoretically larger footprint is the Sierra Club. Like members of the WWF, Sierra Club members can choose to engage strictly in impersonal, institutional modes by simply responding to calls for action in an environment of anonymity with respect to other members. But the Sierra Club's traditional chapter-based structure also provides a variety of opportunities for members to meet with one another at the local level and to engage in social as well as political activities, especially small group outings in nature. These activities entail a good deal of personal interaction and only a modest level of entrepreneurial activities; local activities are still managed and organized by local group leaders, but they involve more opportunities for entrepreneurialism than traditional national-scale membership groups. Other such groups include the

American Civil Liberties Union (ACLU) and the Federalist Society, in which members may be highly involved at the chapter level, engaging personally with other members on localized issues, or simply reactive, participating in general campaigns directed by the national organizational leadership, without any form of personal interaction or contribution to the direction or tactics of the action.

In theory, the area occupied by a group might even be discontinuous. An example of this might be the complex footprint of the Howard Dean campaign for president. The official Dean campaign organization in early 2003 would have been located in the lower-right quadrant, the typical location of election campaigns, which are very hierarchically organized and share some features with the military organizations that conduct campaigns of war. It offered mainly institutional engagement and impersonal interaction with some opportunities for volunteering and more personal experiences. By the middle of the year, people not connected officially with the campaign initiated a variety of personal, entrepreneurial modes of engagement on behalf of Dean. These activities involved Meetups that were personal and entrepreneurial, as well as opportunities for individuals to blog and act as mobilizers – activities spread along the upper half of collective action space, where engagement is entrepreneurial (Wolf, 2004). Within a few months during the middle of the year, the Dean campaign embraced and encouraged these independent activities. Without exerting any centralized control over them, the impersonal-institutional campaign endorsed and supported the unofficial entrepreneurial-personal activities. By late 2003, the official and unofficial Dean campaigns had amalgamated into a complex collective action process with elements across the collective action space.

When we turn to the empirical analysis of our three organizations in the next chapter, we will look carefully at the shape of their footprints in both dimensions. Before doing so, it is worth exploring briefly how collective action space can be interpreted in terms of two well-known bodies of theory: social-capital theory and organization theory.

Collective Action Space and Social-Capital Theory

The argument by Putnam (1995, 2000) about the decline of social capital in the United States is readily interpretable in terms of interaction and engagement. The basic social-capital argument represents the observation that people who participate in more personal organizations (toward the left of the collective action space) are likely to derive a different set of resources than those engaged exclusively to the right, where interaction is impersonal. When social capital refers to the institutions, relationships, and norms that shape the quantity and quality of a society's social interactions, there is a basic assumption that within an organization, members' experiences are homogenous. Definitions such as that proposed by Putnam – "connections among individuals – social networks and the norms of reciprocity and trustworthiness that arise from them" (2000, 19) – assume that it is only personal interaction that enables people to build communities and develop a sense of belonging, trust, and commitment. Putnam's argument about the decay of civic organization and the rise of more superficial, interest-based association constitutes the empirical claim that, since the 1950s, many people's experience of organizations has shifted from left to right through collective action space and perhaps downward as well, toward more institutional forms of engagement. Social capital is thus most likely to be developed toward the left of collective action space, where strong ties are most likely to enhance the emergence of shared norms and relational trust. Any organizational movement from these quadrants is therefore thought to reduce social capital because other modes of interaction will be more likely to develop weak or affiliative ties and less likely to evoke a homogeneous value system.

However, the prevalence of contemporary collective action efforts suggests that social capital has developed in other ways that have not yet been identified or fully articulated. In our terms, scholars have largely failed to recognize the distinctions among quadrants with regard to social capital, which has been shown to develop not just as a function of personal interaction but also within an impersonal mode of interaction, and personally or impersonally combined with relatively entrepreneurial forms of engagement.

A related issue is the question of social capital online. A number of authors have taken issue with Putnam's assertion that social capital is unlikely to be built online. Wellman and colleagues (2001), for example, note a positive correlation among Internet use and involvement in online and offline voluntary organizations and political activity. Lin (2001) and others argue that there is "clear evidence that social capital has been on the ascent in the past decade in the form of networks in cyberspace" (211). Resnick (2005) goes even further, suggesting that new technologies enable "sociotechnical capital," in which information technology helps people connect with information and other people, share and exchange resources, and coordinate interdependent action. "Introducer" and "recommender" systems, for example, match people on the basis of common values, matching tastes, and similar sensibilities, all important in the early identification stages of collective action. Similarly, reputation systems help establish trust and credibility, which are important components of collective action. The question, therefore, is not whether social capital can be built online. It is where social capital can be built in collective action space and if and how the use of technology affects people's location in collective action space. Our expectation is that because the current technological environment facilitates relationships in all quadrants within almost any organization, it helps lay the foundation for the development of strong ties in ways that would not have occurred two decades ago.

Collective Action Space and Organization Theory

Theories of organization have a similarly direct relationship to the dynamics of collective action. Toward the end of the twentieth century, scholars and practitioners took note of radically new forms of organization that were developing and that raised several challenges to traditional theory (e.g., Nohria and Berkley, 1994; Powell, 1990). Network forms of organization are now considered to be the archetypal new organizational form, enabling organizations to rapidly adjust and maintain flexibility in order to meet the volatile demands of change within the global system (Stohl, 2001). Contemporary organizations are increasingly turning to network forms that stress complementarity, relational communication, interdependence, and high trust over more contractual or formal relations (Miles and Snow, 1984, 1986; Powell, 1990). These new forms transcend traditional boundaries (e.g., personal, national, and institutional) and are built around symbolic, informational, and material flows that link people together, often for short periods of time. The formal, centralized organizations with identified leaders, prescribed roles, and quantifiable resources that are fundamental to collective action theory are no longer the only, nor necessarily even the primary, means of contemporary organizing.

This evolution is captured in collective action space in the following way. Dynamism in organizational structure represents increasing density upward along the vertical axis of collective action space. Theoretically, the mechanisms for this are twofold: organizations in the bottom half of the collective action space, where engagement is institutional, spread their footprints upward as members seize opportunities for engagement. New organizations emerging in the entrepreneurial upper quadrants may either persist there or disband without experiencing traditional downward movement. This argument is analogous, though not precisely parallel, to the social-capital argument about the historical shift in the United States from left to right within collective action space since the 1960s.

Collective action space also captures potential changes in what had previously been a robust dynamic within traditional theories of organization. That is, virtually all structural-functional theories posit that, given the need for activity coordination and control in maintaining and growing an association (Barnard, 1938), organizations tend to become more formal, bureaucratic, and embedded within and constrained by interorganizational relationships (Aldrich, 1979; Hickson et al., 1979). This suggests that as organizations get larger and older, organizational dynamics typically move from informal face-to-face contexts to more formal and impersonal modes of engagement (Hage, 1980). Accordingly, in that view organizational profiles are continuously moving down and to the right in collective action space.

A predicted downward movement is also potentially embedded in the tenets of institutional theory (DiMaggio and Powell, 1983; Scott, 1995). Institutional theory posits that through coercive, mimetic, and normative mechanisms "organizational environments elaborate rules and requirements to which individual organizations must conform if they are to receive support and legitimacy" (Meyer and Scott, 1983, 149). These dynamics often result in a "startling homogeneity of organizational forms and practices" (DiMaggio and Powell, 1983, 148). In terms of collective action space, these processes suggest that individual collective action organizations, no matter where member interactions originate, should exhibit the tendency – consistent with the aforementioned structural-functional theories – to shift toward institutional and impersonal modes of interaction; that is, downward over time along the vertical axis and away from the entrepreneurial quadrants.

Collective action space enables one to explore whether organizational footprints still conform to these expectations or, rather, operate as we suggest, in the less unidimensional and more complex ways underlying contemporary organizational and network theory. Organizations may be incorporating more entrepreneurial modes of interacting (moving upward along the vertical axis), but they are not necessarily giving up institutional modes. Collective action space captures the degree to which boundaries between modes are becoming blurred, not only in terms of the population of organizations changing locations in faster and more diverse ways than traditional collective action or organizational theory suggest, but also in terms of whether individual organizations and their members are evolving in systematic yet unforeseen ways.

In this manner, theories of collective action, social capital, and organizations intersect in fundamental ways in the two dimensions of collective action space. Combined in this way, these theories suggest a great deal of dynamism and change at present in the landscape of collective action organizations. This dynamism has up to this point been recognized independently in these literatures, or has been attributed loosely to technological change without clear connections to basic behavioral processes enabled by technology that need not be necessarily connected to technology. Most importantly, the dynamics of collective action space reveal that apparently disparate phenomena reported by scholars working in various disciplines and on apparently distinct topics – including social-capital trends, technology and collective action, and organizational change – are potentially different facets of the same underlying process: changes in the modes of human interaction and engagement in collectivities.

So far, we have theorized that features of technological context lead one to expect weakened boundaries among members of organizations and between members and the organizations to which they belong. This idea can be represented in collective action space as a framework for thinking about the experience of people in organizations in which interaction and engagement are central. This framework begins to suggest some expectations for real organizations, as we move from purely theoretical considerations to considering more closely what happens in practice inside contemporary organizations. Collective action space provides an approach to explore a diversity of organizational outcomes, including contribution to organizational goals, identification with the organization, and organizational trust, outcomes that we will pay special attention to as we consider the results of our surveys.

At the most general level, this framework suggests that the dynamics of collective action for individuals are likely to vary substantially within our three organizations, as well as others. Because interaction and engagement are so crucial theoretically to so many theories, it is likely that where people are located in the collective action space will tell us a good deal about what factors shape their contribution to collective action efforts and their identification with and trust in the organization. Although the fractions of people in AARP and the Legion who experience their organization as entrepreneurial and personal are likely to vary substantially, for example, it is likely that their experiences are quite similar to one another, despite the very different objective features of their organizations. It is also likely that within any organization, the characteristics that are associated with more or less contribution to the organization's goals are likely to vary across the collective action space. For example, scholars commonly point to education as a predictor of various forms of contribution. But it is plausible that the association between education and behavior varies greatly as a function of whether one is engaged entrepreneurially or institutionally. In this way, collective action space suggests thinking beyond one-size-fits-all models of people's involvement in collective action within organizations. Overall, collective action space enables us to look at variation within and between organizations as well as to develop a model of collective action that takes into account traditional antecedents of collective action within an environment of weakened boundaries. In Chapter 4, we will see how these expectations play out in real life.

4

The American Legion, AARP, and MoveOn in Collective Action Space

In Chapter 3, we suggested that by considering organizations in a technological atmosphere in which boundary crossing is more fluid, collective action space can integrate a number of theoretical topics in social-capital theory, interest-group theory, and organization theory. We argued that this presents a potentially useful new way to look at organizations that is sensitive to variation in what memberships are like. It avoids stereotyping organizations and their members based on designations derived from structural characteristics, environmental features, or "typical" member profiles. So the question is, what about the memberships of The American Legion, AARP, and MoveOn? What do their footprints actually look like in collective action space? The first step to address these questions is to plot each member of the three organizations on the dimensions of interaction and engagement, so that we can visualize the organizations' areas in the collective action space. Then we will look at how people participate, as well as how much they identify with their organizations and trust them, in order to understand the similarities and differences in memberships across the organizations in our study.

The Study

To analyze the memberships of the organizations, we draw on data from surveys of these memberships. To conduct the membership surveys, we worked with leaders of each organization to obtain complete membership lists and treated these lists as three populations to be sampled. We surveyed members of the organizations by using a standard computer-assisted telephone-interviewing procedure based on randomly drawn telephone numbers of members and a Web-based online survey to which we invited participants through unique e-mail invitations from randomly drawn e-mail addresses. This allowed us to obtain independent probability samples of members of each organization.

Our sample of The American Legion members includes a total of 2,535 responses, 761 of which come from the telephone survey and 1,774 of which come from the e-mail survey. For AARP, we were unable to obtain a random sample of e-mail addresses,[1] so we included only the telephone responses, which number 854. For MoveOn, we obtained 1,714 responses, 403 of which are from the telephone survey and 1,311 of which are from the e-mail survey.[2] Our analysis showed trivially small differences between the telephone samples and the e-mail samples for the main substantive questions we are reporting here, so we pooled the samples across survey modes and created a single sample for each of the three organizations. Throughout this chapter and Chapter 5, we rely on a number of statistical perspectives regarding these three samples. We will use a convention in the narrative of describing values as different from one another only if they meet the standard criterion of p values below .05, taking into account Bonferroni and other corrections as appropriate, but we will not report significance tests in each case in the text, in order to streamline the discussion. If the differences between important values are not significant, we will either indicate this or we will not describe the values as being different in the first place. We have placed some of the statistical detail into footnotes and into the appendices following the last chapter.

Measuring Interaction

Placing members of the organizations in the collective action space requires measuring interaction and engagement. For interaction, we

[1] AARP did not release its full e-mail list but did permit us to solicit responses by using advertisements in a newsletter. We obtained more than 3,000 responses to this online survey, which we treated as an exploratory sample for the purposes of measuring bias in self-selected samples. Therefore, none of the analyses presented here are based on this sample.

[2] Surveying was conducted by the Social Science Survey Center at the University of California, Santa Barbara. The simple response rate for the online survey of The American Legion is 36.5%, calculated as the number of responses divided by number of people invited. The simple response rate for the online survey of MoveOn was 13.1%. For the telephone surveys, AAPOR response rates are as follows. For The American Legion: RR2 = 17.6%, COOP2 = 46.0%; for AARP: RR2 = 17.1%, COOP2 = 52.8%; and for MoveOn: RR2 = 20.1%, COOP2 = 56.4%.

developed a set of questions tapping people's perceptions of the personal nature of interaction in the organization of which they were a member. We treated people who reported no interaction with other members as having a completely impersonal experience.

Each participant who reported at least some interaction was asked sets of questions about their interaction and sense of personalness. Because we knew that participants might interact with one another either online, in more traditional face-to-face settings or by telephone, or in multiple ways, and because we wanted to be able to account for any differences between these modes, we asked each respondent two batteries of questions. The first battery included four items about their interaction with others "by talking with them on the phone or seeing them in person at meetings or events." We then asked about how much personal information the person knows about others with whom they interact, how much personal information others know about the respondent, how much they feel that theirs is the kind of organization in which people tend to know one another, and about how much they feel others actually know each other personally. We used some reverse-coded questions to disrupt patterned responses, and we used the average score across these four questions as a measure of the personalness of traditional interaction.[3]

Our second battery of interaction questions was identical, but it was focused on people's interaction online, which we defined in the survey as using things "like e-mail or a chat room, or instant messages, or a web site." The resulting scale constituted our measure of the personalness of online interaction.[4] For both scales, respondents indicated their level of agreement with our statements on a five-point scale, where higher values corresponded to more impersonal interaction.

We were interested to see how strongly correlated personal interaction online would be with traditional interaction by phone or face-to-face. An old line of reasoning about the use of digital media is that it replaces substantive "real-world" interaction with more superficial, highly mediated interaction, or even that it promotes alienation. Little empirical support for that thesis ever existed, but it seemed intuitive to many skeptics and persists in various critiques of digital media today. Research shows that people who are more socially engaged tend to be so online and offline,

[3] Cronbach's $\alpha = 0.75, 0.71, 0.80$, and 0.77, respectively, for The American Legion, AARP, MoveOn, and the pooled samples across all three organizations.

[4] Cronbach's $\alpha = 0.81, 0.79, 0.84$, and 0.84, respectively, for The American Legion, AARP, MoveOn, and the pooled samples across all three organizations.

and that online and offline social-network sizes are correlated positively (Wellman et al., 2001).

Because of these findings, we expected that our own measures of personalness of interaction online and offline would be correlated. The results support this expectation: when face-to-face interaction among people who belong to The American Legion, AARP, and MoveOn tends to be more personal, so does online interaction, with correlations of about 0.5.[5] Other studies have shown that the volume of communication and network sizes are correlated between online and offline worlds. Our results add the finding that the personal character of communication is consistent as well. For people belonging to our organizations, the act of communicating online as opposed to by telephone or face-to-face does not alter their tendencies to be more or less personal with other members of the organization. If one is personal in face-to-face interactions, one is more likely to be so online as well. Our own theory is agnostic about whether interaction occurs online or offline. Ample reason exists to posit that both are meaningful and this, coupled with the correlation between the two measures, prompted us to combine online and offline interaction into a composite measure of the personalness of interaction for each person in the survey.[6]

Measuring Engagement

Engagement, the second dimension of collective action space, captures the range of people's experiences of organizing and decision making in a group, from highly institutional to very entrepreneurial. Theoretically, engagement captures a crucial feature of organizational structure, namely the experience of participants' capacity to shape the goals of the organization and how those goals are pursued. As we saw in Chapter 3, engagement is closely associated with traditional concepts like centralization, formalization, or hierarchy, but it is not the same as any of these. Even some highly centralized organizations have means by which participants might shape the organization's agenda, if not decide explicitly on its strategies and tactics. MoveOn, for instance, offers opportunities for

[5] Correlations are as follows: $r = 0.53$ ($p < 0.001$) for The American Legion, $r = 0.45$ ($p < 0.001$) for AARP, and $r = 0.55$ ($p < 0.001$) for MoveOn.

[6] Cronbach's $\alpha = 0.85$, 0.80, 0.86, and 0.87, respectively, for The American Legion, AARP, MoveOn, and the pooled samples across all three organizations. For people who said they interact by using traditional and online methods, we simply averaged their scores for online and traditional interaction. For people who said that they interact only online or traditionally, we used the corresponding measure alone.

participants to shape the group's direction through surveys, discussions, and local organizing. The American Legion, like other organizations, is federated, so its national structure works with the state and local post structures. Although one might expect The American Legion to operate in a top-down fashion on a military model, there is no regulatory or governance authority at the top. Resolutions adopted by the national organization are ultimately optional at the state and post levels, where compliance is urged but not mandated. This sets up a great deal of opportunity for variability in the degree to which veterans feel they are able to participate in organizational decisions, from the highest-level policies to local direct actions. From the experience of members, it is more instructive to ask how much participants feel they are able to shape their organization than to ask how centralized, hierarchical, formal, or vertically integrated it is.

To measure engagement in our surveys, we asked a single battery of ten questions that tapped people's perceptions of how the goals of the organization are established, as well as choices made about what activities the organization undertakes. We asked about participants' perceptions that goals are determined by the leaders of the organization or influenced by members, and did the same for their perception of the organization's activities. We averaged responses to the ten questions for a composite measure of engagement ranging from 1, indicating more institutional engagement, to 5, which indicates the most entrepreneurial engagement.[7] Appendix A provides further information about measurement of interaction and engagement, how they are distributed, and the geometry of collective action space.

The American Legion in Collective Action Space

Civic groups such as The American Legion are portrayed in much traditional literature in quite specific ways, especially through the assertion that membership experiences are personal. In this view, membership in The American Legion would have several distinct features. Experiences would be chiefly or exclusively personal, which is to say that they are located in the left-hand side of the collective action space. Traditional views of engagement applied to The American Legion would suggest a middle location on the vertical axis, between entrepreneurial and institutional. As a group rooted in local posts, individual members have

[7] Cronbach's $\alpha = 0.88, 0.87, 0.89$, and 0.88, respectively, for The American Legion, AARP, MoveOn, and the pooled samples across all three organizations.

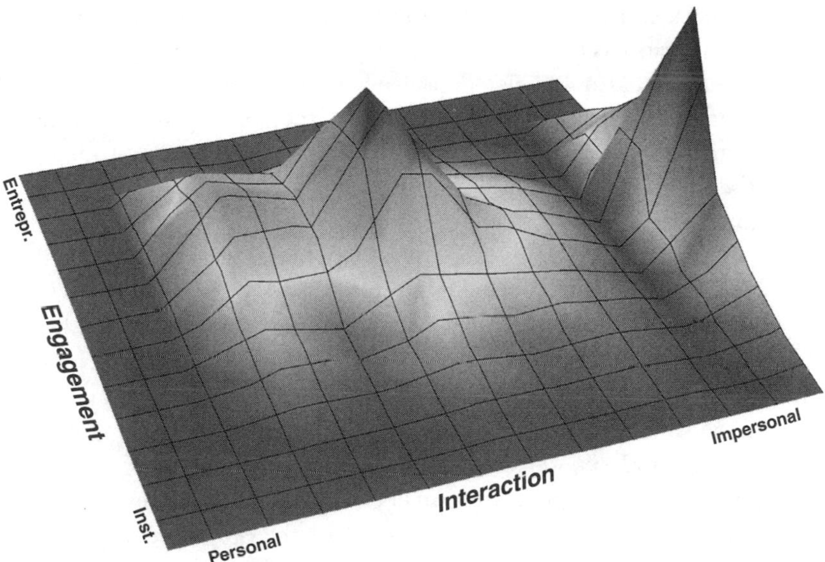

FIGURE 4.1. The American Legion in Collective Action Space

entrepreneurial control over what happens in their organizations. As an organization of veterans organized in ways that reflect military hierarchy – for instance through post commanders – a significant degree of institutionalized engagement might also be found. Therefore, because their interaction and engagement are structured by the organization, members' experiences might be thought to be quite similar and homogenous, and they would be clustered together tightly in collective action space.

But there are also good reasons to think that these stereotypic "ideal types" are wrong, as our discussion in Chapter 3 suggests. The ease of boundary crossing along the interaction and engagement dimensions implies that members of The American Legion may well spread themselves out along both axes, reflecting variation in their motivations for membership and personal communication styles. To the extent that members are able to contribute in some substantial way to the construction of their own membership experiences and to select communication options to fit their own particular circumstances, then the organizational footprint in collective action space should be large, reflecting this heterogeneity.

Our survey evidence bears out this expectation. Figure 4.1 shows the distribution of interaction and engagement, with the x axis representing interaction, the y axis engagement, and the z axis representing the number of members at the intersection of each x, y pair. Looking at the interaction axis, some of The American Legion members do experience their organization as highly personal, in line with the "ideal type" of civic groups. But a great many also experience it as moderately personal, and a substantial cluster find it impersonal, as if they belonged to an interest group rather than a civic association. There are two peaks of members along the interaction dimension, one clustered at the far right, reflecting impersonal interaction, and another centered toward the middle, reflecting the moderate experiences of many members. These are likely members who receive mailings from the Legion or visit its Web site for news and information but do not interact much with other members in highly personal ways. A third set of members is to the left of center on interaction. These are the traditional members who experience The American Legion as quite personal and are likely those who are most closely involved in post activities and experience close ties with other members.

Members of the Legion are considerably less diverse on matters of engagement, consistent with the members of the other organizations in our study. Legion members for the most part find their organization somewhat entrepreneurial, suggesting that they experience not just an opportunity to socialize with other Legion members but also a feeling that they have a voice in the agenda of the organization. To some extent, these are not distinct, inasmuch as there is a modest relationship between engagement and interaction: those who experience their organization as more personal also find it slightly more entrepreneurial, though this effect is not strong.[8] Overall, members of The American Legion reveal themselves to have much less of a classic "civic association" profile than the social-capital literature would suggest and to have, instead, a rather indistinct, hybrid set of features in the collective action space.[9]

AARP in Collective Action Space

Traditional views of interest groups such as AARP are as constrained as those of civic organizations. In the "ideal type," interest groups are comprised of anonymous members who do not interact with other members and have no meaningful regular say in the direction of the organization. Their role is, in effect, to await requests to act and then to make decisions about whether to participate or free ride. Putnam's (2000) caricature of

[8] Pearson $r = 0.25$

[9] For further descriptive data about the footprints of members, see Figures A.1 and A.2 in the appendix.

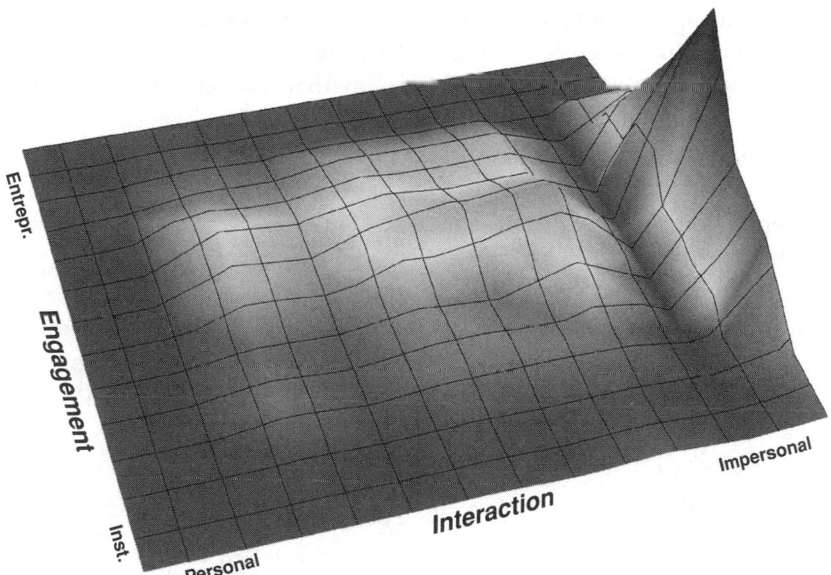

FIGURE 4.2. AARP in Collective Action Space

AARP that we described in Chapter 3 exemplifies this view, in which the vast majority of members does nothing but write checks or occasionally read a newsletter, and certainly never encounters other members. Viewed in that way, members of interest groups such as AARP should be clustered together in the collective action space, located toward the lower-right quadrant, where membership is more impersonal and engagement more institutionalized.

As with The American Legion, however, data show the reality of the situation is quite a bit different from these expectations. AARP members are actually distributed widely and overlap substantially with those of The American Legion, as illustrated in Figure 4.2. As with The American Legion, in Figure 4.2 we see a number of members clustered toward highly impersonal interaction to the far right. This is consistent with the stereotype of interest groups as being composed of members who merely respond to the organization's call to action and whose interaction with one another, should there be any at all, is highly impersonal in nature. However, there is a substantial body of members who also exhibit a degree of personal interaction, as evidenced by the peaks of members spanning from less impersonal toward more personal interaction. These members violate the stereotype prevalent in the literature on interest groups. Although the proportion of members with more personal than impersonal interaction is less than for The American Legion, we nonetheless see similarities in this regard than the literatures on civic associations and interest groups would not lead one to expect.

Similarly, the footprint of AARP members also spreads upward along the engagement axis, indicating that, on the whole, members are more entrepreneurial in their disposition toward the organization's agenda than might be expected. Again, this violates the caricature of members passively awaiting the organization's instructions to do its bidding, indicating rather a degree of entrepreneurialism on the part of members regarding goals and directions. AARP has similarities to civic groups in which members demonstrate that they sometimes do more than merely await instruction from the central organization on what issues to pursue. Here there is evidence that organizational members feel that they have some influence on the organization's agenda. Nonetheless, a senior AARP official commented in our interviews that she could not "think of a situation where . . . there has been a groundswell of a new initiative or something new from the community." In light of our data, this may mean that although some members perceive the opportunity to influence AARP's agenda, this is not a widespread occurrence. Or it may mean that entrepreneurialism is enacted primarily to shape existing initiatives rather than to formulate new ones. As is true of The American Legion, there is a modest correlation between engagement and interaction, showing that those who experience their organization as more personal also find it slightly more entrepreneurial.[10]

MoveOn in Collective Action Space

Unlike with interest groups and civic associations, scholars have not developed clear and uniform expectations about how people experience interaction and engagement in online organizations such as MoveOn. As yet there is no ideal type for these emerging organizational forms. The key characteristic of such organizations is that communication and information sharing is entirely mediated by technologies. For skeptics, this has typically led them to believe that communication among people is impersonal. By contrast, other scholars (e.g., Walther, 1996) propose that by virtue of the unique affordances of computer-mediated communication, relationships can actually exceed their face-to-face counterparts

[10] Pearson $r = 0.20$.

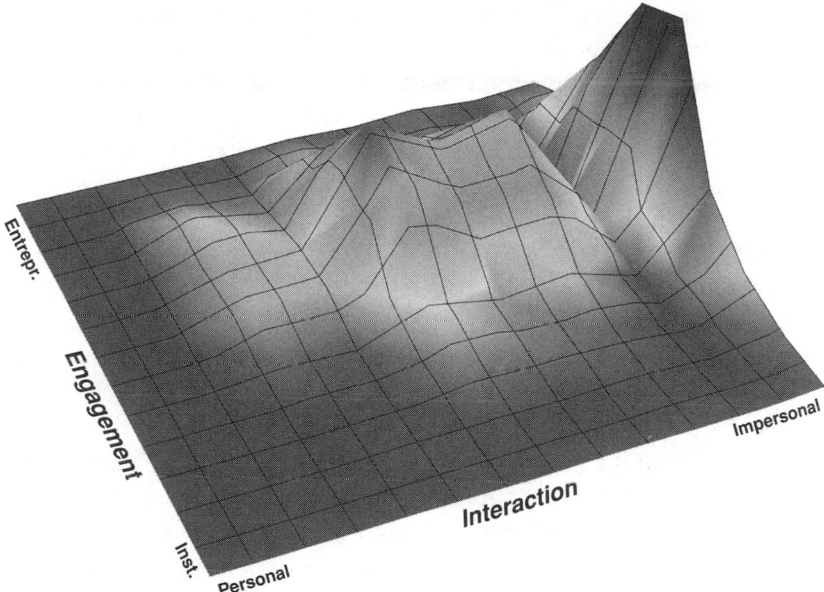

FIGURE 4.3. MoveOn in Collective Action Space

in terms of their personalness and the development of meaningful interaction under certain circumstances. For the most part, a common superficial expectation of online groups is that they are freewheeling and self-organized, due to the use of a readily available communication infrastructure that enables ad hoc connections and wide-scale information sharing to develop swiftly and on a large scale. For the most part, however, such expectations apply more accurately to online networks rather than to formal organizations such as MoveOn.

As Figure 4.3 shows, mapping MoveOn members' interaction and engagement in the collective action space demonstrates several things. First, like the other organizations, there is a group of members whose interaction is entirely impersonal, represented by the peak to the right of the figure. Moreover, in terms of interaction, MoveOn resembles AARP in some respects: members on the whole rate their interaction with other members as mostly impersonal, although there is also a sizable portion of members who report mildly personal interaction with other members. Regarding engagement, however, it becomes clear that MoveOn members view their organizational experience as quite different from that of the members of large organizations with specific interests, such as AARP. In spite of the fact that MoveOn is a very large organization composed of members who have no substantial mechanism for meeting one another or interacting face-to-face, members report overwhelmingly that they perceive ample opportunities to guide the goals and priorities of their organization. In this respect, MoveOn members are similar to members of The American Legion, with its federated structure. In the case of MoveOn, the correlation between engagement and interaction is weakest among the organizations in our study, showing that those who experience their organization as more personal only find it very slightly more entrepreneurial.[11]

The survey results show that it would be inaccurate to ascribe a common set of experiences with others to all members of each organization. Considerable variation exists, and all three organizations evince characteristics of personal and impersonal interaction from the perspective of members. About 35 percent of AARP members and about 40 percent of MoveOn members report more personal interaction than the average member of The American Legion. A comparable number of The American Legion members – about 30 percent – find their organization less personal than does the average member of AARP. The same point arises when one considers how many members in each organization report no interaction with others. We can think of these as isolated citizens, who engage with their organization in various ways without interacting directly with other members. In The American Legion – our face-to-face civic organization – about a quarter of members (26%) have no interaction, compared with 49 percent of AARP members and 31 percent of those in MoveOn.

Although between-group variation in personalness of interaction is larger than within-group variation, the latter shows that people experience each organization along a spectrum that varies quite widely. Each of the three organizations looks at least a little like a traditionally defined civic association and something like a traditionally defined interest group. This confounds traditional classification, and it suggests that in order to understand the experiences people have in these organizations, it is crucial to move beyond across-organization comparisons by examining within-organization variation – which is to say that we need to look at individuals. This constitutes our first key finding from the survey research, which is that organizational structure, strategy, and use of technology do not determine people's experiences of their organizations. People in these organizations are not interchangeable members of unique organizations

[11] Pearson $r = 0.14$.

but are potentially unique members of organizations that overlap in the experiences people have in them. This is a point to which we will return at several places in this chapter and in Chapter 5.

Digital-Media Use in the Three Organizations

It is interesting to ask about use of technology in the three organizations. Unlike many scholars' approaches to technology and civic engagement that have looked for a positive association between digital-media use and engagement, our theory of collective action space does not imply that those who use technology more will necessarily be more entrepreneurial in their relation to the organization or more or less personal toward fellow organizational members. Rather, it suggests that the digital-media context enables people to readily enact their own membership style and personal preferences, whatever that may be, in any particular organizational context. Digital media may help shy, reserved members get more out of membership while remaining that way, or it may encourage or enable them to reach out more fully than they otherwise might. At the same time, digital media may help the outgoing and sociable member connect with others directly, or media use may help that person to pursue a less engaged style of membership than is typical for him or her.

In our surveys, we measured several aspects of people's use of digital media. The first is Internet skill level. Those more proficient at using the Internet are presumably most likely to be affected by it. This has been a core assumption of those concerned with digital divides, where it is believed that those already likely to be advantaged in society socioeconomically are also most likely to use digital media heavily and therefore also to benefit most from it. Following Katz and Rice (2002), to measure Internet skill level we asked people to rate their own perceptions of their skills, rather than attempting to make an objective assessment using a skill test. The result likely conflates people's skills with their confidence or sense of efficacy, but drawing a distinction between these is not important to our analysis and comes with its own set of limitations. We also measured how much people use the Internet at work, and separately when not at work. We asked how many hours per week, at work and not at work, they spent online, using things like e-mail, a chat room, instant messaging, or a Web site. Our results confirmed our intuition that skill and frequency of Internet use are not proxies for each other. The correlation between these is modest: some people who use the Internet a great deal are not particularly confident of their skills.[12] We also asked how many years people had been online, the frequency with which they visit their organization's Web site, and, again following Katz and Rice (2002), whether they had any friends they know exclusively through the Internet. This last measure was intended to capture whether people have developed meaningful social relationships exclusively online, as a sign of depth of their use of the media.

On all of these measures, the three organizations fall into a discernable rank order, with AARP members scoring lowest, The American Legion members falling in the middle, and MoveOn members ranking highest, with more skill, more time online at home and at work, more years online, more exclusively online friends, and more intensive use of their organization's Web site. This rank order comes as no surprise, but what is striking is that the differences are not very great. Although almost all differences on these measures between organizations are statistically significant,[13] they are substantively modest. Given choices of ranking themselves as Beginner, Average, Above Average, or Excellent, the mean members of all three groups rate themselves between Average and Above Average. The American Legion members rate themselves as less than a half standard deviation more skilled online than do AARP members, and MoveOn members think of themselves about a quarter standard deviation more skilled than do Legion members.[14] The picture is quite similar for how long members have used the Internet. For MoveOn and The American Legion, the median member started using the Internet "Between six and ten years ago," while in AARP he or she first went online "Three to five years ago."[15] Similarly, members of each organization report that it is

[12] Pearson's r and Kendall's Tau-b are less than 0.3.

[13] Significant differences in the order indicated were found across all organizations for all measures other than hours online at work (The American Legion and AARP are not different from one another.), hours online when not at work (The American Legion and MoveOn are not different from one another.), and exclusively online friends (The American Legion and MoveOn are not different from one another.), as detailed later in this section.

[14] For The American Legion, the mean score for Internet skill is 2.67 ($SD = 0.90$), for AARP, the mean is 2.26 ($SD = 0.92$), and for MoveOn the mean is 2.86 ($SD = 0.85$; $F = 93.5$ and $p < 0.001$). Internet skill was measured on a 4-point scale in response to the question "What would you say is your Internet skill level?" ranging from 1 = "beginner" to 4 = "excellent."

[15] For The American Legion, the mean score for years online is 4.20 ($SD = 0.91$), for AARP, the mean is 3.87 ($SD = 0.99$), and for MoveOn the mean is 4.42 ($SD = 0.70$; $F = 87.4$ and $p < 0.001$). Years online was measured as a response to the question "When did you start using the Internet?" on a 5-point scale, ranging from 1 = "less than a year ago" to 5 = "more than 10 years ago."

fairly uncommon to have friends they know solely through the Internet.[16] We take this similarity as an indicator of the ubiquity of the technology and its commonness in people's lives. Being a member of a "high-tech" online group like MoveOn does not imply much about computer skill compared with being a member of a traditional organization such as The American Legion.

The areas in which one finds some meaningful divergence among the groups is time online and time spent at each organization's Web site. Not surprisingly, MoveOn members spend more time online outside of the workplace than AARP members, although *not* more than members of The American Legion. When considering time online at work, AARP and American Legion members are nearly indistinguishable, spending about an hour a day online at work, on average. MoveOn members, however, spend a little under twice as much.[17] With regard to time spent at the organization's Web site, MoveOn members do this much more than members of the other two organizations, consistent with the online advocacy efforts spearheaded by MoveOn, and Legion members frequent their organization's Web site more than AARP members go to theirs.[18]

Still, the overall picture that emerges across the three organizations is somewhat contrary to what stereotypes of the organizations might suggest, namely, that MoveOn members are highly technology-savvy, digital-media experts, while the older members of The Legion and AARP are either offline or are technological newbies. The Internet appears in these simple ways to be a rather comparable presence in the lives of people belonging to the three organizations in our study.

To explore whether there is a relationship between people's digital-media use characteristics and their location in collective action space, one can look for a correlation between each characteristic and each of the two axes. As our theory predicts, the data show that there is no

[16] This was measured dichotomously (1 = yes, 2 = no). American Legion members mean value is 1.74 ($SD = 0.44$), AARP mean is 1.86 ($SD = 0.35$), and MoveOn mean value is 1.76 ($SD = 0.42$; $F = 15.51$, $p < 0.001$).

[17] AARP members spend 7.91 hours online weekly when not at work ($SD = 9.13$), American Legion members average 11.88 hours ($SD = 11.48$), and MoveOn members spend 12.08 hours online weekly when not at work ($SD = 11.25$; $F = 31.35$, $p < 0.001$). As for time online at work, American Legion members average 7.7 hours per week online when at work ($SD = 12.2$), while AARP members average 6.6 hours ($SD = 10.9$), and MoveOn members average 12.9 hours per week ($SD = 12.5$; $F = 63.6$, $p < 0.001$).

[18] This was measured on a 7-point scale ranging from 1 = "never" to 7 = "more than once a week." The mean value for MoveOn members was 2.56 ($SD = 1.53$), for The American Legion the mean was 2.01 ($SD = 1.26$), and for AARP the mean value was 1.54 ($SD = 0.86$; $F = 138.43$, $p < 0.001$).

meaningful correlation between interaction and people's years of Internet use, Internet skill, or daily number of hours online. This is true across all three organizations: more intensive use of digital media is not associated with being more personal or having more social interaction in these organizations. The presence of digital media certainly matters in people's relationships to their organizations but not because it tends to make them more or less personal in their interactions with others. This supports a portrait of technology as part of people's routine social lives. Clearly they use it when they interact, but using it more does not make them interact more or interact in a specific manner. Although this does not itself prove our proposition from Chapter 2 that digital media are "disappearing" like plumbing, it does suggest that digital media use is part of the context of people's interaction with one another, rather than a specific force for change in that interaction.

The picture is a little more complex for engagement with the organization, though the conclusions are the same. In MoveOn, again no relationship exists. How entrepreneurial or institutional MoveOn members are is unrelated to their general Internet experience, even though virtually all of people's experience of engagement with MoveOn occurs online. In The American Legion and AARP, people's Internet skills are weakly associated with their engagement: people with more skill are slightly more institutional in their form of engagement, with correlations of about 0.1.[19] In The American Legion, the same is true for the number of years online, and in AARP for the number of hours of daily Internet use.[20] Yet on the whole, only about 1 percent of the variation in people's location on the engagement axis of collective action space is associated with their technology use. This supports our general concept that use of digital media does not affect where a person is located in the collective action space. Technology is part of the context of interaction and engagement, but it does not shape how entrepreneurial or personal people are.

Approaching Collective Action in the Three Organizations: Focusing on the Individual

So far, we have identified where people are situated in the collective action space, and we have seen that their location is not a function of

[19] For AARP, $r = -0.13$, $p = 0.003$ and for MoveOn, $r = -0.11$, $p < 0.001$.

[20] If a Bonferroni correction is made for the fact that these results come from 18 significance tests, however, then hours of daily Internet use is not significant for AARP.

technology use, though people are using digital media in their interaction and engagement – in MoveOn's case, that is their primary way of interacting and engaging. Ultimately, however, we want to know about people's involvement, which brings us directly to issues of collective action.

Involvement in an organization is attitudinal as well as behavioral. To be involved is to work toward goals and collective activities, but it is also to develop procollective attitudes and orientations toward the organization. Although behavior is important, and tends to be the primary focus of much theorizing about collective action, organizations do more than simply mobilize autonomous and anonymous individuals. Organizations help shape people's attitudes and goals and their willingness to be participatory in the future, as well as their propensity to participate in other organizations. People can be changed by their participation in an organization, and this process is potentially as important as simply measuring how many times people take actions. We therefore treat involvement in a collective action organization in terms of three concepts: contributions to the collective goals and activities of the organization, identification with the organization and its goals, and trust in the organization.

Contribution

The first element of involvement in an organization is contribution to the organization's goals, as a direct manifestation of collective action taken by individuals on behalf of the organization. This is a traditional measure of the success of collective action efforts, inasmuch as contribution by a large proportion of potential contributors is typically a strong predictor of the realization of public goods, particularly when resources are distributed among many people rather than clustered among a few. Collective actions weave together individual contributions, and although these contributions may be grounded in a diversity of motivations, goals, and interests, they cohere in a common attempt to produce a public good. To assess the degree to which organizational members participated in contributing to the organization's collective goals and activities, we asked people in our surveys at The American Legion, AARP, and MoveOn to assess how much they "personally contribute to achieve the things provided by [organization]," which we defined to include a range of possibilities, including writing letters, volunteering, giving some time or effort, going to meetings, or donating money other than membership fees.

Across our organizations, members reported a moderate level of personal contribution to organizational goals. On a 10-point scale (where

1 = don't contribute at all to 10 = contribute extensively), the means for The American Legion, AARP, and MoveOn were 4.8 (SD = 2.8), 4.5 (SD = 3.0), and 4.9 (SD = 2.2), respectively.[21] Slightly more than 20 percent of The American Legion and AARP members reported personally contributing a great deal to the organizational goals and approximately 15 percent of MoveOn members reported similar levels of contribution. In contrast, about 17 percent of MoveOn members reported no or very little personal contribution, compared to 28 percent of Legion members and 36 percent of AARP members. So there are great variations in member contributions within each organization. Moreover, it is not surprising that a somewhat larger proportion of AARP and American Legion members report little or no direct contribution to the organizational goals; for some, joining these organizations may be based on the wider variety of goods, services, and social experiences that the organizations offer to their members than those offered by MoveOn, which is primarily an activist organization.

Identification

Although understanding the frequency with which people have contributed toward the goals and actions of their organization is important, it does not necessarily tell the whole story of collective action efforts. Unlike explaining general participation in politics or civic life, where the emphasis is typically on describing the factors that activate a member to take part in some specific action or event, we are concerned with people's sustained involvement in organizations. This means that it is important to understand how people feel about their organization, in addition to how they may participate toward realizing its goals. Leaders of organizations are typically very attentive to developing positive attitudes on the part of members because they assume that such attitudes will sustain membership and collective action in the long run. Contribution to the organization's goals is a complementary outcome to other factors, such as organizational identification and trust, inasmuch as contribution can occur absent of each, particularly when contributions are made in response to organizational calls for action, rather than when they arise from a deep commitment to the organization and its members.

[21] Contribution values for The American Legion and MoveOn were not significantly different from one another ($p = 0.33$), whereas contribution values for AARP were significantly lower than those of The American Legion ($p < 0.01$) and MoveOn ($p < 0.001$).

Organizational identification addresses a person's perception of self in relation to the organization. Although relatively new to the study of collective action, organizational identification has a rich theoretical background in the study of other topics. Management theorists, for instance, define *identification* as the degree that people use the same attributes to define the organization and to define themselves (Dutton, Dukerich, and Harquail, 1994). Identification, according to this conceptualization, is "a property of individuals" (Ravasi and van Rekom, 2003, 124), and from this perspective one would expect goal agreement to be an important contributor to identification across organizations, irrespective of individual perceptions of organizational interaction and engagement. Moreover, the closer in alignment an individual's motivation for joining a group is to the perceived mission of the group, the higher the level of identification. This might be reflected, for example, in a veteran who joins The American Legion out of interest in contributing to his community, experiences the Legion's commitment to that goal, and as a result identifies more closely with the organization. In the long run, this means that the veteran may be more likely to participate in other Legion activities and goals.

Organizational identification is also studied from the perspective of social identity. Theorists posit that organizational identity is a shared perception of the attributes and acceptable behaviors of group membership (see Ashforth and Mael, 1989; Tajfel, 1978). Identification is constructed and has its effects through a process of self-categorization that accentuates attitudinal, emotional, and behavioral similarity to the group prototype – one's cognitive representation of the features that best define the group in the salient social comparative context. In this case, stereotypical views of the organization would be central to a member's level of identification. For example, a person with a perception of MoveOn members as progressive, hip, culturally adept, and socially concerned, and who feels these attributes reflect him- or herself as well, would be more identified with the organization than someone who did not perceive consonance between the organization and his or her own self-image.

Building upon Simon's (1976) conceptualization of identification, Tompkins and Cheney (1983) note that "A person identifies himself with a group when, in making a decision, he evaluates the several alternatives of choice in terms of their consequences for the specified group" (205). The more members view the welfare of their organizational group as relevant, the more likely they will make decisions based on the consequences affecting that group. This conceptualization emphasizes the importance of interaction. The communication of organizational values, goals, and decision premises serves as the persuasive conduit by which members internalize and process their own identities with that of the organization (Cheney, 1983a; Tompkins and Cheney, 1983). People with greater identification tend to see issues in different ways than those with less, making choices in terms of consequences for themselves as well as for the organization. From this perspective, one would expect a relationship between an individual's communicative experiences and their level of identification.

For these reasons, we conceptualized identification as an outcome. We asked about it in our surveys using a three-item measure adapted from Cheney (1983a, 1983b). The measure inquires about how much respondents feel that they have a great deal in common with others, how much they say it is easy to identify with the organization, and how much they find that their values are shared with others in the organization.[22]

The results show that members of all three organizations exhibit high levels of organizational identification, ranging from 3.70 for AARP (*SD* = .78) to 3.81 for The American Legion (*SD* = .78) to 4.10 for MoveOn (*SD* = .65) on a 5-point scale in which higher scores correspond to higher identification.[23] Less than 10 percent of the members of either The American Legion or MoveOn do not identify at least somewhat with the organization, and only 14 percent for AARP report strong or some disagreement with the extent to which they identify with the organization. Here again, we see that within-group variation is as great as or greater than across-group variation.

Trust

Across the social sciences it is agreed that trust is essential for understanding collective behavior. Trust is central to human transactions (Weber, 1930); individuals and groups demonstrate widespread preference for exchanges with trusted individuals over transactions based upon institutional arrangements (Granovetter, 1985), and trust is integral to the maintenance and efficiency of communities (Coleman, 1988; Fukuyama, 1995; Putnam, 2000). Trust reduces transaction costs (Levi, 1988; Williamson, 1985) and is a basic coordination mechanism (Bachmann and Zaheer, 2006). When MoveOn asks a member to host an organizational event and open his or her home to unknown others (a risky behavior), the

22 Cronbach's $\alpha = 0.85, 0.78, 0.86$, and 0.85, respectively, for The American Legion, AARP, MoveOn, and the pooled samples across all three organizations.

23 Mean values for all organizations are significantly different from one another at the $p < 0.001$ level.

individual's decision to do so may be based partly on organizational incentives, but without a high degree of organizational trust it is unlikely to happen. Trust therefore shapes the viability and sustainability of collective action.

The empirical connection between trust and cooperative behavior has been well established across theoretical traditions (McMillan, 1991; Ostrom, 1997). Organizational studies suggest that trust encourages individuals to remain in an organization (Shockley, Morreale, and Hackman, 2010) and influences members' perceptions of the organization and its leadership (Kramer and Cook, 2004). When tens of thousands of AARP members canceled their memberships during the health-care reform debates in 2008, the decline in membership was associated with their loss of trust in AARP to represent their interests (Harris, 2009). Those who trust an organization have a stronger belief in the organization's ability to attain goals that are consistent with their own objectives and thus are more willing to engage in risk-taking behaviors (Schoorman, Mayer, and Davis, 2007). Moreover, there is some evidence that trust facilitates adaptive deference to organizational authorities (Kramer and Cook, 2004). In general, once trust is established and an organization is viewed as trustworthy, the organization is more likely to get a positive response when members are asked to contribute voluntarily to organizational goals.

Trust has been conceptualized as a general predisposition of individuals (Rotter, 1967), a collective attribute based on the relationships among people in a social system (Lewis and Weingart, 1985), and a dimension of relationships that varies within a person, across relationships, and among contexts. Because we are concerned with members' experiences within the context of a specific organizational frame, we follow Tilly (2005), who regards "trust as a relationship with practices attached" (12), noting that although trust may remain within a dyadic relationship, it is more likely part of a larger network of similar relations.

When viewed relationally, organizational trust develops over time through interaction with known and unknown organizational members. Trust is therefore rooted in the communicative experiences of members, facilitating and facilitated by interpersonal relationships and network development (Lambright, Mischen, and Larmaee, 2010; Ring and Van de Ven, 1992). Within our study, we view organizational trust as members' expectation that the organization's future actions will benefit, or at a minimum not harm, them. It is the optimistic belief that an organization will act in the best interests of the individual and the collective and do so reliably, with integrity, fairness, predictability, and benevolence (Castaldo, Premazzi, and Zerbini, 2010). Because we are most interested in the general perception of trust and its relationship to organizationally sponsored collective action, we assessed trust in the survey through the use of a version of the general social trust measure, by asking "generally speaking, would you say that [organization] can be trusted or you can't be too careful with [organization]?"

Despite evidence of increasing mistrust in institutions across the United States (Heclo, 2008), the memberships in all three of our organizations exhibit very high levels of organizational trust. On a 1 to 4 scale (with 4 being the highest level of trust) the mean scores were 3.62 for The American Legion ($SD = .76$), 3.36 for AARP ($SD = 1.04$), and 3.51 for MoveOn ($SD = .73$).[24] Of Legion members, 59 percent reported that the organization can almost always be trusted, 48 percent of MoveOn members agreed, and 38 percent of AARP members responded in the same manner. AARP exhibited a greater degree of variance than the other two organizations. In every case, however, a very large majority of the members felt their organization could consistently be trusted.

Explaining Contribution, Identification, and Trust

A primary goal of our analysis is to explain the factors that contribute to these three indicators of involvement – contributions to the organization's goals, organizational identification, and organizational trust. In doing so, we treat each of these independently, though they are clearly linked conceptually. It is likely that people who contribute more to their organizations come to trust them more, just as people who are more trusting are more likely to contribute. The same is likely true of identification and contributions, as well as identification and trust. We are not interested, however, in attempting to untangle the complex interrelationships of these three indicators of involvement or attempting to collapse them together and treat them as a single concept. Throughout our analyses we will therefore approach each of these three indicators of behavioral and attitudinal involvement with an organization as separate and meaningful in its own right.

The correlations among these three are consistent with this perspective. Identification and organizational trust are only modestly correlated, with $r = 0.25$ across the three organizations combined. Those who are more

[24] Mean values for all organizations are significantly different from one another at the $p < 0.001$ level.

identified with their organizations are more trusting of them, but the data reinforce the theoretical view that scholars have of these as distinct concepts. Organizational trust is more weakly correlated with contributions to collective goals and activities with $r = 0.10$. One can contribute without necessarily trusting an organization. This fact is a good corrective to any overdrawn conclusion that the health of collective action in the United States hinges crucially on changes in levels of trust in organizations. Identification is more strongly related to contribution behaviors, with $r = 0.33$. One need not identify with an organization to contribute, but it helps. To the reformer wishing to restore the health of American civil society, as much thought should be put into questions about how people develop identification with organizations that reflect their own self-concepts as into matters of improving trust.

When scholars explain indicators of involvement such as these, they traditionally employ factors like age, education, and political interest, which offer variations on what might be termed the *standard model*. The standard model of contribution proceeds in terms of two sets of factors, one individual level and one focused on mobilizers. At the individual level, participation in politics, for example, is predicted by a well-studied set of general attributes, including education, age, interest, efficacy, and related characteristics whose specific contributions depend on the type of participation in question (Lewis-Beck et al., 2008; Verba, Schlozman, and Brady, 1995). The social-capital literature also highlights the importance of general social trust and network ties within communities (Putnam, 2000), and one can think of this literature as elaborating on the standard model.

When we analyze how such characteristics affect members' contributions to the collective goals of the three organizations in our study, as well as their identification and trust, demographics and general social trust explain almost nothing. The same is true about whether people have contacted a public official, have expressed themselves to a news outlet, have attended community meetings about local issues, and if they belong to other community groups. One cannot really say anything meaningful about collective action outcomes within these organizations from looking at the kinds of characteristics that social scientists use to explain voting and other forms of political participation.

This should in some ways come as no surprise because participation models have been developed for explaining different kinds of outcomes, namely those not embedded within any particular organizational context. Yet so much of politics and civic engagement in the United States is driven by organizations of various kinds – and so many Americans belong to more than one organization – that the poor fit of standard models to contribution in the organizational context is troublesome. To do better, one clearly needs to probe beyond these demographic factors in order to understand how people's motivations and goals shape their experiences of the organization.

Motivations: Instrumental, Social, Influence-oriented

No social scientist would doubt that motivation is crucial to behavior, yet it is quite uncommon to find a quantitative analysis of political or civic behavior in which motivations make an appearance. Quite often, motivations are assumed rather than treated as variables. The most commonly assumed motivation is instrumental. Influenced by rational choice conceptions of action, it is normative to assume that people act for some concrete gain. In the case of collective action organizations, membership is therefore a function of selective incentives: what the organization can provide back to the citizen in exchange for membership. For our purposes, we measured instrumental incentives by asking people to rate the importance to their decision to belong to the organization of obtaining benefits such as discounts, and getting useful information about things that matter to them. We made a scale from these two questions and labeled it "instrumental motivation."[25] Someone high on this scale belongs to their organization in part at least because of the short-term benefits or selective incentives that come with membership.

An additional and separate motivation for belonging is social. Some people are likely to join an organization because it gives them access to other people with whom they otherwise would not have the occasion to interact. People may belong because they have an orientation toward their community or the organization as a venue for interaction, expression, or service. It should go without saying that people with this kind of motivation for belonging are likely to approach participation and contributions to collective outcomes differently than those with instrumental motives. They may be seeking to contribute, or they may be drawn into action or stronger identification with the organization through their contacts with others. They are likely to experience the organization with fewer boundaries between themselves and others, as well as between themselves and the organization.

[25] Cronbach's $\alpha = 0.76$.

Social motivation can be thought of as adjacent to the concept of social capital. When scholars measure social capital, they are classically interested in the skills and social networks that people develop and with the norms of reciprocity that are associated with those. According to Putnam's canonical view, in both cases, skills, networks, and norms are characteristics that are strengthened or built from repeated interactions with others in a formalized setting of some kind. Social motivation is different: it taps into the reasons why a person might join an organization in the first place and why he or she might remain a member over time. In our surveys, we measured social motivation with a scale formed from three questions asking people how much their motivation for belonging to the organization involves connecting with other people whom they like to interact with, how much it is because of the chance to participate in organizational activities, and how much it is because the person wants an opportunity to serve his or her community.[26]

A third potentially important motivation for joining a collective action organization exists: because one wants the organization to represent one's interests in an influential way. This might be thought of as the original motivation: one joins an environmental organization because one wants to stand up and be counted as an environmentalist and believes that the Sierra Club, Greenpeace, or some other organization will do a particularly good job of making a difference. The point of much of collective action theory since Olson has been to argue that this motivation is insufficient. The shrewd calculator of Olson's world might know the organization is effective at advocating for issues of importance to him but will also realize that he or she can save the cost of joining and just as well enjoy the benefits of others' membership and the organization's advocacy nonetheless. Much has been written about the insufficiency of this stark portrait of behavior. We examined this in our survey by asking people how important it was to their motivation for belonging that their organization have the influence to represent them well on issues they care about. We call this influence orientation, and together with instrumental motivation and social motivation, it allows us to assess a broad range of theoretically interesting reasons as to why people belong to The American Legion, AARP, and MoveOn.

[26] Cronbach's $\alpha = 0.88$, 0.88, 0.81, and 0.86, respectively, for The American Legion, AARP, MoveOn, and the pooled samples across all three organizations.

Goals

In political-economic conceptions of collective action, such as Olson's, action is always goal oriented, and that goal is always the achievement of personal desires. That approach is agnostic about which goals a person might hold, and it is difficult to theorize individual-level goals that vary for largely the same reasons that studying potentially idiosyncratic motivations is challenging. Because we conceptualize attitudes at the individual-organizational level, it was relatively straightforward to ask people about how their own goals align with those of their organization. Using this approach, we need not identify what those goals are, and can instead focus on the extent to which citizens perceive that their own goals are reflected in what the organization does. We measured goal alignment by asking the extent of each respondent's agreement with the goals of the organization and then by asking about effectiveness in two ways. We asked each person's assessment of their organization's influence to achieve the member's goals and whether they see the organization as effective. We combined these items into a single variable.[27]

Digital-Media Use

What does technology use contribute to this picture? We argued in Chapter 2 that technology is crucially important as context, and not simply as a set of tools potentially used by organizations to engage with their members to varying degrees. A considerable body of studies has been reported showing some small positive relationship between Internet use and rates of various forms of participation, most of which are focused on campaigns and elections. For example, Prior (2007) finds positive main effects from Internet access on voter turnout in 1992, 1994, and 1996. Bimber (1999, 2003) finds small but significant effects of Internet use on campaign donations in 1998 and 2000, attending a political event in 2000, and communication with government. Jennings and Zeitner (2003) report a positive association between political involvement and political Internet use in a long-term panel study. Cantijoch (2009) shows that involuntary exposure to political information online is related to protest-oriented politics. Mossberger, Tolbert, and McNeal (2008) find positive effects from Internet use on political discussion, political knowledge, and political interest, with strong effects among younger citizens, and find positive effects from use of chat rooms and political use of

[27] Cronbach's $\alpha = 0.84$, 0.81, 0.81, and 0.83, respectively, for The American Legion, AARP, MoveOn, and the pooled samples across all three organizations.

e-mail on turnout. Xenos and Moy (2007) provide evidence that Internet use has a direct effect on information acquisition and use, that is, political knowledge or opinionation, independent of political interest, and that Internet use interacts with interest for a positive effect on civic participation, political participation, and political talk. Anduiza, Gallego, and Jorba (2009) also find relationships between Internet use and political information acquisition. Wojcieszak (2009) reports participation in extremist online discussion groups is associated with general political participation, controlling for ideology, news, and general political discussion. Excellent reviews of the participation literature are available (Boulianne, 2009; Mossberger, Tolbert, and McNeal, 2008; Xenos and Moy, 2007). Research has not, however, shown any upward trend in the role of technology in people's participation. Instead, it appears that the relationship is idiosyncratic, varying trendlessly across behaviors and across time (Bimber and Copeland, 2011).

We expected a similarly small and idiosyncratic relationship with involvement when digital-media use is treated in a variable-analytic way. We used our measures of people's number of years of Internet experience, their Internet skill, and their hours online, and the question about how frequently people visit the Web sites of their own organizations. This allowed us to say something about people's general experience with digital media as well as their use of it in connection with their organization.

These various elements constitute our basic explanatory structure: a set of individual attributes and attitudes – including demographics and other elements of the standard model, motivations and goals, and the use of digital media – as predictors of the three elements of involvement: contributions to organizational goals, identification, and trust. This model is depicted in Figure 4.4.

Collective Action within and across the Organizations

To begin the exploration of what explains members' involvement in The American Legion, AARP, and MoveOn, it is useful to look at each organization separately and to set aside for the moment our consideration of the dimensions of collective action space in favor of in-depth explorations of the factors related to involvement in our organizations. We used hierarchical regression analyses to do this (results are shown in Appendix B). By including traditional demographic and attributional measures (i.e., the standard model) as the first factor, we are able to compare our models

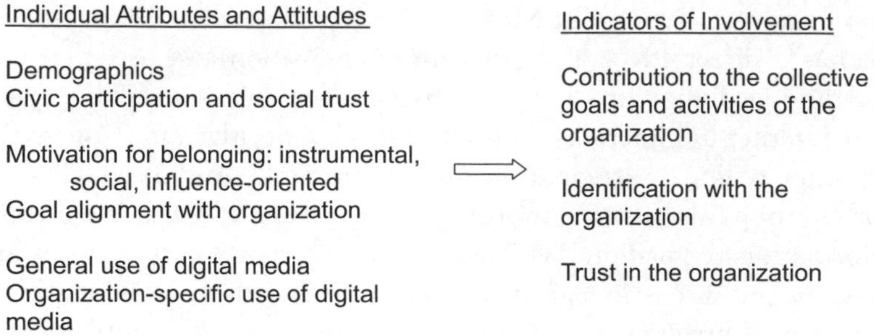

Individual Attributes and Attitudes		Indicators of Involvement
Demographics Civic participation and social trust Motivation for belonging: instrumental, social, influence-oriented Goal alignment with organization General use of digital media Organization-specific use of digital media	⟹	Contribution to the collective goals and activities of the organization Identification with the organization Trust in the organization

FIGURE 4.4. Basic Model for Explaining Involvement in the Collective Action Organization

to those typically used by behavioral scientists to study collective action. Our second set of variables includes individual attitudes that are specific to the focal organization and associated with instrumental, social, and influence-oriented motivations and goal alignment. The third level of predictors includes the measures of individual use and experience with technology as well as how frequently the individual accesses the organization's Web site.

Although we find slight variations among these three very different organizations, there are striking similarities in the results. First, in all cases, our final regression models are best at predicting organizational identification and worst at predicting trust. However, the difference in explanatory power between contribution and identification is relatively modest, ranging between 2 percent and 10 percent. Second, across all organizations, individual demographic attributes do very little to explain the involvement measures, while individual attitudes are far more powerful predictors of our relevant outcomes. Third, technology skills, experience, and use have little predictive power across all the organizations and across all three indicators of involvement.

The American Legion

Among Legion members, who contributes to the goals of the organization? Leaving for now the two dimensions of collective action space and focusing on each organization separately, we find that people's contributions toward the activities and actions of The American Legion exhibit many of the characteristics that one would expect from traditional perspectives on civic engagement. Members who are involved in other community activities and civic acts are also more likely to contribute to the Legion's organizational goals. This matches the traditional expectation that people in any one civic organization are likely to be active in others. Our results show that members who belong to other associations, attend community meetings, and contact public officials with issues of concern are more likely to contribute toward the Legion's goals. In addition, higher levels of general social trust are associated with organizational trust, a traditional relationship derived from the theory of social capital.

The demographics of American Legion participation hold two surprises. Lower educational levels are indicative of greater contribution to the organization's goals, although this relationship disappears when motivations and goals, as well as technology use, are included in the equation. Also, identification and organizational trust are not associated with age (although contribution is, positively). Both of these findings run counter to standard ideas about political participation, which suggest that older people and better educated people are more involved. Nonetheless, demographics, civic participation, and trust alone account for only a small amount of people's involvement – in statistical terms, between 2 percent and 6 percent of the variance.

The picture is very much the same for explaining veterans' organizational identification and trust, except that the statistical models explain even less. These standard-model attributes contain almost no meaningful information about how much a Legion member identifies with the group or trusts the organization. Because these are attitudes specific to the organization, this is not surprising. One would not expect to be able to tell very much about a person's specific attitudes toward a particular organization on the basis of general attributes such as expressiveness to public officials, age, or education. The slightly greater predictive power of these attributes on contributions suggests that behavioral tendencies, such as being participatory, are somewhat more likely to be generalized across a person's whole set of activities than are attitudes such as identification and trust, which are more attached specifically to an organization.

If this is correct, then if we add to the analysis our attitudinal measures (instrumental motivation, social motivation, influence motivation, and goal alignment with the organization), the result should be a much better ability to explain behavior as well as attitudes. This is exactly what happens. Goal alignment and the three motivations are associated with these outcomes, and adding them tells a great deal about each. With these accounted for, in statistical terms the model explains 41 percent of variance in contributions, 46 percent of variance in identification, and 15 percent for organizational trust. (See Tables B.1a, B.1b, and B.1c in Appendix B for the details of the analyses.) This is about as well as one would hope that a regression model would do in the social sciences, especially in the case of contributions and identification. What is more, when these factors are included, education is no longer significant in any of the equations. This implies something important, namely, that in this organization, the effect of education works substantially through people's goals and motivations and how they perceive these to align with the organization.

Regarding organizational trust for members of The American Legion, although explanatory power increases greatly when one considers motivation and goals rather than only demographics and other civic involvement (the variance explained increases to 15% from a negligible 2%), organizational trust is still far less predictable than either of the other outcomes associated with collective action. The results do, however, fit the general pattern in which most of the variation is explained by attitudinal variables rather than by the standard demographic factors. As later analyses will show, across all three organizations, trust operates independently of the social motivations that may drive organizational membership.

So far the findings regarding The American Legion support our general expectation that understanding involvement in an organizational context requires understanding how people feel about the organization at hand. Behavioral social scientists typically think about collective action in terms of generic participation models rather than contributions that are organizationally specific. Here we are focused on an individual's choice to participate in the context of a particular organization, so attitudes toward that organization are highly relevant.

We also wanted to know what role technology plays in this story. For that, we added measures of technology use, including how many hours people report going online when not at work, self-reported Internet skill, how long people have used the Internet, and how frequently they visit the Web site of The American Legion. The results are consistent with what much of the literature on the Internet and political participation more generally has found, namely, that these factors explain a little bit of additional variance in contributions to the collective goals of the Legion. In statistical terms, these increase the variance explained from 41 percent to 44 percent.

As has been true of the general debate about digital media and participation, these figures can be read in two ways. To those looking for evidence that digital-media use increases people's political or civic engagement, there is evidence here of a tiny effect, as is also true for AARP and MoveOn, which we will come to in a moment. Given how many other variables are accounted for in the model, this might be read as an interesting vindication of the idea that media serve as a concrete tool that increases people's participation, even when we already account for a full range of their attributes and inclination to be involved. Yet it is also the case that the only technology variable that is associated with contributions is how frequently people visit the Legion's Web site. People's general intensity of Internet use is not associated with how much they contribute. To us, this constitutes further evidence that, for the most part, digital media are part of the background and civic plumbing of people's lives. Whether people are Internet novices or old hands, feel skilled or not, or spend hours each day online or very little time at all has no relationship to their actual contributions to the collective goals and activities of the Legion.

Yet how often they visit the Legion's Web site does have such a relationship with level of contribution, and this dynamic is one that recurs throughout much of our data: people who are more contributory use the organization's Web site more. Are they more contributory because they visit the Legion online? Do the information and the activities available online motivate people to contribute? It is at least as likely that those who are inclined to be involved, those who already contribute a great deal, are attracted to and use the digital tools offered by the Legion. Moreover, the Web site may be the actual location of individual contributions, if people are taking action online. Our data cannot tell us which is the foundation of the relationship, but what we can say is that when people are active in achieving the goals of their organization, they tend to use the digital-media tools made available by those organizations, even though how much or how skillfully they use the Internet explains nothing.

This view of technology is further supported by the dynamics of identification and organizational trust. For these outcomes, the technology variables accomplish virtually nothing in the way of explanation. In The American Legion, people do not build or lose identification or trust through the use of technology. This is true of general use of digital media and specific use of the Legion's Web site. In the case of identification, a weak negative relationship exists with overall hours online. Heavy Internet users in the Legion are slightly less likely to identify with it, but this effect is so weak as to have no substantive meaning.

AARP

The story of AARP follows many of the contours of that of The American Legion. A handful of standard characteristics, such as belonging to community organizations and expressing opinions to media, combine to explain a very small amount (6%) of members' contributions to the collective goals and activities of AARP in Model 1. Interestingly, neither education nor social trust is associated with contribution to AARP's goals, but unlike the Legion, age is positively associated with contribution (prior to the inclusion of other variables) but not to the other two measures of involvement. Although AARP is often still thought of as an organization of "retired" people, many members are in their fifties, and enough diversity in age exists for the traditional relationship between age and participation to appear.

As with The American Legion, when motivations and goals are added to the picture, a great deal more comes into focus. Social motivation and goal alignment account for much of the variation in members' contributions, raising the power of the statistical model from 6 percent to 40 percent. Technology use raises this again modestly, to 42 percent, largely on the effect of members' use of the AARP Web site. (Table B.1b in Appendix B shows the details.)

The role of social motivation at AARP is striking. The traditional portrait of interest groups holds that people are induced to contribute through exhortation and selective incentives. According to the AARP Web site, the top reasons for joining AARP include saving with valuable discounts, enjoying "award-winning publications," and getting a second membership free. Effecting social change and having a voice in Washington are also featured but not nearly as prominently. Nonetheless, AARP members are contributing to organizational goals as a function of relatively community-centered motivations, just like members of The American Legion. Social motivations – not instrumental or influence motivations – drive AARP members' contributions to their organization's goals. Social motivation and goal alignment are also associated with organizational identification but only goal alignment is associated with organizational trust.

The technology variables play a somewhat different role for AARP members in terms of identification and trust. (See Tables B2.B and B2.C in Appendix B.) The degree to which members frequent the AARP Web site is not associated with identification or trust. However, AARP members who report higher levels of Internet skill are less likely to identify with and trust AARP (although the contribution to these outcomes is rather small; r^2 values increase by .01 and .02, respectively).

MoveOn

Involvement in collective action at MoveOn may present the most interesting case of the three organizations, especially to anyone still suspecting that online participation is superficial or cheap. For starters, the traditional attributes that do so poorly at predicting contributions in

The American Legion and AARP actually are more revealing in the case of MoveOn – a modest but respectable 11 percent of variance is explained by them. Older members contribute more, as do those who are involved civically in other ways, through other organizations, attending community meetings, contacting public officials, and expressing themselves to the media. Education is not associated with contributions, however. Among the three organizations, MoveOn is the one whose members are most likely to be self-selected for activism and who have an interest in being involved. The only reason for "joining" MoveOn is to act, unlike AARP, which so effectively uses selective incentives, and The Legion, which draws on a powerful, common life experience to construct membership. So even among the self-selected activists within MoveOn, some relationships still exist between overall civic involvement and contributions to MoveOn's activities.

Like the other two organizations, goals and the various forms of motivation are also important, raising the explanatory power of the model of contributions to collective goals from 11 percent to 25 percent, as well as from a few percent to 38 percent for identification and 13 percent for organizational trust (see Tables B.3A, B.3B, and B.3C in Appendix B). Despite the apparently different missions of the three organizations, much of people's behavior and attitudes can be distilled down to how well members' goals align with those of their organization, and the extent to which they join for a range of reasons that directly motivate them. Specifically, goals predict each indicator of involvement, and people in MoveOn contribute to, and identify with, their organization when they are motivated for social reasons and because they believe that the organization has the clout to represent their personal interests (i.e., influence motivation). Yet these same motivational factors do not influence their trust of MoveOn. Again the story is the same as in the other two organizations. Age, education, trust, and how involved people are civically explain a modest amount of people's behavioral and attitudinal involvement in these organizations, though these are traditionally considered crucial predictors of participation. What this means is that one cannot say very much about a person's specific involvement in any organization from knowing only characteristics that predict average levels of involvement. To know how someone is going to act within a particular organizational setting, one needs to understand what motivates that person and how his or her goals align with those of the organization.

One might expect the story of technology use to differ for MoveOn compared to the Legion and AARP, but it does so in only trivial ways. By definition, all members of MoveOn are at least nominal Internet users, which is not the case for the Legion and AARP. Despite being homogenous in this regard, members who are more contributory also use the Web tools of MoveOn more. Unlike the other organizations, greater Internet skill is also associated with more contributions to MoveOn's goals. Yet combined, the technology variables explain only an additional 3 percent of variance in contributions and no additional variance in identification or organizational trust. The behavior of MoveOn members supports what we conclude from the more traditional organizations: when people are involved, they use digital media, but in general how much they use general media tells us almost nothing about how involved they are.

Once again looking at our other two dependent variables, the story is somewhat similar to the other organizations, although for identification and organizational trust, individual attributes make negligible contributions (2% and 3%, respectively). As we suggested in the preceding text, goals are important for both, whereas social motivation and influence motivation are only important for organizational identification.

Conclusion

In this chapter we have seen that the three organizations, taken individually, tell us at least three key things. The first and most important is that the dynamics of members' involvement behaviorally and attitudinally are remarkably similar across these apparently different organizations. This fact gives specific meaning to the point that individual-level variation is at least as important as organizational-level variation. This supports our general theoretical perspective, which holds that boundaries are quite porous within organizations, and so people play a larger role in creating their own experiences of membership than has previously been believed.

The second point is that people's motivations and goals tell us a considerable amount – much more than people's age, education, and social trust, for example. These say more even than knowing how involved people are in their communities. The picture that emerges is therefore not surprising: when people act, and they do so in varying ways, it is their organization-specific motivations and goals that matter most, not how old they are, how much education they have, or in some cases, how involved they are generally in other settings.

The third point to emerge from comparing organizations is the story of technology, in which we find clues that technology is present in people's actions, but how much they use technology in general tells us quite little.

In the case of behavior, how much they use technology generally says more than nothing but not much more. In the case of identification and organizational trust, their use of technology does tell us nothing about members' involvement. Yet people who use the Web sites of all three of these organizations more are also more contributory toward their organization's goals. To us, technology appears to serve more as a contributor to the general context for behavior than as a tool that boosts participation in collective action in proportion to how much people employ it.

In this chapter we have focused on developing portraits of the memberships of the three organizations in some detail, setting aside for the moment the theory of collective action space. This focus shows the importance of looking at collective action at the level of an individual within an organizational context, which might be thought of as the "individual-organizational" level of analysis. It is now time to extend that idea more fully, using collective action space, in order to see what happens when we think about people in The American Legion, AARP, and MoveOn, not as distinct memberships but as a single population distributed across the space, differentiated by interaction and engagement within their organizations.

5

Exploring Collective Action Space

In the beginning of Chapter 4, we explored how the members of The American Legion, AARP, and MoveOn are distributed rather widely within the collective action space. We then observed which characteristics of members are associated with their contributions to collective goals, identification, and organizational trust across each organization separately. In the present chapter, we look at these relationships from the perspective of collective action space. Rather than treating the members of each organization as distinct from one another, we combine them based on their shared location within the space, so that their interaction and engagement become the primary features defining them as members.

Recall that in the collective action space, interaction with organizational members addresses the degree to which people have personal interactions with other members. We argued that an environment saturated with digital media provides greater opportunities to choose whether to interact personally with others using tools within and outside of organizations, and Chapter 4 showed that there is a great deal of variation within each organization. The second dimension, engagement with the organization, addresses the degree to which members actively participate in the direction, decision, and goals of the organization. We theorized that diminished boundaries and increased agency allow those who are inclined toward entrepreneurialism to find ways to influence the organization, or at least to feel this is the case. Once again, Chapter 4 showed a great deal of within-organization variation on this dimension.

Within the collective action space, it is useful to simplify people's location by grouping them according to the four quadrants formed by the intersection of the two axes. This is a shorthand way of differentiating people into four theoretical categories and, although it comes at the expense of specificity by reducing the data about each individual through their placement within a group, we believe it provides a meaningful way to distinguish among the various attributes suggested by the collective action space. For the purposes of this chapter, that is therefore what we have done.

We took all the survey respondents from each organization and assigned them one of the four quadrants based on their scores on interaction and engagement. We used the midpoints of our measurement scales, which happens to be a value of three on scales of one to five.[1] Dividing at the midpoints of the dimensions provides a way to describe the location of any individual as well as the complex shapes in Figures 4.1, 4.2, and 4.3 in a succinct way. It is common in the social sciences to consider how two variables work together by "interacting" them statistically, which is to say multiplying them together. That approach is not suitable for collective action space, because theoretically we do not expect interaction and engagement to moderate one another. Rather, we expect distinct effects in

[1] To do this, we created a nominal variable that can take on four values in order to indicate in which quadrant the person falls. Aggregating people this way involves discarding some information, because each person in a quadrant receives the same score regardless of how far from the origin or just where in the quadrant he or she is located. We expect, however, that this loss of information is a worthwhile trade-off in obtaining locational information that is theoretically relevant to the collective action space. There are several ways to assign a quadrant score, depending on what point is designated as the origin. The first is to use the midpoints of the measurement scales, which is (3, 3) and assign quadrant values around this point. This creates an objective, nonrelative quadrant system defined by the measurement instrument. A second approach is to use the mean or median score on each variable for the populations of interest. This creates a relative quadrant system indexed to the values of the population of interest. In the case of a single group, the origin would be the mean of that group's sample. In the case of multiple groups, the origin would fall at the grand mean across groups.

Because we are interested in objective comparisons of the values of interaction and engagement across our three organizations, using the midpoint of the measurement scales is the appropriate approach. Assigning a value for the quadrant variable, which is nominal, is therefore straightforward. Those people who scored greater than 3 on interaction and engagement are categorized as individualists, those scoring less than 3 on interaction and greater than 3 on engagement are enthusiasts, and so on, as defined later in this chapter. Note that this procedure excludes people who fall directly on either axis. Excluding these responses reduced analyses implicating quadrants in our American Legion sample by 520 responses; 110 respondents were dropped from AARP; and MoveOn's sample was reduced by 250 participants. These people receive no quadrant value, because their location is ambiguous.

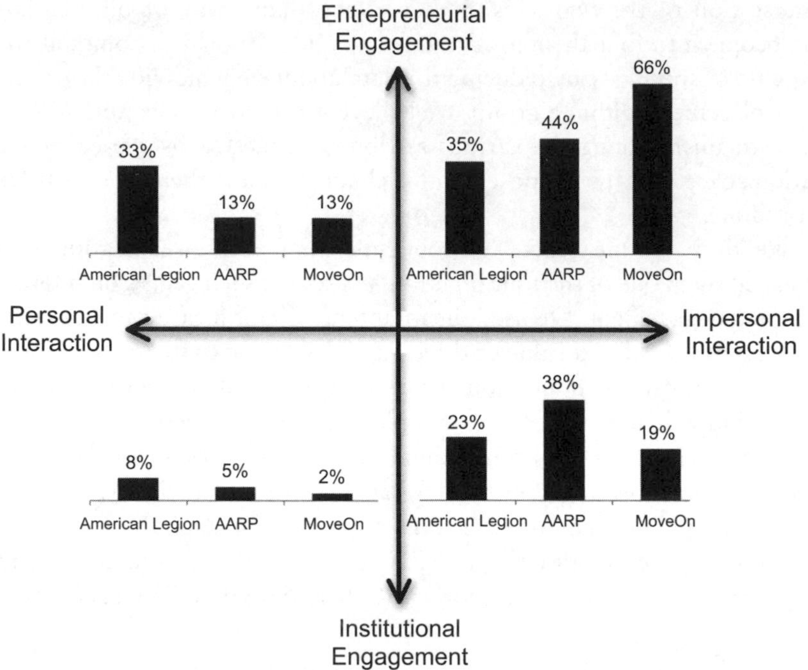

FIGURE 5.1. Distribution of Members in Collective Action Space

each quadrant, because, for instance, being personal and entrepreneurial is not the same as its diagonal opposite, impersonal and institutional.[2]

The result of categorizing the members of the three organizations in this way is shown in Figure 5.1, which gives the fraction of each organization's members that are located in each quadrant. One can readily see that a majority of MoveOn members falls in the upper-right quadrant, which is impersonal and entrepreneurial. These people view MoveOn as open to their input and contribution, but they do not experience much personal interaction with other members. This is consistent with what one might expect of MoveOn, as a large and disaggregated interest group that is

[2] To illustrate this point, consider the trivial case of a person located in the collective action space at (1, 5; where the x axis represents interaction and the y axis represents engagement) and another at (5, 1). The first is located in the quadrant with personal interaction and entrepreneurial engagement, while the second is located in a quadrant with impersonal interaction and institutional engagement. Both individuals have an interaction product of 5, but their experience of their organization is quite different theoretically. For any location in the space, there is a theoretically infinite set of locations with the same product, located along the curve $x^*y = c$, where c is the product of engagement and interaction for any point of interest.

nonetheless receptive to its members' input about its direction and goals. Relatively small, yet not insignificant, numbers of MoveOn members find the organization on the whole to be institutional and impersonal, to the lower right, and somewhat fewer find it entrepreneurial and personal, in the upper left. As is true for all three organizations, very few MoveOn members feel their organization is institutional yet personal.

American Legion members are more evenly divided, with roughly one-quarter to one-third each finding their organization personal-entrepreneurial, impersonal-entrepreneurial, and institutional-impersonal. More than two-thirds of members believe that the Legion is entrepreneurial, perhaps due to its federated form that, in spite of its large size and hierarchical structure, allows for a reasonable level of member input on its agenda and goals. As with MoveOn, relatively few members – only 8 percent – find the Legion personal and institutional, although this proportion is greater than for the other organizations.

The figures for AARP show it to be strongly impersonal, with less than one in five members rating it as personal rather than impersonal. Although a large proportion of members report that AARP fits in the quadrant of the quintessential interest group (i.e., impersonal and institutional), slightly more find AARP to be entrepreneurial and impersonal, indicating a somewhat surprising belief on the part of members that the organization remains receptive to member input.

Participatory Styles in Organizations

If our expectations about the importance of interaction and engagement are correct, then it should be the case that distinct clusters of characteristics are associated with these four quadrants. It may also be true that the underlying dynamics of contributions to collective goals, identification, and organizational trust work differently across the quadrants. For instance, the theory of social capital holds that people who are more civically involved and who have more social trust are likely to be more participatory in organizations such as these, which should manifest itself in increased contributions to the organization's goals. Yet it seems likely on theoretical grounds that the importance of such attributes is different for people who have personal relationships and entrepreneurial engagement than for, say, those whose experiences of their organization are impersonal and institutional. It is likely that distinct styles of participation or contribution may be associated with the quadrants, regardless of what organization is concerned.

A number of scholars have used concepts similar to "participatory styles" to address changing political practices in the last few decades, especially the turn away from institution-focused, duty-driven participation toward expanded, noninstitutional approaches to involvement in public life (Bennett, 1998, 2008; Bennett, Breunig, and Givens, 2008; Dalton, 2008a; Dalton, Scarrow, and Cain, 2004; Inglehart, 1997; Zukin et al., 2006). One important finding from that work is that relationships between individual-level characteristics and collective behaviors can vary greatly between traditional institution-centric action and those actions associated with new norms of engagement in which, for instance, education, age, and race do not necessarily exhibit their traditional patterns (Dalton, 2008a, 2008b).

We apply this idea to the four quadrants, using our survey data to explore the nature of participatory styles in our organizations, which align with these quadrants. Used descriptively, our survey questions allow us to see how levels of organizational trust, for example, vary across the quadrants and how community involvement is different as well. Combined into regression models, the data also allow us to explore relationships between concepts such as community involvement and people's contributions to the collective goals of their organization and to see how these vary across the quadrants.

The result of this effort is twofold. First and most important is the fact that we find four distinct participatory styles in the organizations that map to each quadrant. The theoretically derived quadrants do exhibit empirical differences. These exhibit a wide range of interesting variation in the relationships among people's attitudes, attributes, and behaviors. One of these styles, which we call enthusiasts, exhibits a classical relationship between social capital and contributions to collective goals, while another, traditionalists, does not. One style, minimalists, exhibits a large number of characteristics of the ideal type of an interest-group member. Another style, individualists, appears superficially alienated or disengaged but is actually positive and involved when one looks deeper. In the main part of this chapter, we explore these four styles as the chief empirical manifestation of collective action space. Following that exploration, we take up the question of how much these styles actually help explain indicators of involvement in the form of people's contributions, identification, and organizational trust.

We used the same approach to regression analyses as in Chapter 4 separately on each of the four participatory styles derived from the quadrants of the collective action space. The goal was to see which factors

TABLE 5.1A. *Predicting Contribution to Organizational Goals and Activities across Organizational Participatory Style*

	Individualists		Enthusiasts		Traditionalists		Minimalists	
	Beta	Sig.	Beta	Sig.	Beta	Sig.	Beta	Sig.
(Constant)		0.00		0.34		0.35		0.40
Education	0.02	0.48	0.08	0.03	−0.04	0.58	−0.01	0.70
Year Born	−0.11	0.00	−0.04	0.31	−0.08	0.33	−0.03	0.41
Express Opinion	0.05	0.04	0.05	0.10	0.05	0.47	0.09	0.01
Contact Official	0.12	0.00	0.07	0.07	0.07	0.29	0.07	0.05
Attend Meeting	0.04	0.15	0.06	0.08	0.09	0.17	0.03	0.46
Associations	0.06	0.02	0.05	0.11	0.06	0.42	0.00	0.99
Trust	−0.03	0.16	0.00	0.98	0.03	0.61	0.04	0.24
American Legion	−0.06	0.11	−0.07	0.21	−0.06	0.52	−0.24	0.00
MoveOn	−0.03	0.51	−0.13	0.02	−0.10	0.31	−0.06	0.20
Instrumental Motivation	0.01	0.73	−0.11	0.01	−0.08	0.33	−0.01	0.72
Social Motivation	0.33	0.00	0.46	0.00	0.53	0.00	0.44	0.00
Influence Motivation	0.03	0.38	0.01	0.72	0.13	0.11	0.01	0.88
Goals	0.12	0.00	0.11	0.00	0.02	0.83	0.14	0.00
Internet Skill	0.07	0.02	−0.02	0.65	0.01	0.94	0.08	0.05
Hours Online	0.00	0.87	0.02	0.64	−0.12	0.12	0.02	0.62
Years Online	−0.01	0.66	0.03	0.43	0.07	0.41	−0.02	0.63
Visit Web Site	0.10	0.00	0.28	0.00	0.23	0.00	0.08	0.01
r^2	*0.27*		*0.42*		*0.50*		*0.36*	

predict each of our measures of involvement and how these relationships vary by quadrant. The results are shown in Tables 5.1a, 5.1b, and 5.1c. This method yielded observations about the characteristics of each participatory style, which, because organizational affiliation was included in the regression models, are not merely a function of demographic differences that might be disproportionately represented in the participatory styles. We also compared the mean values of relevant factors measured in our study across each participatory style, in order to draw conclusions about which differences across styles were significant. These results are summarized in Appendix C. We now consider each of the four quadrants and its participatory style in turn.

Personal Interaction and Entrepreneurial Engagement: Enthusiasts

In the upper-left quadrant are people whose experience of interaction is personal, and who are engaged in entrepreneurial ways. They are, in a

TABLE 5.1B. *Predicting Identification across Organizational Participatory Style*

	Individualists		Enthusiasts		Traditionalists		Minimalists	
	Beta	Sig.	Beta	Sig.	Beta	Sig.	Beta	Sig.
(Constant)		0.49		0.41		0.29		0.13
Education	0.03	0.23	0.09	0.03	0.02	0.77	0.01	0.66
Year Born	0.01	0.82	0.00	0.90	0.09	0.22	−0.04	0.28
Express Opinion	−0.02	0.46	0.01	0.71	0.01	0.89	0.00	0.90
Contact Official	0.08	0.01	0.07	0.08	0.00	0.94	0.02	0.49
Attend Meeting	−0.01	0.68	−0.07	0.04	0.13	0.04	0.01	0.86
Associations	0.00	0.95	0.03	0.42	0.02	0.78	−0.02	0.41
Trust	−0.01	0.80	−0.03	0.42	0.01	0.82	−0.04	0.21
American Legion	−0.07	0.06	−0.03	0.60	−0.07	0.45	−0.03	0.41
MoveOn	0.10	0.02	0.02	0.73	0.07	0.41	0.18	0.00
Instrumental Motivation	−0.02	0.49	−0.07	0.12	−0.03	0.67	0.01	0.86
Social Motivation	0.15	0.00	0.21	0.00	0.22	0.00	0.12	0.00
Influence Motivation	0.15	0.00	0.08	0.05	0.30	0.00	0.15	0.00
Goals	0.35	0.00	0.40	0.00	0.44	0.00	0.45	0.00
Internet Skill	−0.01	0.72	−0.08	0.07	−0.15	0.06	−0.04	0.33
Hours Online	−0.02	0.32	−0.03	0.50	0.07	0.29	−0.04	0.19
Years Online	−0.01	0.82	0.01	0.80	−0.05	0.45	−0.01	0.75
Visit Web Site	0.02	0.53	0.09	0.02	−0.05	0.46	−0.01	0.76
r^2	*0.31*		*0.33*		*0.60*		*0.47*	

variety of ways, the most civically appealing of the four styles and might be thought of as the civic heroes of collective action space. They are sociable in a number of ways. Beyond scoring as "personal" on our interaction scale, they (along with traditionalists) have more friends who belong to their organization than do people of the other quadrants. They report that they would feel more positively than members of other participatory styles if they discover that a stranger they have just met also belongs to their organization. This sociability appears for them to be valuable and transcends organizational boundaries: enthusiasts are also more likely than others to report finding the contacts they have made through the organization to be useful to them outside the organizational context.

People who report personal interaction and entrepreneurial engagement have the highest goal alignment with their organization, which means that they are not only sociable, but also they are connected to the direction and goals of their organization. Their reasons for belonging are

TABLE 5.1C. *Predicting Organizational Trust across Organizational Participatory Style*

	Individualists		Enthusiasts		Traditionalists		Minimalists	
	Beta	Sig.	Beta	Sig.	Beta	Sig.	Beta	Sig.
(Constant)		0.06		0.59		0.14		0.24
Education	−0.03	0.31	−0.05	0.32	−0.23	0.01	0.05	0.23
Year Born	−0.03	0.27	0.01	0.90	−0.12	0.19	−0.03	0.45
Express Opinion	0.02	0.59	0.01	0.77	0.18	0.01	−0.06	0.14
Contact Official	0.06	0.07	0.03	0.48	−0.05	0.51	0.04	0.32
Attend Meeting	0.01	0.70	0.02	0.60	−0.07	0.32	0.00	0.99
Associations	−0.02	0.58	−0.04	0.37	0.05	0.54	0.00	1.00
Trust	0.05	0.07	0.02	0.63	0.06	0.41	0.03	0.36
American Legion	0.08	0.06	0.13	0.07	0.07	0.52	0.15	0.00
MoveOn	−0.01	0.86	0.02	0.77	0.14	0.21	0.13	0.02
Instrumental Motivation	−0.06	0.10	−0.09	0.06	0.07	0.43	−0.06	0.17
Social Motivation	0.04	0.24	0.04	0.35	−0.07	0.47	−0.03	0.54
Influence Motivation	0.05	0.13	0.11	0.02	0.02	0.86	0.10	0.03
Goals	0.29	0.00	0.26	0.00	0.49	0.00	0.31	0.00
Internet Skill	0.02	0.64	0.01	0.89	0.13	0.18	−0.10	0.03
Hours Online	−0.01	0.68	−0.03	0.54	0.09	0.25	−0.01	0.70
Years Online	0.06	0.07	0.02	0.72	0.03	0.73	−0.05	0.30
Visit Web Site	−0.01	0.81	0.02	0.72	−0.06	0.48	0.04	0.31
r^2	*0.12*		*0.14*		*0.40*		*0.17*	

highly civic and social, and they have been involved in their organization for a longer period of time than either individualists or minimalists. Instrumental motivations are not of primary importance for enthusiasts and are negatively related to their personal contributions to the organization's goals, although the perceived clout of the organization (i.e., influence motivation) is positively related to their identification with and trust in the organization. These sociable, involved, and civically motivated members exhibit a kind of exuberance toward their organization that is not present among the other three participatory styles that we will describe, and for these reasons we call them enthusiasts. They contribute a great deal toward their organization's goals, more than either individualists or minimalists (each of which is described in detail later), and they are more identified and have more trust in their organization than others.

Because enthusiasts are so plugged in to their organizations, they look superficially like the high social-capital ideal type described by Putnam

(2000). Yet it turns out that one of the central predictions of social-capital theory – the idea that people's involvement in their communities and social trust generalizes across people's civic lives – does not apply to them. Enthusiasts who report greater social trust, are more involved in other community associations, attend town meetings more often, or express their views to news media or public officials are no more likely to contribute to the goals of their organization than other enthusiasts, regardless of which of the three organizations they belong to. Enthusiasts have relatively high levels of social capital, but variation in that capital across enthusiasts says nothing about how contributory they are inside The American Legion, AARP, and MoveOn. Contrary to the idea that social capital is a general civic lubricant that spreads across contexts, enthusiasts act as if their organization is isolated from their broader civic lives. Enthusiasts report greater levels of organizational identification than those with other participatory styles, but those enthusiasts who attend community meetings regularly are less identified with their organization than other enthusiasts, suggesting perhaps that their role is more as agents of social change than as supporters of the status quo. This relationship is not found among people with any of the other participatory styles.

Enthusiasts therefore demonstrate that the highest level of organizational identification is not always a prerequisite or concomitant of contributions to collective goals and activities. There may be several reasons for this feature of the enthusiast style, in which a high degree of energy for participating is not necessarily associated with the highest levels of identification. For example, it may be simply that enthusiasts who are engaged in many organizations face multiple competing opportunities for identification. Or, it may be that general sociability combined with civic motivation means that organization-specific identification is not as important to them. They care about community and like interacting with others. An organization that gives the context in which to act is all they need to contribute, whether they identify with the organization a great deal or a little.

It is also interesting that the enthusiasts' ages are not related to their collective contributions, but education is, as it is also related to identification. Being involved entrepreneurially is likely more cognitively demanding than being involved institutionally. So higher levels of education make it more probable that individuals have the skills and intellectual capital to engage in activities that contribute to the overall direction and decisions of the organization. It may also be that identification with the organization for enthusiasts is also contingent on the exercise of these skills and application of knowledge. As we will see in the following text, this is not true about identification for people whose involvement is institutional.

The portrait of enthusiasts that emerges in these three organizations confounds a classic idea about participation and civic engagement and shows the potential peril of using mean levels of involvement for an individual in predicting what that person might do in any particular context. For example, to assume that enthusiasts, with their plugged-in nature in our organizations, exhibit the same pattern of involvement in their other organizations is to fall prey to an individual-level ecological fallacy. Being a civic joiner in general does not make one a joiner in every context, at least if one is an enthusiast in the collective action space.

This might suggest that there is something unpredictable about enthusiasts, but that is not the case, at least where contributions to organizational goals are concerned. In contrast to identification and organizational trust, where we can still explain 33 percent of the variance in identification and 14 percent for organizational trust (lower than for any other style except individualists), our regression model produces an r^2 of .42 for explaining contributions to collective goals of enthusiasts – a strong value in any effort to model civic or political behavior, and the second highest of the four quadrants in the collective action space. The most important factor in enthusiasts' contributions is the extent to which their motivations for belonging are social – a relationship that occurs for all the participatory styles. Moreover, their social motivation stands in stark contrast to their instrumental motivations, which are negatively related to contributions. Therefore, the more one has joined an organization for reasons that involve social and civic involvement, the more one will contribute to the goals of that organization – and this tells us a great deal more than knowing that person's demographic characteristics, social trust, and involvement in their communities.

Following motivation in importance for enthusiasts is an interesting and important factor: how frequently enthusiasts visit the Web site of their organization. We saw this relationship across organizations in Chapter 4, where use of the organization's Web site was associated with contributory behavior in all three organizations. We interpreted this relationship before as reflecting at least two underlying processes. People who are inclined to contribute are more likely to go to the Web site for information or guidance about how to do so, and people visiting the Web site may be prompted by something they see there to become more involved than

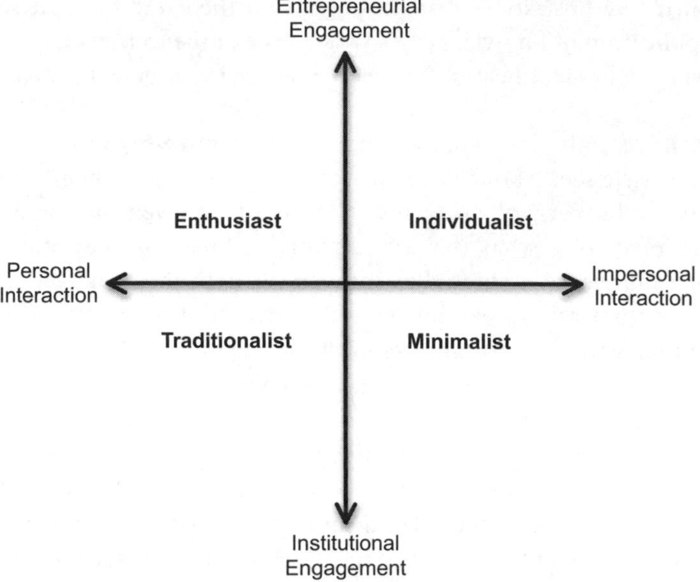

FIGURE 5.2. Participatory Styles in Collective Action Space

they would have been otherwise. This relationship is not a function of organization, occurring across all four participatory styles, but for enthusiasts it is a little stronger than for people in the other participatory styles. The association between Web site use and contribution to collective goals is a little more than half as important as social motivation, well ahead of goal alignment. Being personally involved with others in one's organization and being entrepreneurially engaged with the organization entail using the online tools of the organization. This represents a refinement of the general finding in studies of digital-media use and participation that political interest moderates use of technology in shaping participation. Figure 5.2 shows the location of enthusiasts in the upper-left quadrant of the collective action space, along with the other three participatory styles.

Impersonal Interaction and Institutional Engagement: Minimalist

Diagonally opposite enthusiasts in collective action space is the participatory style we call minimalist, whose interaction is impersonal and whose engagement is institutional. If enthusiasts are civic heroes with some of the highest levels of contributions, identification, and organizational trust, then minimalists are their uncivic, less engaged opposites. They contribute the least, identify the least, and trust their organizations the least. They are thoroughly unsociable compared to enthusiasts. They score low in how many friends they know who belong to the organization and are the least pleased of the four styles to discover a new acquaintance who also belongs. Whatever relationships they do have are bounded within the organization. Minimalists are least likely to find organizational contacts to be useful outside the organizational context. They also frequent their organization's Web site significantly less often than people with any of the other participatory styles.

Minimalists are moderately engaged with their communities, scoring in the midrange on questions about community involvement and political expressiveness. Minimalists also fit the theory of social capital somewhat, but not as well as the third participatory style, individualist, to whom we will turn in a moment. Minimalists who express their political views more are also more likely to contribute to their organization, yet like enthusiasts neither their social trust nor their involvement in community issues or associations carries over into their contributions to their organization. Again, one cannot say that because a minimalist is involved in his or her community that he or she will also be involved in his or her organization. Minimalists' nominal connection to their organization is not the product of being new to it, as one might imagine. They have belonged to their organization about as long as individualists, who are more contributory, identified, and trusting.

In theory, the lower-right quadrant of the collective action space is the domain classically occupied by members of interest groups, who have a nominal and even strategic approach to membership, belong anonymously, and in effect wait for calls to action by the organization, which is positioned to act instrumentally on behalf of its members. The data do and do not support this image. On one hand, minimalists are not highly motivated by social opportunities and contribute very little to the organization's goals, suggesting a kind of instrumental relationship to their organization. On the other hand, minimalists clearly extend beyond interest groups because they are spread across all three organizations in our study and they are the least concerned with the organization's ability to influence issues important to them. Moreover, their instrumental motivation is equal to that of the traditionalists and is lower than that of enthusiasts and individualists.

Like other styles, minimalists' organizational identification is built almost exclusively on goal alignment and social motivation, whereas organizational trust is associated only with goals. The more minimalists perceive alignment between their goals and those of their organization, the more they trust their organization. For them, it appears, trust goes along with goals and compatibility. Minimalists are also the only participatory style in which we find technology associated with trust. The relationship is negative, however. The stronger a miminalists' Internet skill is, the lower his or her trust in the organization.

Impersonal Interaction and Entrepreneurial Engagement: Individualists

The prototypical person located in the upper-right quadrant of the collective action space, where interaction is impersonal and engagement is entrepreneurial, breaks even more traditional ideal-type rules than enthusiasts or minimalists. They look superficially like civic misfits, but just as with enthusiasts, the picture is a good deal more subtle. In many ways, people with this style are individualistic, idiosyncratic, and difficult to predict. We therefore call them individualists.

Individualists are younger than people with the other participatory styles and have been involved in their organization for somewhat less time. Consistent with their impersonal interaction, individualists have relatively few friends who are members of the organization, but they are significantly more positive than minimalists when they meet members of their organization outside the organizational context. Yet individualist relations remain bounded within the organization. They do not find organizational contacts to be particularly useful to them personally. Moreover, they are relatively low in community involvement, and their motivations for belonging are not very civic, being just ahead of minimalists. In these ways, individualists appear relatively disengaged from social and community networks with respect to their membership in their organization, and even isolated.

Yet people with this style do not fit the ideal type of the disengaged, uncivic citizen. They are surprising in a number of ways. Their level of general social trust is similar to that of enthusiasts and traditionalists and higher than minimalists. So they are not joiners, but neither are they mistrustful. Individualists are actually relatively positive about their organization's goals – more so than traditionalists and minimalists. This illustrates that entrepreneurialism is associated with goal alignment. Not only are their goals aligned with their organization, but also the more civically motivated they are, the more contributory they are. They belong for a reason, and they act in accordance with their goals. Unlike enthusiasts, whose outside activities tend to lessen their level of identification, individualists' civic engagement outside the organization does not detract from their organizational identification. Despite their appearance of detachment in traditional terms of civic engagement, individualists are purposeful members, neither alienated nor adrift. Their organizations cannot tell them what do, but they are generally aligned with their organizations' purposes.

Another surprising feature of individualists is that more than in the other styles, the more civically involved they are generally, the more they contribute to their organization. This happens despite the fact that to begin with they are relatively low in social capital. This shows that the general spillover effects of social-capital–like qualities and participation may occur at least as strongly if not more so for people who have lower levels of social capital. For individualists, a little goes a long way.

As one might expect, individualists are not readily explained using regression models. Whereas we can account for 42 percent of the variance in enthusiasts' contributions and 36 percent of minimalists', we can explain only 27 percent for individualists. This pattern holds true for our other indicators of organizational involvement as well. The r^2 scores for organizational identification (.31) and organizational trust (.12) are the lowest across all four participatory styles. It is easier to explain an enthusiast or a minimalist than an individualist.

Individualists' use of technology reflects the general pattern that appeared across the organizations in Chapter 4. Their general Internet skill has a weak association with their contributions to outcomes, while their use of the organization's Web site has a somewhat stronger one. This is the only participatory style for which any of our general Internet use measures shows a relationship with contributions to collective outcomes.

What this means is that among the members of our three organizations, the small effects of general Internet use on contributions to collective outcomes is isolated in this one participatory style. Individualists, who do not have personal relationships in their organization but perceive their experience as entrepreneurial, are slightly more likely to contribute to the organization's goals and activities to the extent that they are more skilled online. This helps shed some light on the debate about the modest relationship between general Internet use and civic engagement that has gone on in the literature for several years. One branch of reasoning has shown that this relationship is moderated by factors such as political interest or preferences for entertainment (Prior, 2007; Xenos and Moy, 2007). Consistent with that conclusion, but extending it in a different way, our findings suggest that general Internet skill has some association with involvement in organizations, but the relationship is weak and contingent. It varies across participatory styles and across indicators of involvement.

Personal Interaction and Institutional Engagement: Traditionalists

The final participatory style in collective action space occurs in the lower-left quadrant. An interesting and even odd style, it combines personal interaction with institutional engagement. People with this style get to know others in their organization but are relatively passive toward it. We label them traditionalists, and their experiences are subtle.

Traditionalists appear to be civic followers, rather than civic activists. Along with enthusiasts, they have been members of their organization longer than the other participatory styles, making them established and settled in the roles they have created for themselves. They are civic and social, but they exhibit a good deal of reserve about their organizations. They are quite likely to attend public meetings, in equal measure to enthusiasts and more often than people with other participatory styles. Although traditionalists are social, they are satisfied to let their organization go its own way, experiencing it as institutional. In spite of being involved in their communities, that involvement does not carry over into their contributions to their organization. Like enthusiasts, their civic involvement does not generalize well from other contexts to their membership in The American Legion, AARP, or MoveOn. What they do inside their organization is not associated with what they are doing in other organizations or their communities at large. And, despite their long memberships and personal interaction with others, they are not very positive about their organization's goals.

Perhaps the most intriguing aspect of traditionalists is that their perception of goal alignment is not associated with their contributions to collective goals. They are the only participatory style for which this is true. The independence of their goals and contributions suggests that their sense of membership is not particularly instrumental or strategic. Instrumental motivation for membership is the lowest among all groups (though roughly equivalent to minimalists), and only the minimalists have less interest in the influence of the organization as a basis for membership. It is as if they belong to their organization because they feel it is the right thing to do, or because it is appealing for reasons other than the achievement of collective goals. Their membership is not habitual or lacking in motivation. It is their social motivations that are singularly and highly important to traditionalists. They belong to make a difference, and they do so. Traditionalists are the most contributory of the four styles (though just barely ahead of enthusiasts) and the most predictable.

Traditionalists' organizational identification also operates somewhat differently. Like the other indicators of involvement, our models do a far better job predicting their level of identification ($r^2 = .60$), more than 10 percent higher than for the minimalists, for whom in turn we find an r^2 that is about 15 percent higher than that of the enthusiasts or individualists. Traditionalists' identification is strongly predicated on the degree of goal alignment with the organization, as well as on their influence motivation and social motivation. They are the only participatory style in which contacting officials outside the organization is not associated with their degree of identification with the organization and, in contrast to individualists and enthusiasts, neither is how frequently they visit the Web site. For people whose engagement is institutional – minimalists and traditionalists – identification is independent of what they do at the organization's Web site. Their sources of identification lie elsewhere, while for the two entrepreneurial styles, identification is associated with people's use of their organization's Web site.

Finally, what is most striking is how much more organizational trust is predictable for traditionalists than for any other participatory style. In the case of trust, there is a .23 difference in r^2 between traditionalists and the next highest style, minimalists. Unlike our other two components of involvement, which are based on recollections of past behavior (contribution is based upon what members have done in the past) and present attitudes (identification is based on how a member affiliates at the time), organizational trust is grounded in members' perception of future behavior. Because trust in general is forward looking, it is not surprising that goal alignment is associated with trust in our study, in all four participatory styles. However, it may come as a surprise to some that general social trust is not related to organizational trust for any of the participatory styles. Trust seems to be an organization-specific construct, not one that generalizes well.

Digital-Media Use and Participatory Styles

Chapter 4 showed how people's use of digital media is surprisingly similar across The American Legion, AARP, and MoveOn. Some simple measures of skill, experience, use, and time online suggested that digital media have a roughly similar presence in the lives of members of these organizations, and we also saw that where people are located in collective action space is not related to these factors. For us, this is evidence of the contextual character of digital media: they are present in people's experiences of their organizations, but they are not associated with being more or less personal, or more or less entrepreneurial. Given what we found when we looked within each organization, it is not surprising that the picture looks the same when we look at the data by participatory style.

Though it might be tempting to imagine that people who are online more are more likely to be enthusiasts because the technology somehow pushes them toward more personal relationships and more entrepreneurial activity, this is not the case. People with all four participatory styles are online about eleven hours per week, and the differences between them are not significant.[3] Something comparable is true of Internet skill, where people with all four participatory styles rate themselves as roughly "above average," and of the number of years of Internet experience, where all report having started using the Internet between six and ten years ago.[4] With respect to these general technology use characteristics, a person's participatory style is not a function of how much or how skillfully they use technology. Exploring technology further requires placing it in the larger context of people's other attributes, behaviors, and characteristics.

Nonetheless, to probe the possibility that technology use is related to one or the other dimension of collective action space further (e.g., interaction or engagement), we analyzed the data by combining people across organizations into those groups reporting entrepreneurial engagement versus institutional engagement and impersonal versus personal interaction. This meant lumping individualists and enthusiasts together, both of whom have entrepreneurial engagement, and comparing them to traditionalists and minimalists, both of whom have institutional engagement. It also meant looking at the personal interaction styles (enthusiasts and traditionalists) compared to the impersonal ones (individualists and minimalists). With the types of engagement and interaction isolated, we then

[3] Mean hours online for individualists is 11.0 (SD = 11.0), for enthusiasts it is 11.5 (SD = 10.7), for traditionalists, the mean is 11.0 (SD = 9.7), and for minimalists it is 11.7 ($SD = 10.6$; $F = 0.69$, $p = 0.56$).

[4] Differences here reach statistical significance but are not substantively important. For Internet skill, means and standard deviations are as follows: individualists: 2.67 (SD = 0.89), enthusiasts: 2.60 (SD = 0.91), traditionalists: 2.67 (SD = 0.95), and minimalists: 2.74 ($SD = 0.92$). $F = 2.9$, $p = 0.04$. For years of Internet experience, means and standard deviations are as follows: individualists: 4.23 ($SD = 0.86$), enthusiasts: 4.14 ($SD = 0.92$), traditionalists: 4.37 ($SD = 0.78$), and minimalists: 4.30 ($SD = 0.83$). $F = 5.5$, $p = 0.001$.

compared scores on the relevant technology characteristics (Internet experience, Internet skill level, and time online at home and at work; although we set aside frequency at the organization's Web site because our focus was on technology use behaviors that were not organizationally specific).

Stark differences along the dimensions might indicate that technology use is directly related to modes of interaction or engagement together, even though it is not related to specific participatory styles. For instance, it is plausible that greater technology use may be related to a more entrepreneurial stance toward the organization, as a function of an enhanced end-user enterprise that may enable new and compelling forms of engagement. Similarly, the greater connectivity offered by Internet-based communication tools might result in a higher degree of personal interaction among organizational members. Theoretically, we do not expect that to be the case, because we anticipate that the contemporary media context enables people to enact their own membership style, whatever that may be.

Results support this idea. When comparing people with an entrepreneurial versus an institutional relationship with their organization, we find that the only difference along the engagement dimension is that those reporting an institutional stance have been using the Internet longer than those with an entrepreneurial organizational relationship.[5] The picture is similar for interaction: no differences in technology use occur along this dimension.[6] The findings remain the same when the analyses are performed on members of each organization separately.[7]

5 Mean entrepreneurial online tenure score = 4.20 ($SD = 0.88$), mean institutional online tenure score = 4.31 ($SD = 0.82$; $t = -3.25$, $p = 0.001$). When accounting for the fact that older members are also more likely to experience an institutional vs. entrepreneurial relationship to their organization, it is likely that this finding is at least partially a function of the age of the organizational member, inasmuch as there is a confound between age and Internet experience. It was also the case that those people reporting an institutional relationship to their organization reported modestly greater skills using the Internet (mean entrepreneurial Internet skill score = 2.65, $SD = 0.89$; mean institutional Internet skill score = 2.72, $SD = 0.92$; $t = -2.16$, $p = 0.03$), although the appropriate Bonferroni correction to adjust for multiple comparisons rendered this finding functionally nonsignificant.

6 When comparing those who report personal vs. impersonal interactions with organizational members, those reporting impersonal relations with fellow members have slightly higher Internet skill levels (mean personal Internet skill level = 2.61, $SD = 0.92$; mean impersonal Internet skill level = 2.69, $SD = 0.90$; $t = -2.24$, $p = 0.03$). Once again, however, the appropriate Bonferroni correction for multiple comparisons renders this finding statistically nonsignificant.

7 Once again, there is one finding that is negated by the appropriate Bonferroni correction: for The American Legion only, those with an institutional relationship to their organization show a slightly higher use of the Internet outside of work (mean entrepreneurial

Therefore, in The American Legion, AARP, and MoveOn, technology use is not a proxy for the mode of engagement between people and the organizations or the extent to which their interaction with one another is personal. What modest evidence there is of a correspondence between individuals' technology use and the modes of engagement or interaction actually runs counter to assumptions about that relationship founded in recent accounts that link technology use to individual action. Rather than technology use accompanying specific behaviors, then, technology appears to supply a context for action, which can take on many forms, spanning across entrepreneurial/institutional and personal/impersonal modes – that is, across all four participatory styles. Overall, this is fairly compelling evidence that people's involvement in collective action efforts takes place in a rich technological environment that accommodates a great many possibilities for human association, rather than those actions being driven by a particular set of technological affordances specific to a time or place. The implication, which we discuss further in Chapter 6, is that contemporary technologies appear to liberate, rather than constrain, collective action today.

Explaining Contributions, Identification, and Organizational Trust with Participatory Styles

The four participatory styles represent the empirical face of the collective action space for the members of The American Legion, AARP, and MoveOn. The styles provide a way to move beyond ideal-type images of members of interest groups and civic organizations, as well as beyond the public stereotypes of the three organizations. As we expected from considering the capacity people have to construct membership in ways that they see fit, there is a considerable amount of diversity within these three organizations. On the one hand, it should not be a surprise that organizations with millions of members exhibit diversity in many characteristics. On the other hand, it is significant that theoretical relationships vary so substantially. For traditionalists, goals and behavior are not related, while for the other three participatory styles they are related. For individualists, civic involvement is predictive of contributions to collective goals, while for the other styles that relationship is weak or even absent. As enthusiasts show, being high in social capital does not mean that one's endowment of

use score = 11.16, SD = 10.96; mean institutional use score = 12.55, SD = 10.52; $t = -2.25$, $p = 0.02$).

social capital will relate to what one does in any particular organization. For all participatory styles, digital-media use is implicated in people's collective behavior through use of their organization's Web site, yet only for individualists is there any solid indication that digital-media use in general actually contributes toward being more contributory. The central message of the participatory styles is that understanding collective action in organizations requires moving beyond general models aimed at the median or "typical" member.

Aside from this conclusion, which we will explore further in Chapter 6, one might ask whether knowing people's participatory styles is useful only as a method of classification and theoretical differentiation, or whether it also improves our ability to explain outcomes. That is, beyond knowing the identity of the organization one belongs to, do participatory styles explain involvement in collective action? This question can be answered by applying the regression equations we have been using throughout Chapters 4 and 5 in a slightly different way. In Chapter 4, we saw that standard predictors of participation such as education or civic engagement are not very informative about what happens inside organizations. Applying a similar approach here, we next look at what happens in stages as one models outcomes using standard predictors of participation, then identities of each member's organization, and then their participatory style. We also look at measures of motivation and goals, as well as technology, to see how these work across the participatory styles.

The regression analysis looks at all people in all three organizations – and all four participatory styles – and models contributions to organizational goals, identification, and organizational trust. The first step uses people's age, education, whether they have expressed opinion to news media, whether they have contacted government or attended local meetings, whether they are members of other community groups, and their social trust. Just as we saw when we looked at each organization separately in Chapter 4, these elementary models say very little, accounting for only 1 percent to 7 percent of the variance in contributions, identification, and organizational trust. This is shown in Model 1 in Tables 5.2a, 5.2b, and 5.2c. This is not a very satisfactory result.

A theorist who is heavily indebted to organizational theories of civic engagement might expect that adding information about which organization people belong to would improve this result. MoveOn is an organization defined by participation – the only reason one "belongs" to MoveOn, and the only way to belong, is to participate. By contrast, AARP provides many selective incentives and entices people to join for reasons other

TABLE 5.2A. *Predicting Contributions to Collective Goals and Activities across Organizations*

	Model 1		Model 2		Model 3		Model 4		Model 5	
	Beta	Sig.	Beta	Sig.	Beta	Sig.	Beta	Sig.	Beta	Sig.
(Constant)		0.04		0.01		0.01		0.06		0.00
Education	−0.08	0.00	−0.08	0.00	−0.06	0.00	0.02	0.26	0.02	0.39
Year Born	−0.03	0.13	−0.04	0.05	−0.04	0.05	−0.03	0.06	−0.06	0.00
Express Opinion	0.08	0.00	0.08	0.00	0.08	0.00	0.07	0.00	0.06	0.00
Contact Official	0.13	0.00	0.12	0.00	0.11	0.00	0.11	0.00	0.09	0.00
Attend Meeting	0.09	0.00	0.10	0.00	0.07	0.00	0.05	0.01	0.04	0.02
Associations	0.10	0.00	0.10	0.00	0.07	0.00	0.04	0.01	0.04	0.01
Trust	0.03	0.09	0.03	0.12	0.00	0.91	0.00	0.91	0.00	0.87
American Legion			0.05	0.06	−0.01	0.72	−0.10	0.00	−0.12	0.00
MoveOn			0.06	0.06	0.05	0.11	−0.05	0.08	−0.08	0.00
Individualist					0.10	0.00	−0.05	0.02	−0.05	0.03
Enthusiast					0.31	0.00	0.07	0.00	0.06	0.01
Traditionalist					0.19	0.00	0.08	0.00	0.07	0.00
Instrumental Motivation							−0.02	0.25	−0.03	0.10
Social Motivation							0.44	0.00	0.42	0.00
Influence Motivation							0.03	0.18	0.02	0.43
Goals							0.14	0.00	0.14	0.00
Internet Skill									0.05	0.01
Hours Online									0.00	0.87
Years Online									0.00	0.84
Visit Web Site									0.15	0.00
r^2	*0.07*		*0.07*		*0.15*		*0.36*		*0.38*	

than contributing to its collective goals. As a civic organization with a long history of community involvement, The American Legion is also associated with contributions. To test this, in a second set of models we included dummy-coded variables for The American Legion and MoveOn in order to compare belonging to one of these with belonging to AARP. The result is that both measures are statistically significant, in line with a traditional perspective, yet they are so substantively weak that they say essentially nothing. Knowing which of our three organizations a person belongs to indicates very little about how involved they are in collective action, beyond knowing their education, age, community involvement, and social trust. If one wants to know about collective behavior and pro-collective attitudes among people in these three organizations, one needs to assess other things.

TABLE 5.2B. *Predicting Organizational Identification across Organizations*

	Model 1		Model 2		Model 3		Model 4		Model 5	
	Beta	Sig.	Beta	Sig.	Beta	Sig.	Beta	Sig.	Beta	Sig.
(Constant)		0.40		0.00		0.00		0.05		0.31
Education	−0.03	0.13	−0.09	0.00	−0.05	0.01	0.02	0.26	0.03	0.11
Year Born	0.02	0.31	−0.06	0.00	−0.06	0.00	−0.01	0.39	0.00	0.97
Express Opinion	−0.03	0.20	−0.03	0.11	−0.02	0.18	−0.01	0.65	0.00	0.82
Contact Official	0.12	0.00	0.06	0.00	0.06	0.00	0.04	0.01	0.04	0.01
Attend Meeting	0.01	0.74	0.01	0.65	−0.01	0.55	−0.01	0.60	−0.01	0.60
Associations	−0.01	0.68	0.01	0.66	0.00	0.95	0.00	0.88	0.00	0.85
Trust	0.04	0.07	0.02	0.25	−0.02	0.19	−0.02	0.17	−0.02	0.17
American Legion			0.10	0.00	0.03	0.28	−0.05	0.02	−0.05	0.04
MoveOn			0.31	0.00	0.24	0.00	0.11	0.00	0.11	0.00
Individualist					0.33	0.00	0.08	0.00	0.07	0.00
Enthusiast					0.45	0.00	0.15	0.00	0.14	0.00
Traditionalist					0.14	0.00	0.05	0.00	0.05	0.00
Instrumental Motivation							−0.03	0.14	−0.03	0.12
Social Motivation							0.15	0.00	0.15	0.00
Influence Motivation							0.14	0.00	0.15	0.00
Goals							0.43	0.00	0.43	0.00
Internet Skill									−0.04	0.04
Hours Online									−0.02	0.11
Years Online									0.00	0.86
Visit Web Site									0.02	0.18
r^2		*0.02*		*0.06*		*0.20*		*0.47*		*0.47*

What about participatory style? In a third step, we added dummy-coded variables for participatory styles to our analysis, which is represented in the third model in Tables 5.2a, 5.2b, and 5.2c. The result is substantively important. The explanatory power of the models jumps roughly a factor of two to three, to 15 percent for contribution, 20 percent for identification, and 10 percent for organizational trust. By overall standards of statistical modeling, these are not high values, but they are modestly strong. They show that participatory styles contain a good deal of information about people's involvement. In Chapter 4 we saw the existence of much within-group variation in the three organizations compared to across-group variation. Earlier in this chapter, we saw the manifestation of this variation in the form of four participatory styles that reflect the collective action space. Now we see that these styles are

TABLE 5.2C. *Predicting Organizational Trust across Organizations*

	Model 1		Model 2		Model 3		Model 4		Model 5	
	Beta	Sig.	Beta	Sig.	Beta	Sig.	Beta	Sig.	Beta	Sig.
(Constant)		0.00		0.00		0.00		0.01		0.04
Education	−0.08	0.00	−0.07	0.00	−0.05	0.01	−0.02	0.33	−0.02	0.38
Year Born	−0.03	0.16	−0.06	0.00	−0.07	0.00	−0.03	0.14	−0.02	0.28
Express Opinion	−0.02	0.43	−0.02	0.26	−0.02	0.35	0.00	0.91	0.00	0.99
Contact Official	0.06	0.01	0.04	0.05	0.05	0.02	0.04	0.05	0.04	0.05
Attend Meeting	0.00	0.96	0.00	0.92	0.00	0.98	0.01	0.69	0.01	0.71
Associations	−0.02	0.37	−0.02	0.32	−0.01	0.48	−0.01	0.65	−0.01	0.63
Trust	0.07	0.00	0.06	0.00	0.03	0.06	0.04	0.03	0.04	0.04
American Legion			0.20	0.00	0.17	0.00	0.12	0.00	0.12	0.00
MoveOn			0.19	0.00	0.13	0.00	0.05	0.06	0.05	0.07
Individualist					0.27	0.00	0.11	0.00	0.10	0.00
Enthusiast					0.27	0.00	0.08	0.00	0.08	0.00
Traditionalist					0.02	0.25	−0.02	0.32	−0.02	0.27
Instrumental Motivation							−0.06	0.00	−0.06	0.00
Social Motivation							0.01	0.76	0.01	0.76
Influence Motivation							0.08	0.00	0.08	0.00
Goals							0.34	0.00	0.34	0.00
Internet Skill									−0.03	0.24
Hours Online									−0.01	0.43
Years Online									0.02	0.39
Visit Web Site									0.01	0.65
r^2		*0.01*		*0.03*		*0.10*		*0.20*		*0.20*

related to collective action results – people's contributions, identification, and organizational trust.

When we continue developing the regression model by adding measures for motivation and goals, the value of r^2 rises further to 0.36 for contributions, 0.47 for identification, and 0.20 for organizational trust. This reflects the aggregate of the individual results for each participatory style that we considered earlier. Looked at this way, the data confirm how important motivation and goal alignment are. We saw the importance of these across most of the participatory styles in the preceding text, and here we see that across the styles these two variables are, not surprisingly, important for all three indicators of involvement. Social motivation is the strongest predictor of contribution, whereas goals best predict organizational identification and trust.

The last step in the model is to consider digital-media use. The question is whether measures of digital-media use add anything to our understanding of involvement in collective action, on top of the preceding sets of factors. Chapter 4 showed that the answer is largely negative when data are viewed group by group and where general measures of Internet use are concerned. Here we find something similar when the data are viewed style by style. The media-use factors explain only a negligible amount of variance, and only in the case of contribution to the goals of the organization. The key variable is visiting the organization's Web site, which is quite strongly associated with contributions – roughly as much as is goal alignment. This means that visiting the organization's Web site is one of the three key correlates of contributions. There is also a weaker relationship with Internet skill that explains about one-third as much variance as visiting the organization's Web site. We know from the earlier models that this effect is concentrated among individualists.

Overall, contribution to the organization's goals is best predicted by one's social motivation, the degree to which personal goals align with organizational ones, and, to an important extent, the degree to which one visits the organization's Web site – but not with general Internet skill or use. For identification with the organization as an outcome, goals are the most important predictor, followed by social motivation and influence motivation, which are about equally important. Organizational trust is also a function of whether one's goals align with those of the organization and of the degree to which the organization is perceived to have the clout (i.e., influence motivation) to represent one's interests.

Looking at the memberships of the three groups this way also allows us to make some comparisons across the styles in ways that are not possible by looking at them individually. We saw in the preceding text that traditionalists and enthusiasts are the most contributory and minimalists the least, while enthusiasts are the most identified and trusting and minimalists (along with traditionalists in the case of trust) the least. We could not be sure, however, whether those are due to the styles or are an artifact of other factors associated with each style. We can now sort that out in the combined model, which controls for the potentially confounding factors. Enthusiasts, along with traditionalists, remain the most contributory, and enthusiasts are also the most well identified with their organizations. Individualists appear as the least contributory, even below minimalists. Individualists and enthusiasts appear to be the most trusting. The rank order of the styles in contributions to collective goals is therefore: traditionalists, enthusiasts, minimalists, and individualists.

Conclusion

This chapter has shown that a person's perception of their interactions with others and of their engagement with their organization indicates a great deal about their experiences of collective action in The American Legion, AARP, and MoveOn. Yet at the same time, these two dimensions do not tell us very much by themselves. Knowing only how personal someone's experiences are does help predict their contributions to collective goals and activities but not their level of identification with their organization or their trust in it. Knowing the extent of people's entrepreneurial or institutional engagement says very little by itself.

Combined together into participatory styles, however, the two dimensions reveal an interesting portrait of varying approaches to membership. These styles help us explain outcomes and show how theoretical relationships vary across people within organizations. The next and last chapter will elaborate on these results and reflect on what they indicate about the relationship of the individual to the organization.

6

Participatory Styles, the Individual, and the Contemporary Organization

Involvement in Collective Action Organizations

In Chapter 1, we identified three aspects of involvement in collective action within organizations that would be one focus of this book: contributions to collective goals and activities, identification with the organization, and trust in the organization. We chose these because they are intrinsically interesting for understanding how people are involved with collective action organizations today. Contributions are important for the obvious reason, namely because these are the behavioral outcomes that have traditionally defined collective action. Absent contributions to collective goals and activities, most collective action organizations would cease to exist. We saw in Chapters 4 and 5 that it is possible to explain a good deal of the variation in people's contributions toward collective action if one attends to matters of motivation, goals, interaction, and engagement. These are consistently more important than education, age, and people's broader involvement in community and public life.

As we argued in Chapter 3, we do not think of contributions to collective goals and activities solely as concrete choices to act or free ride, made in light of incentives. In our view, to contribute is to navigate across the boundary between private domains of interest and public ones. This boundary crossing may manifest classically as conscious choices, especially where boundaries are clear and effortful to cross, or boundary crossing may emerge as more seamless expressions of solidarity with others, as the publicizing of private interests or the statement of political or social identity. For these reasons, our second indicator of collective action was identification, which taps into attitudes that go beyond, or that may precede, behavior. We believe identification is important to understanding collective action, because people's involvement in organizations is not unidirectional. Organizations such as The American Legion, AARP, and MoveOn do not simply mobilize autonomous individuals who have fixed private attitudes and political orientations. Organizations shape how people feel about civil society, and one potentially important way is through identification. To the extent that people come to identify with a civic or political organization, they are shaped by their membership in ways that transcend their specific acts of collective action in that one organization.

To identify is to blur a boundary between the self and the collective, by adopting goals and criteria of the organization as one's own. Our research design was not intended to sort out the difference between people joining an organization because they already identify with it and people growing more identified over time as they belong to an organization. Our measurement of identification, however, was focused on the latter, by asking people specifically about attitudes toward the organization that are likely to be developed only after belonging for some time. The data show that across the organizations in our study people do grow somewhat more identified the longer they belong. When participation shapes people's goals by linking them to the organization's goals, the result is a potentially important part of the story of collective action. Our analysis shows that the same model that explains a good deal of people's behavior explains even more of their identification, and again motivation, goals, interaction, and engagement are key to doing so. Organizational identification, a concept adapted from the study of employment relationships, emerges as an empirically tractable and coherent indicator of involvement in collective action.

The third indicator of involvement we considered was organizational trust. We examined trust because it is one of the most universal variables across the social sciences, a kind of all-purpose regulator of social behavior. Especially in the literature on civil society, general social trust has been widely viewed as important to people's involvement in civic life. One surefire way for people to succeed at certain collective action challenges, according to that view, is to bring to the problem sufficient mutual trust. Trust in collective action organizations is an extrapolation of general trust, and we expected that it might work similarly to organizational identification. People are likely to join an organization if they are more trusting of it, and the more they have been involved in their organization, the more likely they are to trust it. In the classic social-capital story, these are mutually reinforcing and crucial to civic engagement.

What we found for our three organizations, however, departs from that story. Organizational trust is idiosyncratic and not well explained by the characteristics and behaviors that define contributions and identification. More importantly, it is clear that trust in an organization is not just a concomitant of effective membership. People can contribute and identify well with their organizations without being particularly trusting of it. The trust boundary therefore appears to be more rigid than those implicating individual resources and identification.

For the members of The American Legion, AARP, and MoveOn, a person's general social trust says very little about their organizational trust. This leads us toward skepticism that trust is as universally important an attitude as is commonly portrayed in theories of civic engagement and participation. The link from general trust to trust in any particular organizational context is tenuous at best, as are the links from other attributes and behaviors to organizational trust. Likewise, the link from organizational trust to behavior is thin in our organizations and, we suspect, in others as well.

It may be, though we cannot show it in this study, that trust matters most for certain formalized problems of action. Some market transactions such as those in the classic account of diamond merchants by Coleman (1988), online auctions in which trust is required to mitigate risk among interactants who are not well-known to one another (Boyd, 2003; Flanagin, 2007), or game-like problems such as the Prisoner's Dilemma are cases in which trust and action may be most consistently linked. It may be that in less formalized problems, such as collective action as nearly costless boundary crossing, that the relationship of trust to behavior is weaker and inconsistent. It may take more trust to donate money than to post to a blog, respond to a petition request, or "friend" an organization in a social media site. It may take little trust to participate in expressive ways compared with more concrete participation in institution-centric, instrumental ones.

Participatory Styles

These observations about involvement in collective action so far are framed in generalities, as if it is sufficient to speak in terms of average citizens or average members of organizations. A major point of the preceding chapters, however, has been to attempt to contextualize collective action in specific organizations, recognizing that a person's overall or average level of participation arises from a composite of specific actions in various settings. This represents a different level of analysis than is typically undertaken in political science and sociology, which tend to limit themselves to general inferences across contexts. A second major point has been to look for signs of agency and autonomy within specific organizational contexts as people express their own styles of participation – a search on our part prompted by the affordances of contemporary technology in people's lives.

There has been a great deal of concern in recent decades with the average citizen, who evinces declining participation in institution-oriented democratic practices. This concern is reflected in the literature on voting (e.g., Wattenberg, 2002, but see MacDonald and Popkin, 2001) and in the broader literature on civic engagement (e.g., Putnam, 2000). A number of scholars have interpreted these changes alternatively in terms of "new politics," changes in participatory norms, or expanded repertoires of action rather than decline (Bennett, 1998, 2008; Dalton, 2008a; Dalton, Scarrow, and Cain, 2004; Inglehart, 1997; Zukin et al., 2006). These scholars recognize a shift from institutional-centric practices toward non-institutional ones: protesting, petitioning, political consumerism, enthusiasm for direct democracy in the form of ballot initiatives, and other forms of direct expression and action. In new norms of civic engagement, venerable factors such as education and age do not exhibit their traditional patterns, and the overall portrait is not one of decline but of altered norms of citizenship and engagement, originating from the emergence of postmaterial values during the 1960s and 1970s (Dalton, 2008a, 2008b).

We are supportive of this alternative view, although our research for this book was not designed to look for secular trends across populations. Instead, we were interested in cross-sectional variation in participation at the present time. We suspect that the long-term trends underway in recent decades are not simply replacing one dominant set of norms with another, such as expressive civic individualism displacing dutiful institutional orientation. We suspect that an important part of the contemporary picture of civic engagement is a flowering of varieties of involvement that coexist. Newer expressive, individualistic norms of involvement mean precisely that people are more able to go their own way rather than conform to dominant customs and practices. The challenge then becomes understanding what contributes to making a person a minimalist in one setting but an enthusiast or individualist in another. Our work suggests that the kind of citizenship norms and practices under discussion recently by scholars of participation do not vary simply across individuals, where one person is more duty-driven and institutionally focused while the next is more expressive and directed away from institutions. We suspect that any one person may enact somewhat different norms and practices in different settings.

This expectation comes from the finding that motivations and goals are so important in our findings and that in our approach these are a function of how a person feels about a specific organization such as AARP or MoveOn. The expectation also comes from the importance of interaction and engagement in our study, theoretically and empirically, which is again a function of the organizational setting in which a person is located. Although it is undoubtedly true that some citizens possess values that are, on the whole, more postmaterial, duty-driven, or civically inclined than others, it is also clear to us that how norms and values are expressed in civic or political practice is a function in part of organizational setting, and more specifically of how people's participatory styles emerge within specific contexts. Those contexts provide a great deal of latitude, especially because of technology, but they matter.

The digital-media environment does nothing for civic involvement if not contribute to this variety of styles. By breaking down boundaries of all kinds and expanding individual agency, it accelerates the trend toward more heterogeneous approaches to collective behavior. In this study, we saw what heterogeneity can look like within a single organization in the form of individualism, enthusiasm, traditionalism, and minimalism.

One striking illustration of this from Chapter 5 is the way that social capital works differently across participatory styles. A standard assumption in social-capital theory is that being more participatory and more broadly involved in civic affairs is a general trait that carries across people's civic lives: a person who is a joiner in one group is also a joiner in all his or her groups. We did not survey individuals about their entire portfolio of memberships to look for such variation, but we see evidence about it from the other direction. Only for individualists does participation in community meetings and organizations and expressiveness to news media or public officials carry over into involvement in the organizations in our study. This leads us to refine the idea that social capital generalizes, by specifying that this is true for people in our organizations who are entrepreneurially engaged but whose interaction is impersonal. For others, this is not the case. The relationship of social capital – that is, general social trust and involvement in community associations – is mediated by how a person enacts their membership in an organization. People have a good deal of latitude in how they do this.

This also implies that the landscape of collective action and social capital is more complex than portrayed in the declinist thesis. As much academic attention has been dedicated to debating Putnam's thesis of decline as to any other claim in the social sciences in recent decades. Many observers have suggested that social capital either does not work as Putnam suggests or is not in decline in the way he portrays. For example, Hero (2007) has shown that social capital has not conferred the same benefits on African Americans as whites. Romer, Jamieson, and Pasek (2009) examine variation across age in the relationship of media use to social capital. Paxton (1999) presents data suggesting that social capital has not declined in the universal way Putnam depicts. Our findings of a differential relationship of social capital to collective action involvement across participatory styles provide two additional dimensions of variation to the picture of how social capital is related to behavior – interaction with others and engagement with the organization.

To the extent that the pattern we find in The American Legion, AARP, and MoveOn holds in other organizations – a question to which we return shortly– then one implication is that efforts to explain civic engagement and participation in the contemporary media environment should move beyond one-size-fits-all models that, in effect, explain the average citizen rather than the distribution of many citizens. Our position that people vary empirically in participatory styles in ways that align theoretically with interaction and engagement cuts against the grain of most literature on individual-level participation, which has generally avoided categorizing people in favor of explaining the average person.

For us, there are four average citizens found across The American Legion, AARP, and MoveOn. Enthusiasts are entrepreneurial and personal in their organization, are sociable, highly identified, and plugged in, yet their contributions to collective outcomes are isolated from what they do civically in other contexts. One cannot predict what an enthusiast will do in one of our organizations by looking at how involved she or he is in others. Minimalists are another kind of member entirely. They are uncivic, weakly identified, and untrusting of their organization. A minimalist looks like the classic portrait of an interest-group member from the literature of a decade ago, except that they can be found in all kinds of organizations. They exist as passive targets of strategic mobilization by leaders, in effect waiting for messages from groups asking them to write to a member of Congress or express their views in some other way (Goldstein, 1999; Rozell and Wilcox, 1999). Individualists break rules of theory and look like no particular ideal type. Individualists appear disengaged, like organizational slackers, because their civic motivations are relatively low, and they are not much involved in their communities. Yet their goals align with those of their organization. Their technology use and skill is no greater than the other three styles, but they are the only people for whom general Internet skill is associated with their contributions to their organization. Technology use facilitates contributions to collective goals for people whose membership is impersonal and entrepreneurial. Traditionalists, by contrast with all three of the other styles, are civic followers. They are joiners and are sociable, but they do not attempt to shape what their organizations do.

To say that participatory styles are crucial to making sense of the membership of organizations is not to say that they explain everything. Although participatory styles affect how education, goals, and other forms of civic involvement translate into involvement in collective action in the organizations in this study, they do not have much bearing on the importance of the overriding characteristic of people's motivation. Motivation represents the other end of the engine of participation from skills, networks, norms, and other outcomes of civic engagement. Motivation tells us why people belong to a specific organization, regardless of what skills, networks, or norms they might accumulate through their activities. People who join an organization with an orientation that is social and civic will be more involved than those less oriented in that way, regardless of every other attribute that one might consider, from their general social trust to how participatory they are in other organizations. This is true of all participatory styles: whether one is an individualist or traditionalist, enthusiast or minimalist, motivation is the most important driver of involvement.

This finding stands in some contrast to the expectations from traditional collective action theory about the importance of instrumental reasons for joining organizations. In that view, organizations should be filled with instrumentalists, each seeking to maximize his or her benefits in relation to costs. Yet our organizations contain people with a mix of motives. Although our research design did not allow us to compare people who joined the organization to those who did not, among those who do belong, the most participatory and identified members are those whose motives were social in nature, not those who joined to obtain benefits or information (i.e., instrumental motivation). Evidence from our study shows that those with more instrumental motivations are actually somewhat less likely to trust their organization, contribute toward the collective good (among enthusiasts and The American Legion members), or identify with their organization (among The American Legion members). Across all four participatory styles, regardless of organization, the only motivation that predicts contributions to collective goals and activities is social motivation.

Although we did not investigate where motivations come from or how the motivation to continue belonging to an organization over time is shaped by participation, we can say with some assurance that social motivation is crucially important to people's involvement, and it has been largely overlooked or set aside in research, presumably because it is so hard to measure in general. One of the great advantages of studying people in specific organizational contexts, however, is that measuring motivation is relatively straightforward. Confronted with a need for predicting the involvement of a new group of members of some organization, and able to ask them only one thing, we would pass over their general civic involvement, trust, and education and instead would ask about why they joined. Asked to advise some new organization about what kinds of people to attract as members, we might answer as follows: if what you want are a great many passive dues payers to fund central initiatives, then follow the advice of Olson and legions of others by offering people selective incentives to join. If what you want are participants who contribute their time, energy, and voice, then attract people who have social motivations and will join because they wish to connect with others, participate in the organizations' activities, and have a desire to serve their community. Do not necessarily worry about building identification and trust.

The Three Organizations in Perspective: Organizations Matter

What then of organization? Throughout this book we have focused primarily on individuals and their participatory styles and given less attention to the more typical focus of research on organizations, for example, their structure and strategies. So one might ask, does structure matter? Or does everything boil down to the interaction between organizations and individuals that produces participatory styles?

Without question, organizations such as The American Legion, AARP, and MoveOn cannot be reduced to collections of participatory styles. These organizations pursue dramatically different public agendas, and their values and objectives overlap comparatively little – topics that have not been part of our analysis in this book. At the time of this writing, The American Legion's national office was involved in congressional consideration of ending the ban on the military's "Don't Ask Don't Tell" policy toward gays and lesbians, was advocating for better health care for veterans, and was involved in efforts to sustain public interest in a constitutional amendment protecting the flag. AARP was urging members to write to Congress asking for Social Security benefit increases and was posting a memorial at its Web site honoring John Lennon. MoveOn was running a petition calling on Congress not to extend tax breaks on people making more than $1 million per year. It was not our purpose in this book to give accounts of specific advocacy efforts or campaigns by these organizations, which change with each passing month, but instead to ask questions about how their memberships think about the organizations and to understand the structure of membership, regardless of the changing agenda.

Beyond bringing different objectives and goals to the public sphere, organizations matter specifically because of their structures and how these interact with participatory styles. Just as studies of participation in public life have typically avoided categorizing individuals except by race, age, or socioeconomic characteristics, studies of organizations in public life have generally taken the opposite approach by engaging in overcategorization. A great deal of work across theoretical traditions rests on sharp distinctions among types of organization, especially in work on social capital and civil society. A distinguishing feature of collective action space is that an organization's location is not derived from classical a priori categorizations based on organizational structures or the average member's profile. Rather, the space provides a theoretical framework for identifying participatory styles of organizational members based upon the emergent communicative dynamics of organizing, independent of their organization's "ideal type" or specific member demographics.

Knowing about participatory styles permitted us to locate and characterize the three organizations in our study in new ways. In Chapter 3 we suggested that traditional explanations of collective action tend to reflect what Granovetter (1985) described as either "undersocialized" or "oversocialized" accounts of human action. In undersocialized accounts, action results from the pursuit of self-interest by rational, atomized individuals. The explanatory focus is on selective incentives and cost-benefit ratios. In oversocialized accounts, normative patterns and behavioral prescriptions associated with social roles, status, and class have been internalized to such a degree that ongoing social relations have only peripheral effects on individual or collective action. From this perspective, knowing an individual's social class, educational level, and other demographic data as well as the institutional positioning and structure of the membership organization are enough to predict individual behavior.

Our theoretical position hardly lifts people out of their organizations. It enables us to embed someone's patterns of action in concrete ongoing systems of social relations within a specific organizational context. A compelling finding from this study is that members' organization-specific attitudes are by far the most critical factor in predicting their various levels of involvement with the organization. In our view, organization does matter, but it cannot be understood in isolation from the agency and communicative construction of membership that people bring to their involvement in collective action. Our data, derived from three very different organizations, with vastly different reputations, structures, membership rules, and institutional positioning, enable us to compare and contrast the relative influence of individual characteristics, organizational structure, and emergent communicative processes and social relations. In Chapter 4 we compared each organization to the others, and in Chapter 5 we compared people with each of the four participatory styles to one another, regardless of their organization. Our findings suggest that for each organization, neither individual characteristics nor the organization itself are very useful in predicting involvement. Further, neither was very helpful for explaining the ways in which individuals participated in their organizations. There were some general characteristics of the "average" member's experience of the organization that conformed to the "ideal organizational type," but there were also significant percentages of members whose participatory styles departed radically from experiences stereotypically associated with The American Legion, AARP, and MoveOn.

As we saw in Chapter 4, all three organizations have members with each of the four styles. As one would expect from the stereotypes, the average American Legion member reports significantly higher levels of personal interaction than do those of MoveOn and especially AARP. In contrast, the average AARP member experiences significantly higher levels of institutional engagement, where American Legion and MoveOn members are more entrepreneurial in their engagement. These means are clearly consistent with the classical theoretical expectations associated with civic and interest-group organizations discussed in Chapter 1. Nonetheless, only 42 percent of American Legion members were more personal than the midpoint on our scale for interaction. Moreover, about 35 percent of AARP members and 40 percent of MoveOn members reported more personal interaction than the average member of The American Legion.

About two-thirds of The American Legion members are individualists or enthusiasts; both styles are entrepreneurial in their approach to engagement. What this suggests is that the Legion is an organization more distinguished by members' engagement than members' interaction. We think of the Legion as an engagement-dominant organization, because it is more distinctive due to how members engage than how they interact. This is not to say that the personal nature of links among members of the Legion is unimportant, but it is to say that the important feature of its location in collection action space is its entrepreneurialism.

In AARP, 80 percent of members are either individualists or minimalists, both of which are impersonal in their interaction. AARP is an interaction-dominant organization, in which the distinguishing fact of its location is its impersonal interaction. This is consistent with part of the traditional story of interest groups, though the fact that more members are entrepreneurially (58%) engaged than institutionally engaged violates the interest-group ideal type.

The distinctive nature of MoveOn cannot be understood in terms of either dimension alone. Almost two-thirds of its members are individualists, meaning they are impersonal in their interaction and entrepreneurial in their engagement. MoveOn is as impersonal as AARP but is as entrepreneurial as the Legion. Almost 80 percent of MoveOn members report levels of engagement at the midpoint or above on entrepreneurial participatory styles, compared with about 70 percent of American Legion members and 60 percent of AARP members. As we wrote in Chapter 1, unlike the clear communicative expectations associated with interest groups and civic associations, probabilities about how people experience interaction and engagement in online organizations such as MoveOn have not yet developed within the scholarly literature, so there is no ideal type against which MoveOn can be compared. It is, in a way, typifying a new category.

It is worth noting, given the age skew of AARP and the Legion, as well as the gender skew of the latter, that neither age nor sex differences are important to our conclusions. We separated men and women and examined them, and their individual stories with respect to participatory styles and involvement in collective action are essentially the same, except that women across all three organizations exhibit a somewhat higher level of organizational identification. MoveOn has members of all ages, AARP has members generally age fifty or older, and the American Legion has a range of ages but is dominated by older veterans. To make sure that these different age profiles were not influencing our results, we compared across ages in the groups in various ways, such as dividing MoveOn into people older and younger than fifty, in order to make a comparison group with AARP. We again found no major differences, and so we conclude that our results are reasonably robust with respect to age.

So if one looks at The American Legion, AARP, or MoveOn through its average member, one sees profiles that seem to conform to the ideal civic and interest groups, in the oversocialized view. But when one considers the entire collective action space, differences transcending organizations are apparent. Regardless of organizational type, the variance within a particular organization is quite large compared to that among organizations. Organizations do matter, and they potentially make a huge difference in the consequences of a particular participatory style, because organizations create the context that gives meaning to the forms of member interaction and engagement. But it is important to recognize how important different participatory styles can be within an organization.

The interaction of participatory style and organization can be seen in the following. Across organizations, enthusiasts and traditionalists, both of whom have personal interaction, consistently have the highest level of contribution to collective action. Individualists and minimalists, who have impersonal interaction, contribute the least. But this pattern varies in magnitude across the organizations. Minimalists in MoveOn are about half a standard deviation less contributory than enthusiasts, while minimalists in The American Legion are nearly a whole standard deviation less so. Participatory styles make a bigger difference for the traditional civic organization, with its community-based norms and its hierarchical organization, than for the flat, lean online MoveOn. The same pattern appears for organizational identification and organizational trust, where the difference between the least and most identified styles is about half the size in MoveOn as it is in the other two groups.

One potentially useful way to conceptualize differences across the organizations is through the idea of expectancy. The American Legion is typically perceived as an organization whose members, through the post system, develop close personal relationships with other members. However, for some members this expectation is violated – namely for individualists and minimalists – and these people are significantly less likely to contribute than similar types of members of AARP. It may be that this expectancy violation exerts a negative boomerang effect on some American Legion members, prompting them to fall to lower levels of contribution to the group's goals than people belonging to other organizations. By contrast, because being impersonal is the traditional expectation for interaction by members of AARP, members' locations in these quadrants do not negatively affect the degree of organizational contribution.

Moreover, when we look at enthusiasts we see that not only do expectations seem to matter but also the direction of the violations matters. Enthusiasts from AARP are much more likely to contribute than enthusiasts from MoveOn. In this case, there is a violation of expectations toward greater personal interaction and entrepreneurial engagement, which actually increases the likelihood of contribution for those people.

The same type of violation may be less likely to be evidenced with MoveOn because it is a relatively new organization that has not yet developed a strong prototypical profile of member interaction or engagement. We suspect that if organizational expectations develop and become normative, a stronger relationship between collective action type and organizational membership may emerge when expectations are violated with them as well.

When we consider the heightened role "branding" now plays in advocacy organizations, the implications of these findings are far-reaching. Since the 1990s, the marketing strategy of branding has become a common tactic for advocacy organizations as they strive to create a unique niche within today's competitive environment (Lecy, Mitchell, and Schmitz, 2010). Brands are about creating public recognition for what an organization stands for, the organization's focal issues and positions, the ways they carry out their missions, and their styles of interaction with multiple publics. Technology is viewed as an enabler of branding (Wright, 2002), and comprehensive media branding strategies are highly touted (Ratnatunga and Ewing, 2005). Strong branding brings high levels of public recognition and consistent expectations for the organization and its members. Despite the negative publicity that advocacy organizations like Amnesty International, for instance, received for the commodification of their logo and image (Barakso, 2010), the research literature suggests that organizations will benefit from strong branding through increased donor and membership involvement.

However, our findings suggest that the relationship is far more complex than previously believed. Each of our organizations has a unique brand, particularly in terms of its relationship with its members, and those members whose experiences were inconsistent with that brand image tended to be the members who were less likely to be involved. The increased capacity for individuals today to interact and engage organizations in their own ways rather than in the manner typically determined by the organization suggests that the unequivocal benefits of homogenous branding, at least in terms of what members can and should expect, may need to be reconsidered.

In the case of organizational identification, it is interesting that individualist members of the Legion are less likely to identify with their organization than members of AARP. Here again, normative expectations seem to be operating: location in this quadrant strongly violates The American Legion's norm of members' personal involvement, and thus it is not surprising that being in this position as a Legion member is more negatively associated with identification than it is for AARP members, more of whom are individualists. In contrast, individualists who belong to MoveOn identify more with their organization than the individualists in AARP. Although norms for modes of interaction and engagement are not particularly well developed for MoveOn, the rhetoric of the organization is far more entrepreneurial than it is for AARP, suggesting the diminished identification for AARP members in this quadrant. However, minimalist members of MoveOn are also more identified than those of AARP, in spite of the fact that MoveOn members in this quadrant might be experiencing a negative expectancy violation.

Technology and End-User Enterprise

We framed the problem of collective action early in this book from the perspective of technology and the digital-media environment. But we did not take the traditional path of searching for a correlation between variation in technology use and variation in extent of civic or political behavior. We did not expect, for example, that on average people who use technology more would also be more likely to exhibit more of some behavior – like voting, protesting, writing to public officials, or, in our case, being more involved in their organizations. In the early days of the Internet, there were some good reasons for thinking that this might be true, because the technology was novel, available to only some citizens who shared particular traits, and used by only some elites and organizations.

Today technology is different. Thinking about the affordances of digital media, and what these mean for individuals and organizations, led us to expect weakened boundaries of various kinds and enhanced agency for people. We expected this to be more important as a contextual influence on people's involvement in collective action than as an explanation of why some people are more involved than others. The end-user enterprise and contemporary ubiquity that come from these affordances imply something quite different than the assertion that particular behaviors (e.g., enhanced civic engagement) might result from greater technology use. Rather, in the contemporary environment people are now more able than ever to act however they see fit, readily acting beyond the constraints imposed by a context for collective action once largely dominated and controlled by organizations. This might entail being more involved, for some people, but it is not likely to mean that for everyone. Prior (2007) has shown that digital media increase choice, and that people use that choice to do different things: some use it to avoid news and public affairs, and some use it to go deeper into them. We have argued that technology expands agency, and that people use this agency to enact different styles of participation, rather just uniformly becoming more involved. For some people in some organizations, end-user enterprise may mean being an effective activist, organizer, and entrepreneur who knows many others personally – an enthusiast. For others, or for the same person in another setting, end-user enterprise may translate to a more satisfying experience as a minimalist who avoids personal interaction and engagement with their organization, but who can monitor activities, news, and opportunities in order to act as they arise. The end-user enterprise associated with digital media means that people have more degrees of freedom as they approach collective action, even within quite traditional organizational contexts. These additional degrees of freedom mean more variety of practice.

These ideas are implicitly longitudinal rather than cross-sectional, and our argument about technology as context is specifically counter to the idea that the most important implications of technology for behavior are to be found by comparing those who use a particular technology more with those who use it less or not at all. We therefore did not attempt in designing our study to test directly the hypothesis that the diversity of participatory styles we find in organizations is chiefly the product of technology. To do that would have required at least two snapshots of our organizations, with a baseline portrait from the early 1990s – or the late 1990s in the case of MoveOn, which was established at that time. This we could not do. We suspect but cannot prove that a comparison of portraits across time would show a spreading of the footprints of membership in each organization over time, with more variance as time went on until some equilibrium was reached – or is reached in the future.

Yet clearly the existence of multiple participatory styles is not solely the product of digital media, as analyses in Chapters 4 and 5 have demonstrated. The leader of any collective action organization would readily say that his or her membership is diverse, containing activists and more passive members, outspoken participants and quiet lurkers, and reliable contributors of money and those who never open their pocketbooks. In even the smallest groups, people adopt varying roles. The questions about collective action prompted by digital media help shed light on this fact, in particular by illuminating the importance of how personally people interact with others and how entrepreneurially they engage with the organization. Digital media enhance people's agency to construct membership in ways they see fit, but we suspect that most organizations have always exhibited much more variety than the ideal-type characterizations such as civic organization and interest group depicted. Undoubtedly, there have always been enthusiasts in AARP alongside minimalists, as well as individualists in The American Legion who coexisted with traditionalists.

One important set of implications about technology from our study comes from MoveOn. As the technology-dependent case among our three organizations, to compare it with The American Legion and with AARP is to compare an organization that relies on technology for everything – an organization that has no other medium of communication with its members than digital media – with organizations that, like most, existed long before digital media and have layered new technology into old practices of communication and membership. Few political professionals who have seen MoveOn in action doubt that it has clout in organizing collective action. In that sense, MoveOn is proof of concept that online organizations can be efficacious socially and politically. MoveOn has spawned several other organizations that have applied its model successfully. The group Color of Change is one, advocating for the political voice of African Americans. It was cofounded in 2005 by James Rucker, who was the director of Grassroots Mobilization for MoveOn before starting the new organization, which currently reports having eight hundred thousand members. The international group Avaaz, which pursues progressive topics on the global stage, was also modeled after MoveOn. It started in 2007, and at the time of this writing reported about ten million members in 193 countries. Like MoveOn, it polls members (in fourteen languages) about what issues to work on, rather than setting a top-down agenda, and it can raise money, deliver large numbers of petitions, and mobilize people for phone calls and protests. Unlike many traditional transnational organizations, Avaaz operates without regional or national bureaucracies or staff, instead relying on technology to allow a nimble staff with a small budget of only about $4 million annually to orchestrate actions by many people who are widely distributed – as MoveOn has proven can be done for more than a decade within the United States.

Our analysis shows that people's involvement with MoveOn is as rich and complex as in the case of the more traditional organizations, and we suspect the same would be true for Color of Change, Avaaz, and other organizations inspired by MoveOn. Though it is an online organization, people identify with MoveOn and contribute toward its collective goals and activities, and these outcomes are associated with underlying motivations and other characteristics in ways that match quite closely what happens in The American Legion and AARP. A comparable richness in participatory styles exists within MoveOn, though these styles do play a less powerful role in driving outcomes. It may be that the porousness of MoveOn's boundaries as an online organization without membership criteria means that participatory styles matter somewhat less for what people do than in more traditional organizations. It is clear in any case, however, that technology-based membership looks a great deal like traditional forms of membership, and that participatory styles in this unusual "virtual" organization made possible by digital media are the same styles one finds in "physical" organizations. Though few technology experts would find it the least surprising, it may still come as something of a surprise in some corners of the political and civic world that "virtual" is "real."

MoveOn sees advantages of this kind of relationship with members. In the words of a senior MoveOn staffer, "The obvious difference with our not being a bricks-and-mortar organization is that people's conception of what it means to be a member of MoveOn, of what MoveOn is, is very different. There's no headquarters. There's no place where you can go where MoveOn is. So that means that MoveOn can just as easily be in your home and at your desk with you – it can *be* you – as it can be some building somewhere, because it is *not* some building somewhere. It is something that you as a member carry with you."

Beyond MoveOn, the central implications of our study for technology are captured in the observation that how much and how skillfully people use digital media generally indicates little about the extent of their involvement in these three organizations. Framed this way, the finding makes sense intuitively because one might expect that organizational context is determinant of what members of an organization do. Yet a decade-long search for effects of technology use on civic engagement has occurred across the social sciences, and much of the engagement of interest does occur within organizational contexts – a well-known fact that is often set aside. Across many organizations and many opportunities for involvement, people who are more involved digitally are modestly more involved civically. More civically and politically interested people are affected positively by the availability of technology, though the relationship is very small and contingent (Bimber and Copeland, 2011).

Our project considered this issue from within the three organizations, and it shows that people's general use of technology does not exhibit much of a relationship with their involvement in these organizations. In almost no case does the amount of time one spends online generally have any association with involvement in one of the three organizations. Minimalists and individualists show a modest relationship between overall Internet skill and contributions to the collective goals of their organizations. These two styles share the characteristic of impersonal interaction, which suggests that for people who are not interactive with others personally (either face-to-face or online), more skill and comfort with the Internet are associated with somewhat more involvement with their organization.

In this way, we find support for our expectation from Chapter 2 that while technology use is enormously relevant to civic life, it is as context for action rather than as a factor whose variation across individuals tells us important things about why some people are more involved than others. The fact that in our organizations people who are more involved use the online tools of their organization more is consistent with this idea. When people are involved in The American Legion, AARP, and MoveOn, they are likely to use the Web sites and other digital tools of the organizations. There is also a sense at The American Legion and AARP that the new generation of members will be more likely to drive grassroots advocacy through digital exchanges.

Scholars of technology have long wrestled with an endogeneity problem around this kind of observation. Does an association between technology use and a behavior mean that using the technology causes more of the behavior, or that an inclination to the behavior drives people to the technology? The answer can vary across problems, but likely the answer is also commonly "both." Where digital media and collective action are concerned, the main features of the problem are that collective action opportunities are ubiquitous, and technology is ubiquitous, not only for individuals but also for organizations. The tools and opportunities afforded by mobile phones, social software, and other digital media are embedded in social life and implicated in the repertoire of communicative practices that people experience regardless of their own utilization or skill. When the technology is ubiquitous and its association with a common behavior is substantively modest at very best, then we are disinclined to think that the project of untangling the direction of causal arrows is likely to be theoretically illuminating.

The recent revolutions in Tunisia, Egypt, Libya, and elsewhere in North Africa and the Middle East are cases in point about problems of directionality. The headlines, at the time of the protests, were filled with stories of a pan-Arab youth movement founded on Facebook, and terms such as "Revolution 2.0," "Facebook Revolution," and "Wikipedia Revolution" were bandied about. The general theme of much news coverage and expert commentary in early 2011 was of the power of the Internet to challenge authoritarian regimes. But the crucial point is that not every protestor was online, blogging, tweeting, and checking or updating Facebook. The Egyptian revolution was not a revolution of millions of Wael Ghonims, the Google employee who managed the crucial Facebook page and who helped plan the protest. Facebook mattered to the people in Tarir Square in Cairo not because everyone there used it, but because Facebook was part of the context of organizing and acting. Enough people used these technologies to shift the terms of revolution, diminish the power of state-controlled media, and set the pace of events. All who participated in the overthrow of dictators benefited from the new media context for revolution, whether they used Twitter and Facebook a great deal, a little, or not at all. For us, and we believe for the members of The American Legion, AARP, and MoveOn, technology is a significant part of the context in which to become involved and to express participatory styles; it is not chiefly a powerful covariate that can explain differences in levels of involvement.

The Organization and the Individual

The digital-media environment in which collective action now almost universally takes place is one in which organizations are in flux. As we observed at the beginning of this book, enormous attention has been focused in recent years on collective action occurring either without organizations or with organizations playing a role that is less than central. Major themes in that work, including our own, include horizontal communication among citizens without the need for central brokers, new agendas that arise from citizen-activists rather than traditional elites in organizations, and organizational hybridity and flexibility. As researchers and as citizens, we continue to be fascinated and hopeful about the power of these new changes.

This potential for organizational diversity and individual control, coupled with the variety in participatory styles and the implications of end-user enterprise that arise from the current media environment, will continue to raise the question of how formal organizations cope with the enhanced agency available to their members. In the end, collective action organizations rely on having members, at least nominally, in order to achieve their goals, discern and derive meaning, and justify their very existence. On the surface, though, contemporary technological tools provide people the means to bypass organizations altogether.

In studying three formal organizations, one each from the era of newspapers, the broadcasting age, and the early years of the Internet revolution, we have examined many of these issues. We found that individual agency is associated not so much with one or another form of organization as with great variety in membership experiences. Organizations like those in our study should not be overlooked in the enthusiasm over Twitter protests and self-organized action through other social media. For the people who belong to The American Legion, AARP, and MoveOn, it is clear that their organizations matter enough to them for continued involvement.

We also suggested at the outset of this book that although we believe that organizations still matter, they do so in more subtle ways than scholars have previously believed. Rather than offering fixed and inflexible templates for involvement, organizations offer much broader opportunities for people to define their roles and to establish their own participatory styles than one might have imagined. One can be an enthusiast or a minimalist in any of our organizations, and the consequences of those choices are substantial for researchers' efforts to explain involvement. This means that scholars interested in collective action, civil society, interest groups, and social movements should look beyond old classifications of organization by looking inside at the diversity of relationships that they can support.

We argued in Chapter 2 that individuals matter, and that in particular a key feature of the digital-media environment – agency – means that individual-level variation is very important. Individual characteristics such as motivations, goals, and communicative preferences can matter greatly, not simply because one specific technology or another facilitates a particular form of involvement, but because the aggregate technological environment facilitates individuation. The challenge of understanding collective action in organizational contexts is therefore one of understanding individual-level variation within any one organization and organizational-level similarities across organizations. The participatory styles that are represented in the collective action space provide a way to approach people's involvement while accounting for both these facets of collective action.

The collective action space provides a general framework for thinking about involvement, but in this book we have examined concrete evidence about it only for three organizations. This raises the question: does it work beyond The American Legion, AARP, and MoveOn? None of these organizations is exactly representative of a larger class. Few organizations are in fact "typical," and so it would be fruitless either to go in search of the perfectly representative organization or to suggest that any of these three represents others well. The American Legion is not like other civic organizations, because it is an organization of veterans and operates a national-level advocacy program. AARP is unlike other interest groups because of its size, the extended program of selective incentives it uses to attract members, and broad focus on policies related to age. MoveOn is the original archetype of a small but growing class of organizations whose future in flux. Consequently, we have been careful in this book to avoid arguing that what we have found empirically generalizes to all organizations. It is central to our assumptions that a given person is likely to have different experiences and relationships with different organizations, and that these are not discernable with standard socioeconomic measures or general attributes such as social capital. So in this very important way, organizations are a key element of collective action space: we always consider a person's inclination to be involved in collective action in the context of a specific mobilizing organization. In this sense, our theory returns us to the two basic elements of the standard model of political participation: the individual and the mobilizer. We have attempted to tie these together conceptually in a new way. Our theoretical approach is general, because one can locate any organization in collective action space; having done that, one can inquire whether members have distinct profiles and patterns of involvement across the space, but the answer is not knowable without more research. We have two expectations, however, one more solid and one more speculative.

The first is that participatory styles will vary across the four quadrants of collective action space for most, if not all, organizations and for nonorganizations as well. This reflects our trust in the vast bodies of scholarship that have come before us identifying interaction among people and the degree of entrepreneurial or institutional engagement as fundamental aspects of people's experiences of collective action. It would be surprising if how personal and entrepreneurial a person is does not play a key role in their contributions and identification – and perhaps in their trust as well – in most organizations. It seems likely that these dimensions would capture important aspects of membership in the National Rifle Association and Amnesty International, the Red Cross and the Masons, the Sierra Club and a Tea Party group. We suspect as well that they capture what happens in networks and ad hoc groups. We can ask of members of networks of activists how personally they know others, as well as how entrepreneurial they find the network to be, and we would expect on theoretical grounds that the answers people give would say a great deal about how much they contribute, how identified they are, their levels of trust, and how factors such as involvement in their communities translate into what they do in their networks.

The second expectation, which is more speculative, is that the empirical portraits of participatory styles that one would find in other organizations are not likely to differ greatly from what we have found in the Legion, AARP, and MoveOn. Although these organizations cannot be said to represent others, they are about as different as large organizations can be from one another. This suggests to us that our findings may well be robust across other large organizations, though this remains an empirical question. It may be, for example, that smaller organizations work differently. All three of our organizations are very large. Very small organizations, especially those not extending beyond the local, in which all members are likely to know one another and to be involved in activities, are likely to work quite differently, with less variation on each axis and perhaps with different meanings attached to the four participatory styles.

Perhaps the greatest limitation of looking at collective action in the way we have in this book is that we have been unable to say what any individual's entire portfolio of involvement looks like. The concept of participatory styles entails a hybrid individual-organizational level of theorizing and measurement. This means that we can use any particular style, such as minimalist, to describe an individual in an organization, but we cannot conclude that the same person would exhibit the same style in other contexts. A person might have a portfolio of styles that describes his or her involvement in various organizations and situations. Because being an enthusiast requires a good deal of time and attention, each person's time budget, energy, dedication to civic issues, and agenda of interests are likely to limit the number of enthusiast relationships he or she may undertake.

It is likely, though our study cannot show it, that individualism and traditionalism may more strongly reflect personality traits and orientations to the world, and people inclined toward these styles of participation may well exhibit them more universally. Still, styles are always a reflection of how an individual acts and crosses boundaries within an organizational context. Some organizations are likely to elicit more individualism or more traditionalism than others. One can imagine Amnesty International or the Libertarian Party as especially supportive of the former, and a religious values organization such as Focus on the Family as supportive of the latter.

Our data collection looked outward from each organization, so to speak, and stopped at each member's involvement in his or her organization. A next step for analysis would be to look further, by examining all of the most important memberships that each citizen in a large sample has, and then assessing the footprint of the individual in collective action space. Some people may evince similar styles in many organizations, while some may interact and engage quite differently across contexts. To look at collective action space from that perspective would shed even greater light on the dynamics of involvement.

Without question, the organizational context for collective action is growing richer and more ramified as digital media change the character of the public sphere. People are involved across organizations and groups, among networks of individuals, and among networks of organizations. They may be involved through sustained memberships or in one-off acts. Their communication environment involves complex horizontal communication, messages to and from elites, and new classes of intermediaries such as bloggers. The time spans involved in collective action may be long, as in the case of social movements or presidential election campaigns, or they may last only hours as messages calling for a specific action flash through the digital environment. Purposeful membership, a meaningful sense of identity, and a coherent way to navigate the porous boundaries of the contemporary media environment are not, we suspect, always clear to people. With roles less clearly defined for them by organizations and institutions, and with new technology-enabled agency that permits people to construct their forms of involvement with considerable discretion, citizens confront an abundance of choice.

That choice, we also suspect, is empowering and disorienting in these transitional years as new technologies and new ways of belonging continue to multiply in advance of the development of new norms and customs about how the practices of collective action should work. Understanding how people navigate this world requires considerably more than knowing their demographics or counting how many hours they use one technology or another. It requires, at the very least, ways of understanding how motivations combine with opportunities, expectations, and communication in specific contexts, such as a membership organization, and then seeing how these are expressed in the styles of involvement that people construct as they react to their environment – and contribute to it.

APPENDIX A

Interaction and Engagement

Interaction within The American Legion ($\overline{X} = 3.48$, $SD = 1.12$) is more personal than interaction in AARP ($\overline{X} = 4.08$, $SD = 1.04$; $p < 0.001$), by about a half a standard deviation. Similarly, although both are large interest groups, interaction among members within MoveOn ($\overline{X} = 3.93$, $SD = 0.95$) is also more personal than within AARP ($p < 0.01$). So members of The American Legion experience more personal interaction with others in their organization than do MoveOn and AARP members, and AARP members experience the least personal interaction with their fellow organizational members overall. Figure A.1 illustrates the distribution of the perceived personalness of interaction among members within each organization.

In terms of engagement, AARP is the most institutional, with a value right at the midpoint of our scale ($\overline{X} = 3.03$, $SD = 0.64$). The American Legion is somewhat more entrepreneurial ($\overline{X} = 3.17$, $SD = 0.60$), followed by MoveOn ($\overline{X} = 3.35$, $SD = 0.59$). Each of these differences is statistically significant ($p < 0.001$). The span from AARP to MoveOn is about half a standard deviation, which is similar to the spread on interaction. This comports with the general perception of AARP as a large, highly institutionalized, and centrally run organization, with relatively fewer opportunities for member input when compared to The American Legion and MoveOn. MoveOn is traditionally viewed by scholars as quite entrepreneurial, and our data support that perception. Figure A.2 shows these distributions, oriented vertically to reflect the fact that engagement is the *y* axis of collective action space.

As is true of interaction, these differences in scores among the three organizations belie the fact that members are distributed close to normally

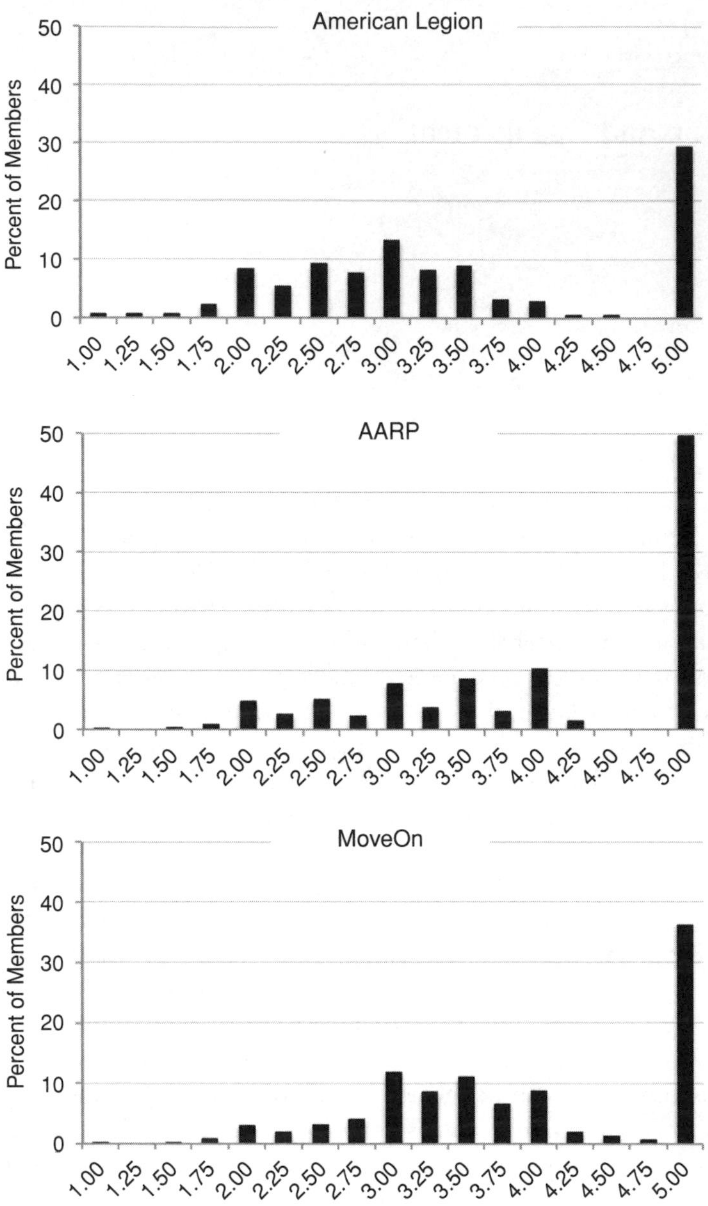

FIGURE A1. Distribution of Interaction

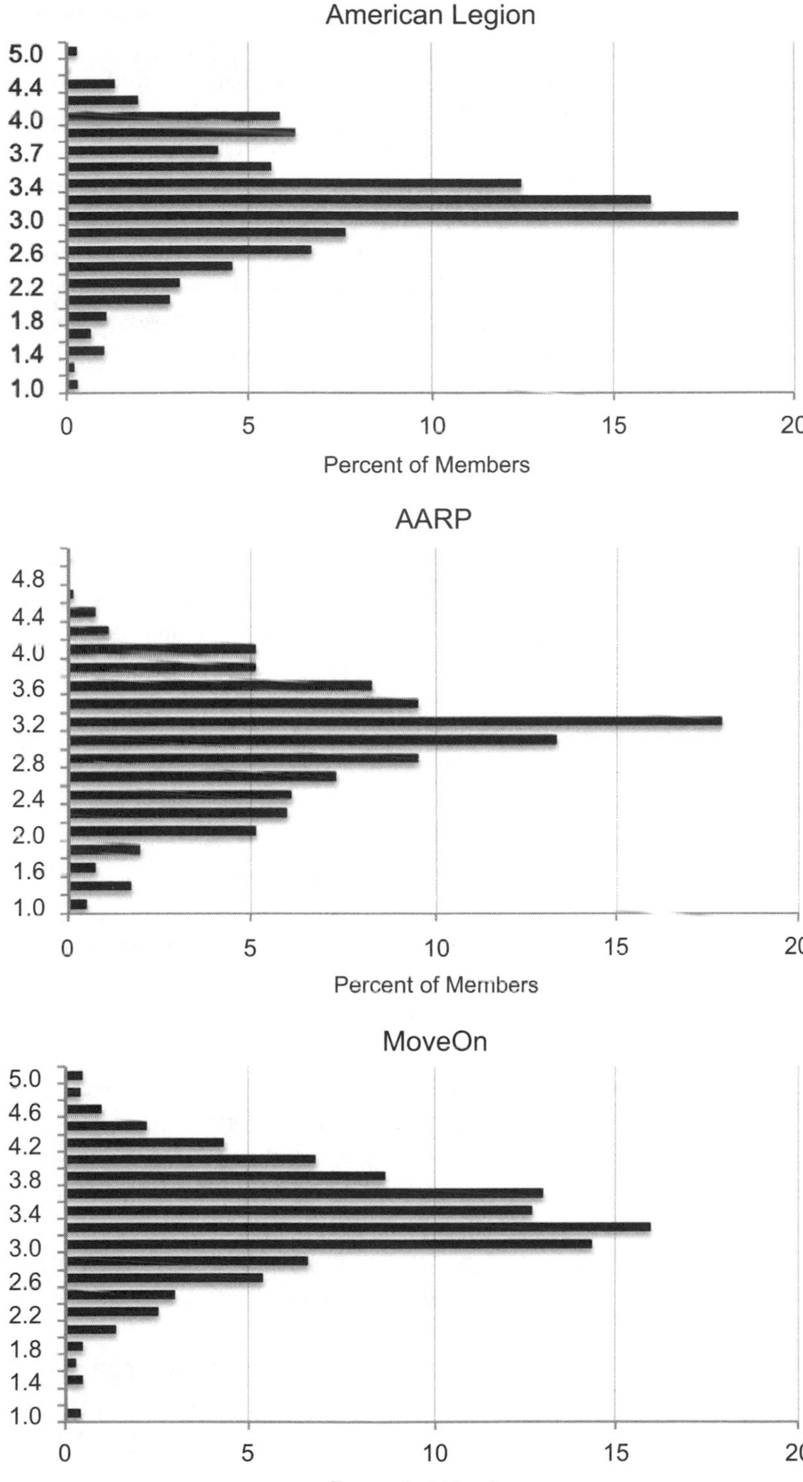

FIGURE A2. Distribution of Engagement

along the engagement dimension. Some Legion members find it to be highly entrepreneurial, as do a few AARP members, while some MoveOn members experience their organization as highly institutionalized. This should come as a surprise to some observers because it is typically assumed that the experience people have of an organization's degree of centralization is chiefly or even solely a function of its objective structure, as might be reflected in an organization chart. These data, however, show that people's perception of engagement varies quite substantially within each organization and, interestingly, to a similar degree across all three, despite their very different objective structures.

Combining Interaction and Engagement to Form the Collective Action Space

Theoretically, collective action space represents the combination of interaction and engagement as the axes of a two-dimensional space. Social scientists usually do not form geometric abstractions for their data, especially in the case of survey research, where linear and, sometimes, nonlinear summations of variables are typically used to predict other variables. We are instead concerned with establishing how interaction and engagement can be combined to represent a meaningful two-dimensional space consistent with our theory. The basis of this combination is the representation of each of the respondents in our survey by a pair of coordinates, representing their individual scores on interaction and engagement. These x,y coordinates are the Cartesian location of each respondent and allow an exploration of subsets of people on the basis of their location in the collective action space.

In order for this approach to succeed, interaction and engagement should be roughly orthogonal in Cartesian terms. In the terms of statistical methods, "orthogonal" is typically interpreted from the perspective of bivariate correlation, where it implies a lack of correlation. Variables that are uncorrelated are said to be orthogonal, which we see visually when a line fit to the two variables portrayed orthogonally to each other has a slope of 0. In terms of correlation or regression, a line fitting variables with a perfect correlation of 1 has a slope of 1. We can therefore appraise orthogonality of interaction and engagement in statistical terms by using simple correlation.

Interaction and engagement show a small correlation for our three organizations, varying from $r = -0.14$ for MoveOn to $r = -0.25$ for The American Legion. This means that the axes are not perfectly independent:

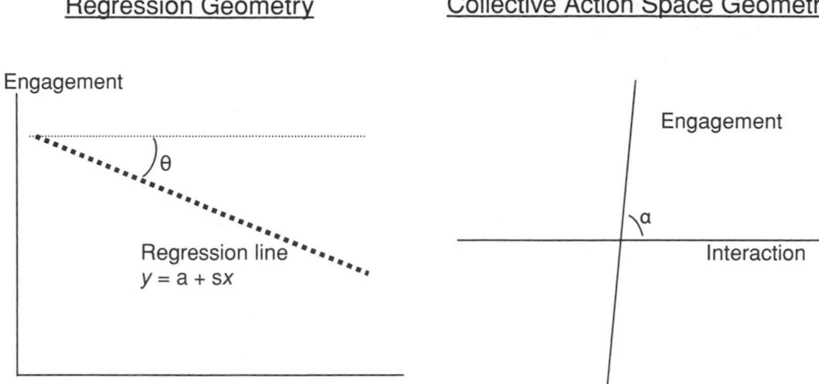

FIGURE A3. Deriving the Angle between Interaction and Engagement

as interaction becomes more personal, engagement becomes slightly more entrepreneurial. From 2 percent to 6 percent of the variance in either variable is connected to variance in the other. So the axes are far closer to perpendicular than to parallel, but some deviation exists from a perfectly rectangular space.

What does this level of orthogonality look like graphically in Cartesian terms, which is how we have theorized them, rather than in statistical geometry? It is possible to convert correlations or regressions into a measure of the Cartesian angle between the two variables by using basic trigonometry. The key to this conversion is the recognition that when statistical correlations are depicted in traditional scatter plots, the variables of interest are plotted perfectly perpendicularly to each other as the *x* and *y* axes – despite the fact that their actual relationship is unknown until the slope of a line fit to each corresponding pair of values is calculated, and in few cases would actually be 90°.

To convert statistical geometry to Cartesian geometry, we need to find the actual angle between the two variables. One technique for doing so is to first imagine a regression line fit to the two variables, in the present case interaction and engagement. The slope, *s*, of the regression line is simply the regression coefficient between the two variables. Alternatively, *s* can be read from the correlation coefficient between the variables, *r*, according to the following formula: $s = r\ (\sigma_{Engagement}/\sigma_{Interaction})$. The next step is interpreting what the slope means. To do that, consider the angle between the regression line and horizontal line, which we call θ, as shown in the left-hand panel of Figure A.3. From simple trigonometry, this angle is the

TABLE A.1. *Summary of Measured Angles between Axes in Collective Action Space across Organizations*

	β	Θ	α
American Legion	−0.14	−7.722	105.4
AARP	−0.12	−6.880	103.8
MoveOn	−0.08	−4.823	99.65
All Three Organizations	−0.11	−6.316	102.6

arctangent of the slope. So $\theta = \arctan(s)$. The link between this statistical geometry and Cartesian geometry, which is shown in the right-hand panel of Figure A.3, is the fact that the angle θ can vary from 0, when there is no correlation between the two variables, to 45°, when the correlation is 1. The Cartesian deviation from orthogonal of the two variables is twice θ, and the angle between the two is $90 - 2\,\theta$. So $\alpha = 90 - 2 \arctan s$.

To see how this works, consider the limiting cases. For perfectly correlated variables with the same standard deviation, then $r = 1$, $s = 1$, $\theta = \text{Arctan}(s) = 45$, and $\alpha = 90 - 2(45) = 0$, meaning the variables are parallel. In the case of perfectly uncorrelated variables, $r = 0$, $s = 0$, $\theta = 0$, and $\alpha = 90$, meaning the variables are perpendicular. Using this approach, we calculate the angle α for each of our organizations separately, and then for the groups combined, as shown in Table A.1. The results show that, in practice, our axes deviate from perfectly orthogonal by about 10 to 15 degrees as a function of the organization. In the analyses in Chapter 5, results are not very sensitive to small changes in how we define quadrants created by these axes, and so we proceed as if they were perfectly orthogonal.

APPENDIX B

Predicting Contribution, Identification, and Trust by Organization

TABLE B.1A. *Predicting Contribution to Collective Goals and Activities for The American Legion*

	Model 1		Model 2		Model 3	
	Beta	Sig.	Beta	Sig.	Beta	Sig.
(Constant)		0.96		0.11		0.00
Education	−0.12	0.00	−0.01	0.57	0.00	0.98
Year Born	0.01	0.65	−0.03	0.09	−0.06	0.00
Express Opinion	0.04	0.18	0.05	0.02	0.03	0.10
Contact Official	0.07	0.01	0.08	0.00	0.06	0.01
Attend Meeting	0.13	0.00	0.07	0.00	0.05	0.02
Associations	0.12	0.00	0.06	0.00	0.05	0.01
Trust	0.05	0.05	0.01	0.68	0.00	0.82
Instrumental Motivation			−0.03	0.13	−0.04	0.03
Social Motivation			0.53	0.00	0.48	0.00
Influence Motivation			−0.01	0.66	−0.02	0.41
Goals			0.15	0.00	0.15	0.00
Internet Skill					0.02	0.43
Hours Online					−0.03	0.15
Years Online					−0.03	0.22
Visit Web Site					0.22	0.00
r^2	*0.06*		*0.41*		*0.44*	

TABLE B.1B. *Predicting Identification for The American Legion*

	Model 1		Model 2		Model 3	
	Beta	Sig.	Beta	Sig.	Beta	Sig.
(Constant)		0.10		0.29		0.61
Education	−0.14	0.00	−0.02	0.29	−0.01	0.61
Year Born	−0.01	0.74	−0.01	0.75	0.00	0.83
Express Opinion	−0.04	0.17	0.00	0.95	0.00	0.90
Contact Official	0.05	0.05	0.05	0.01	0.05	0.01
Attend Meeting	0.05	0.09	0.01	0.69	0.01	0.79
Associations	0.06	0.02	0.03	0.12	0.03	0.11
Trust	0.02	0.42	−0.03	0.10	−0.03	0.08
Instrumental Motivation			−0.04	0.07	−0.04	0.05
Social Motivation			0.23	0.00	0.23	0.00
Influence Motivation			0.07	0.00	0.08	0.00
Goals			0.50	0.00	0.50	0.00
Internet Skill					−0.03	0.29
Hours Online					−0.05	0.01
Years Online					−0.01	0.56
Visit Web Site					0.03	0.16
r^2	*0.02*		*0.46*		*0.46*	

TABLE B.1C. *Predicting Organizational Trust for The American Legion*

	Model 1		Model 2		Model 3	
	Beta	Sig.	Beta	Sig.	Beta	Sig.
(Constant)		0.04		0.25		0.34
Education	−0.09	0.00	−0.03	0.20	−0.04	0.13
Year Born	−0.01	0.56	0.00	0.94	0.00	0.98
Express Opinion	−0.03	0.19	−0.01	0.57	−0.01	0.66
Contact Official	0.00	0.98	−0.01	0.70	−0.01	0.82
Attend Meeting	−0.01	0.78	−0.02	0.48	−0.01	0.57
Associations	−0.02	0.36	−0.03	0.21	−0.03	0.24
Trust	0.10	0.00	0.07	0.00	0.07	0.00
Instrumental Motivation			−0.03	0.21	−0.03	0.27
Social Motivation			0.03	0.29	0.04	0.16
Influence Motivation			0.11	0.00	0.11	0.00
Goals			0.30	0.00	0.30	0.00
Internet Skill					−0.01	0.79
Hours Online					−0.01	0.61
Years Online					0.03	0.25
Visit Web Site					−0.04	0.11
r^2	*0.02*		*0.15*		*0.16*	

TABLE B.2A. *Predicting Contribution to Collective Goals and Activities for AARP*

	Model 1		Model 2		Model 3	
	Beta	**Sig.**	**Beta**	**Sig.**	**Beta**	**Sig.**
(Constant)		0.01		0.95		0.42
Education	−0.06	0.22	0.07	0.07	0.04	0.31
Year Born	−0.11	0.01	0.00	0.96	−0.03	0.39
Express Opinion	0.09	0.05	0.07	0.06	0.06	0.14
Contact Official	0.05	0.29	0.03	0.43	0.01	0.71
Attend Meeting	0.05	0.31	0.02	0.55	0.00	0.93
Associations	0.13	0.01	0.08	0.06	0.08	0.04
Trust	−0.01	0.79	0.00	1.00	−0.01	0.87
Instrumental Motivation			−0.03	0.49	−0.04	0.39
Social Motivation			0.58	0.00	0.55	0.00
Influence Motivation			−0.01	0.89	0.00	0.94
Goals			0.11	0.04	0.11	0.03
Internet Skill					0.08	0.10
Hours Online					0.02	0.58
Years Online					0.03	0.50
Visit Web Site					0.10	0.01
r^2	*0.06*		*0.40*		*0.42*	

TABLE B.2B. *Predicting Identification for AARP*

	Model 1		Model 2		Model 3	
	Beta	**Sig.**	**Beta**	**Sig.**	**Beta**	**Sig.**
(Constant)		0.03		0.28		0.41
Education	−0.07	0.18	0.04	0.32	0.04	0.32
Year Born	−0.08	0.08	−0.03	0.41	−0.02	0.56
Express Opinion	−0.08	0.11	−0.08	0.03	−0.07	0.06
Contact Official	0.07	0.17	0.03	0.38	0.03	0.42
Attend Meeting	−0.02	0.72	0.02	0.65	0.02	0.68
Associations	0.02	0.69	0.01	0.88	0.01	0.82
Trust	0.01	0.89	0.06	0.07	0.05	0.10
Instrumental Motivation			0.00	0.90	0.01	0.89
Social Motivation			0.11	0.01	0.09	0.02
Influence Motivation			0.36	0.00	0.35	0.00
Goals			0.37	0.00	0.37	0.00
Internet Skill					−0.10	0.02
Hours Online					−0.03	0.39
Years Online					0.06	0.09
Visit Web Site					0.06	0.08
r^2	*0.02*		*0.51*		*0.52*	

TABLE B.2C. *Predicting Organizational Trust for AARP*

	Model 1		Model 2		Model 3	
	Beta	Sig.	Beta	Sig.	Beta	Sig.
(Constant)		0.94		0.51		0.21
Education	0.01	0.81	0.06	0.18	0.09	0.07
Year Born	0.01	0.81	0.04	0.41	0.07	0.15
Express Opinion	−0.06	0.22	−0.05	0.24	−0.03	0.46
Contact Official	0.10	0.05	0.10	0.04	0.10	0.03
Attend Meeting	−0.06	0.23	−0.03	0.46	−0.02	0.69
Associations	0.01	0.83	0.01	0.80	0.01	0.83
Trust	0.04	0.40	0.06	0.19	0.06	0.18
Instrumental Motivation			−0.02	0.67	−0.01	0.81
Social Motivation			−0.02	0.68	−0.03	0.58
Influence Motivation			0.03	0.62	0.01	0.82
Goals			0.37	0.00	0.37	0.00
Internet Skill					−0.16	0.00
Hours Online					0.02	0.75
Years Online					0.01	0.78
Visit Web Site					0.01	0.78
r^2	*0.01*		*0.14*		*0.16*	

TABLE B.3A. *Predicting Contribution to Collective Goals and Activities for MoveOn*

	Model 1		Model 2		Model 3	
	Beta	Sig.	Beta	Sig.	Beta	Sig.
(Constant)		0.00		0.00		0.00
Education	−0.01	0.70	0.04	0.16	0.03	0.16
Year Born	−0.10	0.00	−0.08	0.00	−0.11	0.00
Express Opinion	0.11	0.00	0.10	0.00	0.08	0.00
Contact Official	0.18	0.00	0.16	0.00	0.14	0.00
Attend Meeting	0.10	0.00	0.08	0.00	0.08	0.00
Associations	0.07	0.01	0.05	0.04	0.06	0.02
Trust	−0.02	0.41	−0.04	0.12	−0.03	0.20
Instrumental Motivation			−0.03	0.38	−0.03	0.26
Social Motivation			0.31	0.00	0.29	0.00
Influence Motivation			0.09	0.01	0.08	0.01
Goals			0.10	0.00	0.09	0.00
Internet Skill					0.09	0.00
Hours Online					0.02	0.44
Years Online					0.01	0.75
Visit Web Site					0.12	0.00
r^2	*0.11*		*0.25*		*0.28*	

TABLE B.3B. *Predicting Identification for MoveOn*

	Model 1		Model 2		Model 3	
	Beta	Sig.	Beta	Sig.	Beta	Sig.
(Constant)		0.00		0.05		0.03
Education	0.00	0.86	0.05	0.02	0.05	0.03
Year Born	−0.11	0.00	−0.02	0.29	−0.03	0.20
Express Opinion	0.00	0.90	0.03	0.15	0.03	0.13
Contact Official	0.06	0.04	0.02	0.46	0.02	0.41
Attend Meeting	0.00	0.88	0.01	0.54	0.01	0.59
Associations	−0.01	0.79	−0.02	0.48	−0.02	0.47
Trust	0.01	0.71	−0.01	0.56	−0.01	0.58
Instrumental Motivation			−0.05	0.07	−0.05	0.08
Social Motivation			0.11	0.00	0.11	0.00
Influence Motivation			0.22	0.00	0.22	0.00
Goals			0.43	0.00	0.43	0.00
Internet Skill					0.03	0.27
Hours Online					−0.02	0.32
Years Online					−0.01	0.55
Visit Web Site					−0.01	0.73
r^2	*0.02*		*0.38*		*0.38*	

TABLE B.3C. *Predicting Organizational Trust for MoveOn*

	Model 1		Model 2		Model 3	
	Beta	Sig.	Beta	Sig.	Beta	Sig.
(Constant)		0.00		0.00		0.00
Education	−0.06	0.03	−0.04	0.12	−0.05	0.10
Year Born	−0.14	0.00	−0.09	0.00	−0.09	0.00
Express Opinion	−0.01	0.82	0.01	0.68	0.02	0.58
Contact Official	0.02	0.47	0.01	0.82	0.01	0.82
Attend Meeting	−0.01	0.77	0.00	0.99	0.00	0.96
Associations	−0.03	0.25	−0.04	0.19	−0.04	0.17
Trust	0.04	0.19	0.02	0.45	0.02	0.45
Instrumental Motivation			−0.04	0.19	−0.04	0.18
Social Motivation			0.01	0.68	0.01	0.63
Influence Motivation			0.05	0.20	0.05	0.20
Goals			0.32	0.00	0.32	0.00
Internet Skill					−0.02	0.52
Hours Online					−0.03	0.34
Years Online					0.02	0.52
Visit Web Site					0.00	0.97
r^2	*0.03*		*0.13*		*0.13*	

APPENDIX C

Descriptive Statistics for the Participatory Styles

TABLE C.1. *Selected Variables by Participatory Style*

		N	Mean	Std. Deviation	F value	$p<$
Level of Education	Individualists	1669	4.06[a,b]	1.51		
	Enthusiasts	804	3.62[c]	1.45		
	Traditionalists	192	3.92[a,c,d]	1.48	18.70	.001
	Minimalists	884	4.09[b,d]	1.47		
	TOTAL	3549	3.96	1.50		
Year Born	Individualists	1649	1947	14.50		
	Enthusiasts	797	1944[a,b]	13.82		
	Traditionalists	188	1943[a,c]	13.23	11.26	.001
	Minimalists	870	1944[b,c]	13.63		
	TOTAL	3504	1945	14.13		
Social Trust	Individualists	1654	2.75[a]	.68		
	Enthusiasts	800	2.83[a]	.72		
	Traditionalists	188	2.76[a]	.67	17.19	.001
	Minimalists	874	2.59	.74		
	TOTAL	3516	2.73	.71		
Usefulness of Contacts Made through Organization	Individualists	1660	1.90	.68		
	Enthusiasts	813	3.18	.72		
	Traditionalists	193	2.86	.67	379.87	.001
	Minimalists	876	1.71	.74		
	TOTAL	3542	2.20	.71		
Organizational Tenure	Individualists	1643	7.00	.68		
	Enthusiasts	812	13.30[a]	.72		
	Traditionalists	189	14.43[a]	.67	72.05	.001
	Minimalists	875	8.35	.74		
	TOTAL	3519	9.19	.71		

		N	Mean	Std. Deviation	F value	$p<$
Membership in Other Organizations/ Groups	Individualists	1692	1.48	.68		
	Enthusiasts	814	1.32[a]	.72		
	Traditionalists	193	1.30[a]	.67	22.77	.001
	Minimalists	891	1.39[a]	.74		
	TOTAL	3590	1.41	.71		
Attended Meeting	Individualists	1683	.43[a]	.49		
	Enthusiasts	807	.54[b]	.50		
	Traditionalists	192	.64[b]	.48	16.65	.001
	Minimalists	887	.46[a]	.50		
	TOTAL	3569	.47	.50		
Contacted Official	Individualists	1685	.62[a]	.49		
	Enthusiasts	808	.60[a]	.49		
	Traditionalists	192	.68[a]	.47	1.39	.001
	Minimalists	888	.62[a]	.49		
	TOTAL	3573	.62	.49		
Expressed Opinion	Individualists	1685	.28[a]	.45		
	Enthusiasts	808	.29[a]	.46		
	Traditionalists	191	.37[a]	.48	2.76	.001
	Minimalists	887	.31[a]	.46		
	TOTAL	3571	.30	.46		
Organizational and Individual Goal Alignment	Individualists	1699	7.62	1.36		
	Enthusiasts	818	8.10	1.25		
	Traditionalists	196	6.85	1.69	289.00	.001
	Minimalists	885	6.12	1.89		
	TOTAL	3598	7.32	1.67		
Instrumental Motivation	Individualists	1701	6.86	2.64		
	Enthusiasts	814	6.48	2.75		
	Traditionalists	194	5.35[a]	2.72	59.01	.001
	Minimalists	891	5.49[a]	2.81		
	TOTAL	3600	6.35	2.78		
Social Motivation	Individualists	1708	4.99	2.41		
	Enthusiasts	819	6.73[a]	2.30		
	Traditionalists	196	6.38[a]	2.48	205.86	.001
	Minimalists	895	4.02	2.41		
	TOTAL	3618	5.22	2.58		
Influence Motivation	Individualists	1700	8.19[a]	1.97		
	Enthusiasts	818	8.36[a]	1.94		
	Traditionalists	193	7.38	2.42	101.25	.001
	Minimalists	885	6.74	2.89		
	TOTAL	3596	7.83	2.34		

(*continued*)

TABLE C.1 *(continued)*

		N	Mean	Std. Deviation	F value	$p<$
Number of Friends Also Belonging to Organization	Individualists	1601	2.41[a]	1.03		
	Enthusiasts	808	3.04[b]	1.08		
	Traditionalists	192	3.00[b]	1.14	79.86	.001
	Minimalists	819	2.40[a]	1.13		
	TOTAL	3420	2.59	1.11		
Feelings about Meeting a Stranger from Organization	Individualists	1662	7.95[a]	1.86		
	Enthusiasts	814	8.62	1.57		
	Traditionalists	192	7.87[a]	1.97	110.86	.001
	Minimalists	864	6.97	2.11		
	TOTAL	3532	7.86	1.95		
Online Hours Per Week (excluding at work)	Individualists	1424	11.04[a]	11.03		
	Enthusiasts	637	11.49[a]	10.69		
	Traditionalists	162	11.02[a]	9.69	.69	.56
	Minimalists	754	11.68[a]	10.58		
	TOTAL	2977	11.30	10.77		
Internet Skill Level	Individualists	1443	2.67[a,b]	.89		
	Enthusiasts	648	2.60[a]	.91		
	Traditionalists	170	2.67[a,b]	.95	2.86	.04
	Minimalists	764	2.74[b]	.92		
	TOTAL	3025	2.67	.90		
Friends Known Only through the Internet (higher value = fewer)	Individualists	1444	1.79[a]	.41		
	Enthusiasts	649	1.74[a]	.44		
	Traditionalists	170	1.79[a]	.41	1.52	.21
	Minimalists	764	1.77[a]	.42		
	TOTAL	3027	1.77	.42		
Began Using the Internet (higher value = more recently)	Individualists	1444	4.23[a,b,c]	.86		
	Enthusiasts	649	4.14[a]	.92		
	Traditionalists	169	4.37[b,d]	.78	5.52	.001
	Minimalists	764	4.30[c,d]	.83		
	TOTAL	3026	4.23	.86		
Frequency of Visits to Organizational Web Site	Individualists	1442	2.17[a]	1.35		
	Enthusiasts	649	2.46[b]	1.56		
	Traditionalists	170	2.46[a,b]	1.68	25.46	.001
	Minimalists	766	1.86	1.11		
	TOTAL	3027	2.17	1.38		
Contribution	Individualists	1695	4.56	2.44		
	Enthusiasts	818	6.11[a]	2.54		
	Traditionalists	195	6.21[a]	2.95	126.27	.001
	Minimalists	885	4.00	2.63		
	TOTAL	3593	4.86	2.67		

		N	Mean	Std. Deviation	F value	p<
Organizational Identification	Individualists	1708	4.00[a]	.62		
	Enthusiasts	819	4.27	.55		
	Traditionalists	196	3.87[a]	.81	206.76	.001
	Minimalists	893	3.47	.88		
	TOTAL	3616	3.93	.75		
Organizational Trust	Individualists	1715	3.62	.71		
	Enthusiasts	820	3.72	.60		
	Traditionalists	186	3.29[a]	.74	83.79	.001
	Minimalists	897	3.22[a]	.95		
	TOTAL	3628	3.53	.78		

Note: Mean values with shared superscripts (a, b, c, and d) are not significantly different from each other at the $p < .05$ level. Significance in this table should be interpreted in light of the Bonferroni adjustment for experiment-wise error.

References

AARP. (2009). "Annual Report." Retrieved October 8, 2011 from http://pubs.aarp.org/aarpannualreport/aarp2009ar?folio=29#pg1.

______. (2010). "About AARP." Retrieved October 8, 2011 from http://www.aarp.org/about-aarp.

Aldrich, H. (1979). *Organizations and Environments*. Englewood Cliffs, NJ: Prentice-Hall.

American Legion. (2010). "How to Keep and Retain Members." Retrieved October 8, 2011 from http://www.legion.org/membership/retainmembers.

Anduiza, E., Gallego, A., and Jorba, L. (2009). "The Political Knowledge Gap in the New Media Environment: Evidence from Spain." Paper prepared for delivery at the International Seminar Citizen Politics: Are the New Media Reshaping Political Engagement? conference. Barcelona, Spain. May.

Arnold, R. D. (1990). *The Logic of Congressional Action*. New Haven, CT: Yale University Press.

Ashforth, B. E. and Mael, F. (1989). "Social Identity Theory and the Organization." *Academy of Management Review* 14:20–39.

Axley, S. R. (1984). "Managerial and Organizational Communication in Terms of the Conduit Metaphor." *Academy of Management Review* 9(3):428–37.

Bachmann, R. and Zaheer, A., eds. (2006). *Handbook of Trust Research*. Cheltenham, UK: Edward Elgar.

Bagnoli, M. and Lipman, B. L. (1989). "Provision of Public Goods: Fully Implementing the Core through Private Contributions." *Review of Economic Studies* 56:583–601.

Bagnoli, M. and McKee, M. (1991). "Voluntary Contribution Games: Efficient Private Provision of Public Goods." *Economic Inquiry* 29:351–66.

Bagnoli, M., Ben-David, S., and McKee, M. (1992). "Voluntary Provision of Public Goods: The Multiple Unit Case." *Journal of Public Economics* 47:85–106.

Barabasi, A. (2002). *Linked: The New Science of Networks*. Cambridge, MA: Perseus Publishing.

Barakso, M. (2010). "Brand Identity and the Tactical Repertoires of Advocacy Organizations." In *Advocacy Organizations and Collective Action*, ed. A. Prakash and M. K. Gugerty. Cambridge: Cambridge University Press, 155–76.

Barasko, M. and Schaffner, B. (2008). "Exit, Voice, and Interest Group Governance." *American Politics Research* 36:186–209.

Barnard, C. (1938). *The Functions of the Executive*. Cambridge, MA: Harvard University Press.

Barry, B. and Hardin, R., eds. (1982). *Rational Man and Irrational Society*. Beverly Hills, CA: Sage Publications.

Baumgartner, F. and Leech, B. (1998). *Basic Interests: The Importance of Groups in Politics and Political Science*. Princeton, NJ: Princeton University Press.

Bell, D. (1974). *The Coming of Post-Industrial Society: A Venture in Social Forecasting*. Special anniversary ed. New York: Basic Books.

Beniger, J. R. (1986). *The Control Revolution: Technological and Economic Origins of the Information Society*. Cambridge, MA: Harvard University Press.

Benkler, Y. (2006). *The Wealth of Networks: How Social Production Transforms Markets and Freedom*. New Haven, CT: Yale University Press.

Bennett, L. (1998). "The Uncivic Culture: Communication, Identity, and the Rise of Lifestyle Politics." *PS: Political Science and Politics* 31(4):740–61.

______. (2003). "Communicating Global Activism." *Information, Communication and Society* 6:143–68.

______. (2008). "Changing Citizenship in the Digital Age." In *Civic Life Online: Learning How Digital Media Can Engage Youth*, ed. W. L. Bennett. Cambridge, MA: MIT Press, 1–24.

Bennett, L., Breunig, C., and Givens, T. (2008). "Communication and Political Mobilization: Digital Media and the Organization of Anti-Iraq War Demonstrations in the United States." *Political Communication* 25:269–89.

Bennett, L. and Segerberg, A. (2011). "The Logic of Connective Action: Digital Media and the Personalization of Contentious Politics." Paper presented at the 6th General Conference of the European Consortium for Political Research, Reykjavik, August 25–7.

Bimber, B. (1999). "The Internet and Citizen Communication with Government: Does the Medium Matter?" *Political Communication* 16:409–28.

______. (2003). *Information and American Democracy: Technology in the Evolution of Political Power*. Cambridge: Cambridge University.

Bimber, B. and Copeland, L. (2011). "Digital Media Use and Political Participation Over Time in the U.S.: Contingency and Ubiquity." Paper presented at the 6th General Conference of the European Consortium for Political Research, Reykjavik, August 25–7.

Bimber, B., Flanagin, A. J., and Stohl, C. (2005). "Reconceptualizing Collective Action in the Contemporary Media Environment." *Communication Theory* 15:365–88.

Bimber, B., Stohl, C., and Flanagin, A. J. (2008). "Technological Change and the Shifting Nature of Political Organization." In *Routledge Handbook of Internet Politics*, ed. A. Chadwick and P. Howard. New York: Routledge, 72–85.

Blau, P. and Scott, W. (1962). *Formal Organizations: A Comparative Approach*. San Francisco: Chandler Publishing Company.

Blumenthal, M. S. and Clark, D. D. (2001). "Rethinking the Design of the Internet: The End to End Arguments vs. the Brave New World." *ACM Transactions on Internet Technology* 1(1):70–109.

Bornstein, D. (1997). *The Price of a Dream: The Story of the Grameen Bank*. Chicago: University of Chicago Press.

Boulianne, S. (2009). "Does Internet Use Affect Engagement? A Meta-Analysis of Research." *Political Communication* 26:193–211.

Boyd, J. (2003). "The Rhetorical Construction of Trust Online." *Communication Theory* 3(4):392–410.

Buchanan, M. (2002). *Nexus: Small Worlds and the Groundbreaking Science of Networks*. New York: W.W. Norton and Company.

Campbell, A. and Skocpol, T. (2003). "AARP at Risk of Medicare Blowback." *The Times Union*. December 3. Retrieved October 8, 2011 from http://www.timesunion.com.

Cantijoch, M. (2009). "Reinforcement and Mobilization: The Influence of the Internet on Different Types of Political Participation." Paper prepared for delivery at the Citizen Politics: Are Media Reshaping Political Engagement? conference. Barcelona, Spain. May.

Carey, J. (1989). *Communication as Culture. Essays on Media and Society*. New York: Routledge.

Castaldo, S., Premazzi, K., and Zerbini, F. (2010). "The Meanings of Trust: A Content Analysis on the Diverse Conceptualizations of Trust in the Scholarly Research on Business Relationships." *Journal of Business Ethics* 96:657–68.

Castells, M. (1996). *The Information Age, Economy, Society, and Culture – Volume I: The Rise of the Network Society*. Oxford: Blackwell Publishers.

______. (2000a). "Materials for an Exploratory Theory of the Network Society." *British Journal of Sociology* 51(1):5–24.

______. (2000b). *The Rise of the Network Society*. 2nd ed. Malden, MA: Blackwell Publishers.

______. (2009). *Communication Power*. Oxford: Oxford University Press.

Chadwick, A. (2007). "Digital Network Repertoires and Organizational Hybridity." *Political Communication* 24(3):283–301.

Chamberlin, J. (1974). "Provision of Collective Goods as a Function of Group Size." *Political Science Review* 68:707–13.

Cheney, G. (1983a). "On the Various and Changing Meanings of Organizational Membership: A Field Study of Organizational Identification." *Communication Monographs* 50:342–62.

______. (1983b). "The Rhetoric of Identification and the Study of Organizational Commitment." *Quarterly Journal of Speech* 69:143–58.

Cho, C. H. and Gorman, A. (2006). "Massive Student Walkout Spreads across Southland." *Los Angeles Times*. March 28. Retrieved October 8, 2011 from http://www.latimes.com/.

Clausing, J. (1999). "Anti-impeachment Website Tallies Millions in Pledges." *New York Times*. January 8. Retrieved October 8, 2011 from http://www.nytimes.com/.

Clegg, S. and Hardy, C. (1999). *Studying Organization: Theory and Method*. London: Sage Publications.

Coleman, J. (1988). "Social Capital in the Creation of Human Capital." *The American Journal of Sociology* 94:95–120.

______. (1990). *Foundations of Social Theory*. Cambridge, MA: Harvard University Press.

Connolly, T. and Thorn, B. K. (1990). "Discretionary Databases: Theory, Data, and Implications." In *Organizations and Communication Technology*, ed. J. Fulkand and C. Steinfield. Newbury Park, CA: Sage Publications, 219–33.

Cooren, F. (2006). "The Organizational Communication-Discourse Tilt: A Refugee's Perspective." *Management Communication Quarterly* 19:653–60.

Corrado, A. and Firestone, C., eds. (1996). *Elections in Cyberspace: Toward a New Era in American Politics*. Washington, DC: Aspen Institute.

Crowley, J. and Skocpol, T. (2001). "The Rush to Organize: Explaining Associational Formation in the United States, 1860s–1920s." *American Journal of Political Science* 45:813–29.

Curtis, J., Baer, D., and Grabb, E. (2001). "Nations of Joiners: Explaining Voluntary Association Membership in Democratic Societies."*American Sociological Review* 66(6):783–805.

Dalton, R. (2008a). "Citizenship Norms and the Expansion of Political Participation." *Political Studies* 56:76–98.

______. (2008b). *The Good Citizen: How a Younger Generation Is Reshaping American Politics*. Washington, DC: CQ Press.

Dalton, R., Scarrow, S., and Cain, B. (2004). "Advanced Democracies and the New Politics." *Journal of Democracy* 15(1):124–38.

della Porta, D. (2007). "The Global Justice Movement in Context." In *The Global Justice Movement: Cross-national and Transnational Perspectives*, ed. D. della Porta. Boulder, CO: Paradigm Publishers, 232–351.

Department of Transportation. (2003). "Transportation Statistics Annual Report." Retrieved October 8, 2011 from http://www.bts.gov/publications/transportation_statistics_annual_report/.

DiMaggio, P. and Powell, W. W. (1983). "The Iron Cage Revisited: Institutional Isomorphism and Collective Rationality in Organizational Fields." *American Sociological Review* 48:147–60.

Downs, A. (1957). *An Economic Theory of Democracy*. New York: Harper.

Drucker, P. (1999). "Beyond the Information Revolution." *Atlantic Monthly*. October 1–6.

Dutton, J. E., Dukerich, J. M., and Harquail, C. V. (1994). "Organizational Images and Member Identification." *Administrative Science Quarterly* 39:239–63.

Dutton, W. (2007). Through the Network (of Networks): The Fifth Estate. Inaugural lecture presented at the Oxford Internet Institute, University of Oxford. October 15. Retrieved October 8, 2011 from http://people.oii.ox.ac.uk/dutton/wp-content/uploads/2007/10/5th-estate-lecture-text.pdf.

Earl, J. and Kimport, K. (2011). *Digitally Enabled Social Change: Activism in the Internet Age*. Cambridge, MA: MIT Press.

Environmental Defense Fund. (1997). "Annual Report." Retrieved October 8, 2011 from http://www.edf.org/documents/220_AR97.pdf.

———. (2009). "Annual Report."Retrieved October 8, 2011 from http://www.edf.org/documents/10659_EDF_AnnualReport2009.pdf.

———. (2010). "Fact Sheet." Retrieved October 8, 2011 from http://www.edf.org/documents/2978_FactSheet_aboutus.pdf.

FAIR. (2001). "Annual Report." Retrieved October 8, 2011 from http://www.fairus.org/site/DocServer/fair_annual_report_2001.pdf?docID=482.

———. (2008). "Annual Report." Retrieved October 8, 2011 from http://www.fairus.org/site/DocServer/2008_Annual_Report.pdf?docID=3981.

Feenberg, A. (1995). *Alternative Modernity: The Technical Turn in Philosophy and Social Theory*. Berkeley: University of California Press.

Fischer, C. (1992). *Calling America*. Berkeley: University of California Press.

Flanagin, A. J. (2007). "Commercial Markets as Communication Markets: Uncertainty Reduction through Mediated Information Exchange in Online Auctions." *New Media and Society* 9(3):401–23.

Flanagin, A. J. and Metzger, M. J. (2007). "The Role of Site Features, User Attributes, and Information Verification Behaviors on the Perceived Credibility of Web-based Information." *New Media and Society* 9(2):319–42.

Flanagin, A. J., Flanagin, C., and Flanagin, J. (2010). "Technical Code and the Social Construction of the Internet." *New Media and Society* 12(2):179–96.

Flanagin, A. J., Monge, P. R., and Fulk, J. (2001). "The Value of Formative Investment in Organizational Federations." *Human Communication Research* 27:69–93.

Flanagin, A. J., Stohl, C., and Bimber, B. (2006). "Modeling the Structure of Collective Action." *Communication Monographs* 73:29–54.

Friedman, T. (2005). *The World Is Flat: A Brief History of the Twenty-First Century*. New York: Farrar, Strauss, and Giroux.

Fukuyama, F. (1995). *Trust: Social Virtues and the Creation of Prosperity*. London: Hamish Hamilton.

Fulk, J., Flanagin, A. J., Kalman, M., Monge, P. R., and Ryan, T. (1996). "Connective and Communal Public Goods in Interactive Communication Systems." *Communication Theory* 6:60–87.

Fulk, J., Heino, R., Flanagin, A. J., Monge, P. R., and Bar, F. (2004). "A Test of the Individual Action Model for Organizational Information Commons." *Organization Science* 15:569–85.

Gamson, W. (1992). "The Social Psychology of Collective Action." In *Frontiers in Social Movement Theory*, ed. A. Morris and C. Mueller. New Haven, CT: Yale University Press, 53–76.

Gamson, W. and Schmeidler, E. (1984). "Organizing the Poor." *Theory and Society* 13:567–85.

Ganesh, S. and Stohl, C. (2010). "Qualifying Engagement: A Study of Information and Communication Technology and the Global Social Justice Movement in Aotearoa/New Zealand." *Communication Monographs* 77:51–74.

Gerlach, L. (2001). "The Structures of Social Movements: Environmental Activism and Its Opponents." In *Networks and Netwars: The Future of Terror, Crime, and Militancy*, ed. J. Arquila and D. Ronfeldt. Santa Monica, CA: Rand Corporation, 289–309.

Gilbert, M. (2008). "The End of the Organization?" *Nonprofit Online News*. February 7. Retrieved October 8, 2011 from http://news.gilbert.org/EndOfOrg.

Gladwell, M. (2010). "Small Change: Why the Revolution Will Not Be Tweeted." *The New Yorker*. October 4. Retrieved October 8, 2011 from http://www.newyorker.com/reporting/2010/10/04/101004fa_fact_gladwell.

Global Voices. (2008). "Burmese Protests 2007." March 23. Retrieved October 8, 2011 from http://globalvoicesonline.org/specialcoverage/burmese-protests-2007/.

Goldstein, K. (1999). *Interest Groups, Lobbying, and Participation in America*. New York: Cambridge University Press.

Granovetter, M. (1973). "The Strength of Weak Ties." *American Journal of Sociology* 78:1360–80.

______. (1985). "Economic Action and Social Structure: The Problem of Embeddedness." *American Journal of Sociology* 91:481–510.

Hage, J. (1980). *Theories of Organizations: Form, Processes, and Transformation*. New York: John Wiley.

Hardin, R. (1982). *Collective Action*. Baltimore, MD: Johns Hopkins University Press.

Harris, G. (2009). "A Heated Debate Is Dividing Generations in AARP." October 4. *New York Times*, A22.

Head, J. G. (1972). "Public Goods: The Polar Case." In *Modern Fiscal Issues: Essays in Honour of Carl S. Shoup*, ed. R. M. Bird and J. G. Head. Toronto: University of Toronto Press, 7–16.

Heclo, H. (2008). *On Thinking Institutionally*. Boulder, CO: Paradigm Publishers.

Hero, R. E. (2007). *Racial Diversity and Social Capital: Equality and Community in America*. New York: Cambridge University Press.

Hickson, D., MacMillan, C., Azumi, K., and Horvath, D. (1979). "Grounds for Comparative Organization and Theory: Quicksands or Hard Core?" In *Organizations Alike and Unlike*, ed. C. Lammers and D. Hickson. London: Routledge and Kegan Paul, 25–41.

Humphreys, L. (2007). "Mobile Social Networks and Social Practice: A Case Study of Dodgeball." *Journal of Computer-Mediated Communication* 13(1):341–60.

Inglehart, R. (1997). *Modernization and Postmodernization: Cultural, Economic, and Political Change in 43 Societies*. Princeton, NJ: Princeton University Press.

Internet World Stats. (2010). "Internet Usage and Population in North America." Retrieved October 8, 2011 from http://www.internetworldstats.com/stats14.htm.

ITU. (2010). *The World in 2010: ICT Facts and Figures*. International Telecommunications Union. Retrieved October 8, 2011 from http://www.itu.int/ITU-D/ict/material/FactsFigures2010.pdf.

Jennings, M. and Zeitner, V. (2003). "Internet Use and Civic Engagement: A Longitudinal Analysis." *Public Opinion Quarterly* 67:311–34.

Kahn, R. and Kellner, D. (2004). "New Media and Internet Activism: From the 'Battle of Seattle' to Blogging." *New Media and Society* 6(1):87–95.

Karpf, D. (2009). "The MoveOn Effect: Disruptive Innovation within the Interest Group Ecology of American Politics." Unpublished manuscript. Retrieved October 8, 2011 from http://davekarpf.files.wordpress.com/2009/03/moveon.pdf.

Katz, J. and Aakhus, M., eds. (2002). *Perpetual Contact: Mobile Communication, Private Talk, Public Performance*. Cambridge: Cambridge University Press.

Katz, J. E. and Rice, R. E. (2002). *Social Consequences of Internet Use: Access, Involvement and Expression*. Cambridge, MA: MIT Press.

Kaufman, H. (1960). *The Forest Ranger: A Study in Administrative Behavior*. Baltimore, MD: Johns Hopkins University Press.

Knoke, D. (1986). "Associations and Interest Groups." *Annual Review of Sociology* 12:1–21.

Knoke, D. and Wood, J. (1981). *Organized for Action: Commitment in Voluntary Associations*. New Brunswick, NJ: Rutgers University Press.

Kollock, P. (1999). "The Production of Trust in Online Markets." In *Advances in Group Processes*, ed. E. J. Lawler. Greenwich, CT: JAI Press, 99–123.

Kramer, R. and Cook, K., eds. (2004). *Trust and Distrust in Organizations: Dilemmas and Approaches*. New York: Russell Sage Foundation.

La Raza. (2000). *Annual Report*. Washington, DC: National Council of La Raza.

______. (2008). *Annual Report*. Washington, DC: National Council of La Raza.

Lambright, K., Mischen, P. M., and Larmaee, C. (2010). "Building Trust in Public and Nonprofit Networks." *The American Review of Public Administration* 40:64–82.

Lecy, J., Mitchell, G., and Schmitz, P. (2010). "Advocacy Organizations, Networks and the Firm Analogy." In *Advocacy Organizations and Collective Action*, ed. A. Prakash and M. K. Gugerty. Cambridge: Cambridge University Press, 229–51.

Lessig, L. (1999). *Code and Other Laws of Cyberspace*. New York: Basic Books.

Levi, M. (1988). *Of Rule and Revenue*. Berkeley: University of California Press.

Lewis, J. and Weingart, A. (1985). "Trust as Social Reality." *Social Forces* 63:967–85.

Lewis-Beck, M., Jacoby, W., Norpoth, H., and Weisberg, H. (2008). *The American Voter Revisited*. Ann Arbor: University of Michigan.

Lin, N. (2001). *Social Capital: A Theory of Social Structure and Action*. Cambridge, UK: Cambridge University Press.

Lowi, T. (1979). *The End of Liberalism: The Second Republic of the United States*. New York: W. W. Norton.

Lupia, L. and Sin, G. (2003). "Which Public Goods Are Endangered? How Evolving Technologies Affect the Logic of Collective Action." *Public Choice* 117:315–31.

MacDonald, M. P. and Popkin, S. (2001). "The Myth of the Vanishing Voter."*American Political Science Review* 95(4):963–74.

MacManus, R. (2009). "Black Out Your Twitter Photo: NZ Copyright Law Protest Goes Viral." *ReadWriteWeb*. Retrieved October 8, 2011 from http://www.readwriteweb.com/archives/nz_internet_blackout.php.

Madrigal, A. (2011). "Protesters: Mark Zuckerberg Good, Ben Ali Evil." *The Atlantic*. January 18. Retrieved January 20, 2011 from http://www.theatlantic.com/technology/archive/2011/01/protesters-mark-zuckerberg-good-ben-ali-evil/69732/.

Malone, T. and Rockart, J. (1991). "Computers, Networks, and the Corporation." *Scientific American* 265:128–36.

Markus, M. L. (1990). "Toward a Critical Mass Theory of Interactive Media." In *Organizations and Communication Technology*, ed. J. Fulk and C. W. Steinfield. Newbury Park, CA: Sage Publications, 194–218.

Marwell, G. and Ames, R. E. (1981). "Economists Ride Free, Does Anyone Else? Experiments on the Provision of Public Goods, IV." *Journal of Public Economics* 15:295–310.

Marwell, G. and Oliver, P. (1993). *The Critical Mass in Collective Action: A Micro-Social Theory*. New York: Cambridge University Press.

McAdam, D., Tarrow, S., and Tilly, C. (2001). *Dynamics of Contention*. Cambridge: Cambridge University Press.

McMillan, J. (1991). *Games, Strategies and Managers*. Oxford: Oxford University Press.

Melucci, A. (1996). *Challenging Codes: Collective Action in the Information Age*. Cambridge: Cambridge University Press.

Metzger, M. J. and Flanagin, A. J. (2008). *Introduction to Digital Media, Youth, and Credibility*, ed. M. J. Metzger and A. J. Flanagin. Cambridge: MIT Press, 1–4.

Meyer, J. and Scott, W. (1983). *Organizational Environments: Ritual and Rationality*. Beverly Hills, CA: Sage Publications.

Michels, R. (1915). *Political Parties: A Sociological Study of the Oligarchical Tendencies of Modern Democracy*. Translated into English by Eden Paul and Cedar Paul. New York: Free Press.

Miles, R. E. and Snow, C. C. (1984). "Fit, Failure, and the Hall of Fame." *California Management Review* 26(Spring):10–28.

______. (1986). "Organizations: New Concepts for New Forms." *California Management Review* 28(Spring):62–73.

Monge, P. R., Fulk, J., Kalman, M., Flanagin, A. J., Parnassa, C., and Rumsey, S. (1998). "Production of Collective Action in Alliance-based Interorganizational Communication and Information Systems." *Organization Science* 9:411–33.

Morgan, J. (2010). "Twitter and Facebook Respond to Haiti Crisis." *BBC News*. January 15. Retrieved October 8, 2011 from http://news.bbc.co.uk/2/hi/americas/8460791.stm.

Mossberger, K., Tolbert, C. J., and McNeal, R. S. (2008). *Digital Citizenship: The Internet, Society, and Participation*. Cambridge, MA: MIT Press.

Nohria, N. and Berkley, J. D. (1994). "The Virtual Organization: Bureaucracy, Technology, and the Implosion of Control." In *The Post-Bureaucratic Organization: New Perspectives on Organizational Change*, ed. C. Heckscher and A. Donnellon. Thousand Oaks, CA: Sage Publications, 108–28.

Oliver, P. (1993). "Formal Models of Collective Action." *Annual Review of Sociology* 19:271–300.
Oliver, P. E. and Marwell, G. (1988). "The Paradox of Group Size in Collective Action: A Theory of the Critical Mass III." *American Sociological Review* 53:1–8.
Oliver, P., Marwell, G., and Teixeira, R. (1985). "A Theory of Critical Mass I: Group Heterogeneity, Interdependence and the Production of Collective Goods." *American Journal of Sociology* 91:522–56.
Olson, M. (1965). *The Logic of Collective Action.* Cambridge, MA: Harvard University Press.
Ostrom, E. (1990). *Governing the Commons: The Evolution of Institutions for Collective Action.* Cambridge: Cambridge University Press.
______. (1997). "A Behavioral Approach to the Rational Choice Theory of Collective Action: Presidential Address." *The American Political Science Review* 92:1–22.
Paxton, P. (1999). "Is Social Capital Declining in the United States? A Multiple Indicator Assessment." *American Journal of Sociology* 105:88–127.
Powell, W. W. (1990). "Neither Market nor Hierarchy: Network Forms of Organization." *Research in Organizational Behavior* 12:295–336.
Prior, M. (2007). *Post-Broadcast Democracy: How Media Choice Increases Inequality in Political Involvement and Polarizes Elections.* New York: Cambridge University Press.
Pugh, D., Hickson, D., Hinings, C., and Turner, C. (1968). "Dimensions of Organization Structure." *Administrative Science Quarterly* 13:65–105.
Putnam, L., Stohl, C., and Baker, J. (2012). "Bona fide groups: A discourse perspective." In *Research Methods for Studying Groups: A Behind-the-Scenes Guide*, ed. M. S. Poole and A. Hollingshead. New York: Taylor and Francis/Routledge, 210–34.
Putnam, R. (1995). "Bowling Alone." *Journal of Democracy* 6(1):70.
______. (2000). *Bowling Alone: The Collapse and Revival of American Community.* New York: Simon and Schuster.
Puusa, A. and Tolvanen, U. (2006). "Organizational Identity and Trust." *Electronic Journal of Business Ethics and Organization Studies* 11(2):29–33.
Rafaeli, S. and LaRose, R. J. (1993). "Electronic Bulletin Boards and 'Public Goods' Explanations of Collaborative Mass Media." *Communication Research* 20(2):277–97.
Ratnatunga, J. and Ewing, M. (2005). "The Brand Capability of Integrated Marketing Communication." *Journal of Advertising* 34(4):25–40.
Ravasi, D. and van Rekom, J. (2003). "Key Issues in Organizational Identity and Identification Theory." *Corporate Reputation Review* 6:118–32.
Resnick, P. (2005). "Impersonal Sociotechnical Capital, ICTs, and Collective Action among Strangers." In *Transforming Enterprise*, ed. W. Dutton, B. Kahin, R. O'Callaghan, and A. Wyckoff. Boston: MIT Press, 486–99.
Rheingold, H. (2002). *Smart Mobs: The Next Social Revolution.* New York: Basic Books.
Ring, P. and van de Ven, A. (1992). "Structuring Cooperating Relationships between Organizations." *Strategic Management Journal* 13(7):483–98.

Rohlinger, D. A. and Brown, J. (2009). "Democracy, Action, and the Internet after 9/11." *American Behavioral Scientist* 53:133–50.

Romer, D., Jamieson, K. H., and Pasek, J. (2009). "Building Social Capital in Young People: The Role of Mass Media and Life Outlook." *Political Communication* 26:65–83.

Rosenstone, S. and Hansen, J. (1993). *Mobilization, Participation, and Democracy in America*. New York: Macmillan.

Rotter, J. (1967). "A New Scale for the Measurement of Interpersonal Trust." *Journal of Personality* 35:651–65.

Rozell, M. and Wilcox, C. (1999). *Interest Groups in American Campaigns: The New Face of Electioneering*. Washington, DC: CQ Press.

Saltzer, J. H., Reed, D. P., and Clark, D. D. (1984). "End-to-End Arguments in System Design." *ACM Transactions on Computer Systems* 2:277–88.

Samuelson, P. A. (1954). "The Pure Theory of Public Expenditure." *Review of Economics and Statistics* 36:387–90.

Schattschneider, E. E. (1975). *The Semisovereign People: A Realist's View of Democracy in America*. New York: Harcourt Brace College Publishers.

Schoorman, F., Mayer, R., and Davis, J. (2007). "An Integrative Model of Organizational Trust: Past, Present, and Future." *Academy of Management Review* 32:344–54.

Scola, N. (2011). "Why Tunisia Is Not a Social-Media Revolution." *The American Prospect*. January 24. Retrieved January 30, 2011 from http://prospect.org//cs/articles;jsessionid=awJPBevPlbra58sHn3?article=why_tunisia_is_not_a_socia_media_revolution.

Scott, W. R. (1995). *Institutions and Organizations*. Thousand Oaks, CA: Sage Publications.

Shah, D. V., Kwak, N., and Holbert, R. L. (2001). "'Connecting' and 'Disconnecting' with Civic Life: Patterns of Internet Use and the Production of Social Capital." *Political Communication* 18:141–62.

Shirky, C. (2008). *Here Comes Everybody: The Power of Organizing without Organization*. New York: Penguin Press.

Shockley, P., Morreale, S., and Hackman, M. (2010). *Building the High Trust Organization: Strategies for Supporting Five Key Dimensions of Trust*. San Francisco: Jossey-Bass.

Simon, H. A. (1976). *Administrative Behavior: A Study of Decision-making Processes Administrative Organization*. New York: Free Press.

Skocpol, T. (2003). *Diminished Democracy: From Membership to Management in American Civic Life*. Norman: University of Oklahoma Press.

Skocpol, T. and Fiorina, M., eds. (1999). *Civic Engagement in American Democracy*. Washington, DC: Brookings Institution.

Skocpol, T., Cobb, R., and Klofstad, C. (2005). "Disconnection and Reorganization: The Transformation of Civic Life in Late 20th Century America." *Studies in American Political Development* 19:137–56.

Skocpol, T., Ganz, M., and Munson, Z. (2000). "A Nation of Organizers: The Institutional Origins of Civic Volunteerism in the United States." *American Political Science Review* 9:527–46.

Spinard, W. (1960). "Correlates of Trade Union Participation." *American Sociological Review* 25(3–4):237–46.

Stohl, C. (1995). *Organizational Communication: Connectedness in Action*. Thousand Oaks, CA: Sage Publications.

______. (2001). "Globalizing Organizational Communication." In *The New Handbook of Organizational Communication*, ed. F. Jablin and L. Putnam. Thousand Oaks, CA: Sage Publications, 323–75.

Stohl, C. and Cheney, G. (2001). "Participatory Processes/Paradoxical Practices: Communication and the Dilemmas of Organizational Democracy." *Management Communication Quarterly* 14:349–407.

Stohl, C. and Stohl, M. (2007). "Terrorism Networks: Theoretical Assumptions and Pragmatic Consequences." *Communication Theory* 17:93–124.

Sunstein, C. (2009). *Going to Extremes: How Like Minds Unite and Divide*. New York: Oxford University Press.

Tajfel, H. (1978). "Social Categorization, Social Identity and Social Comparison." In *Differentiation between Social Groups: Studies in the Social Psychology of Intergroup Relations*, ed. H. Tajfel. London: Academic Press, 61–76.

Tarrow, S. (1983). *Struggling to Reform: Social Movements and Policy Change during Cycles of Protest*. Ithaca, NY: Western Societies Program, Cornell University.

______. (1994). *Power in Movement: Social Movements, Collective Action, and Politics*. New York: Cambridge University Press.

______. (2006). *The New Transnational Activism*. New York: Cambridge University Press.

Taylor, J. (2004). "Dialogue as the Search for Sustainable Organizational Co-orientation." In *Dialogue: Theorizing Difference in Communication Studies*, ed. R. Anderson, L. Baxter, and K. Cissna. Thousand Oaks, CA: Sage Publications, 125–40.

Tilly, C. (2005). *Trust and Rule*. Cambridge: Cambridge University Press.

Tocqueville, A. (1945). *Democracy in America*. New York: A. A. Knopf.

Tompkins, P. and Cheney, G. (1983). "Account Analysis of Organizations: Decision Making and Identification." In *Communication and Organizations: An Interpretive Approach*, ed. L. L. Putnam and M. E. Pacanowsky. Beverly Hills, CA: Sage Publications, 123–46.

Truman, D. (1951). *The Governmental Process: Political Interests and Public Opinion*. New York: Alfred Knopf.

Van Atta, D. (1998). *Trust Betrayed: Inside the AARP*. Washington, DC: Regnery Publishing.

Verba, S., Schlozman, K., and Brady, H. (1995). *Voice and Equality: Civic Voluntarism in American Politics*. Cambridge, MA: Harvard University Press.

Walker, J. (1991). *Mobilizing Interest Groups in America: Patrons, Professions, and Social Movements*. Ann Arbor: University of Michigan.

Walther, J. B. (1996). "Computer-mediated Communication: Impersonal, Interpersonal, and Hyperpersonal Interaction." *Communication Research* 23:3–43.

Wattenberg, M. (2002). *Where Have All the Voters Gone?* Cambridge, MA: Harvard University Press.

Weber, M. (1930). *The Protestant Ethic and the Spirit of Capitalism*. Trans. T. Parson. New York: Charles Scribner's Sons. (Original work published in 1904).

Weiser, M. (1991). "The Computer for the 21st Century." *Scientific American* (February):94–104.

Wellman, B. A., Quan-Haase, J., Witte, J., and Hampton, K. N. (2001). "Does the Internet Increase, Decrease, or Supplement Social Capital? Social Networks, Participation, and Community Commitment." *American Behavioral Scientist* 45:437–56.

Williamson, O. (1985). *The Economic Institutions of Capitalism*. New York: Free Press.

Wojcieszak, M. (2009). "Carrying Participation Offline: Mobilization by Radical Online Groups and Politically Dissimilar Offline Ties." *Journal of Communication* 59:564–86.

Wolf, G. (2004). "How the Internet Invented Howard Dean." *Wired*. January. Retrieved October 8, 2011 from http://www.wired.com/wired/archive/12.01/dean.html.

Wright, A. (2002). "Technology as an Enabler of the Global Branding of Retail Financial Services." *Journal of International Marketing* 10(2):83–98.

Xenos, M. and Moy, P. (2007). "Direct and Differential Effects of the Internet on Political and Civic Engagement." *Journal of Communication* 57:704–18.

Yuan, Y., Fulk, J., Shumate, M., Monge, P. R., Bryant, J. A., and Matsaganis, M. (2005). "Individual Participation in Organizational Information Commons: The Impact of Team Level Social Influence and Technology-Specific Proficiency." *Human Communication Research* 31(2):212–40.

Zald, M. and McCarthy, J., eds. (1987). *Social Movements in an Organizational Society*. New Brunswick, NJ: Transaction Books.

Zander, E. (n.d.) "The Invisible Internet." Tomorrow's Professor Mailing List, Stanford Center for Teaching and Learning, Stanford University. Retrieved October 18, 2011 from http://cgi.stanford.edu/~dept-ctl/tomprof/posting.php?ID=311.

Zickuhr, K. (2010). "Generations 2010." Retrieved October 8, 2011 from http://pewinternet.org/Reports/2010/Generations-2010.aspx.

Zukin, C., Keeter, S., Andolina, M., Jenkins, K., and Delli Carpini, M. (2006). *A New Engagement? Political Participation, Civic Life, and the Changing American Citizen*. New York: Oxford University.

Index

Other Books in the Series (*continued from page iii*)

Myra Marx Ferree, William Anthony Gamson, Jürgen Gerhards, and Dieter Rucht, *Shaping Abortion Discourse: Democracy and the Public Sphere in Germany and the United States*

Hernan Galperin, *New Television, Old Politics: The Transition to Digital TV in the United States and Britain*

Tim Groeling, *When Politicians Attack: Party Cohesion in the Media*

Richard Gunther and Anthony Mughan, eds., *Democracy and the Media: A Comparative Perspective*

Daniel C. Hallin and Paolo Mancini, *Comparing Media Systems: Three Models of Media and Politics*

Daniel C. Hallin and Paolo Mancini, eds., *Comparing Media Systems beyond the Western World*

Robert B. Horwitz, *Communication and Democratic Reform in South Africa*

Philip N. Howard, *New Media Campaigns and the Managed Citizen*

Ruud Koopmans and Paul Statham, eds., *The Making of a European Public Sphere: Media Discourse and Political Contention*

L. Sandy Maisel, Darrell M. West, and Brett M. Clifton, *Evaluating Campaign Quality: Can the Electoral Process Be Improved?*

Pippa Norris, *Digital Divide: Civic Engagement, Information Poverty, and the Internet Worldwide*

Pippa Norris, *A Virtuous Circle: Political Communications in Postindustrial Society*

Adam F. Simon, *The Winning Message: Candidate Behavior, Campaign Discourse*

Bruce A. Williams and Michael X. Delli Carpini, *After Broadcast News: Media Regimes, Democracy, and the New Information Environment*

Gadi Wolfsfeld, *Media and the Path to Peace*